Learning the Anglican Story

FOUNDATIONS FOR
CHRISTIAN MINISTRY

LESLIE P. FAIRFIELD

SERIES EDITOR, JOEL SCANDRETT

Whitchurch
Publishing

Trusted Resources from Trinity School for Ministry

Foundations for Christian Ministry
Learning the Anglican Story

Copyright © 1990, 2003, 2020 Trinity School for Ministry

Published by Whitchurch Publishing
311 Eleventh St.
Ambridge, PA 15003
1-800-874-8754
www.tsm.edu

Cover design by Rebecca Murden
Book design by Christopher Klukas

ISBN: 978-1-947562-03-5

This book is a part of the *Foundations for Christian Ministry* (FCM) curriculum. FCM is a non-degree curriculum designed to train laypeople for Christian life and ministry, and can be undertaken as parish-based, small-group, or individual study. The purpose of FCM is *to encourage and strengthen Christian formation, discipleship, and witness for all members of Christ's body through study that is biblically sound and theologically orthodox.*

From the Series Editor

Greetings in the name of the Lord Jesus Christ! It is my privilege and delight to introduce you to this rich resource for Christian discipleship: *Foundations for Christian Ministry.* This multivolume curriculum is designed to deepen and strengthen your grasp of Holy Scripture, of the essential realities of the Christian faith, of Christian moral reasoning, of the Church's life and history, and of the Christian's calling to ministry in the Church and the world.

As we stand at the beginning of the twenty-first century, the global Church faces a world that appears increasingly hostile to the Christian faith. Yet as in ages past, Christian disciples are called faithfully to bear witness to the saving love of God in Jesus Christ and to be agents of the kingdom of God in the world. In such a time as this, we can no longer afford to rely upon the trappings of Christian culture or to be content with a simplistic understanding of our faith. Rather let us all, as the apostle Paul prayed for the Christians in Ephesus two millennia ago:

> *. . . no longer be children, tossed to and fro by the waves and carried about by every wind of doctrine, by human cunning, by craftiness in deceitful schemes. Rather, speaking the truth in love, we are to grow up in every way into him who is the head, into Christ (Ephesians 4:14-15).*

My prayer is that the Triune God will use this resource to *transform* your understanding of Christ (Romans 12:2), to cause you to *grow* in maturity in Christ (Ephesians 4:14-15), and to *equip* you as agents of Christ's ministry and mission in the world (Hebrews 13:20-21). To him be all praise and glory!

Joel Scandrett

The Rev. Dr. Joel Scandrett
Director of the Robert E. Webber Center
Series Editor, Foundations for Christian Ministry

Table of Contents

Introduction: How the Course Works

Course Structure

This book consists of twelve chapters. Each chapter has a similar structure with specific objectives. The text of the chapter is interspersed with questions designed to integrate and internalize the content of the lesson. Review questions are included to test the specific objectives. Several *For Thought and Application* questions end each chapter. At the end of the course is a summary review, which will enable students to discover just how many of the overall course objectives have been met, and how much of the course content has been assimilated.

Home Assignments

The success of the group meetings hinges on each individual's faithful preparation in between meetings. Expect to spend at least one and a half hours in study for each chapter of this book.

The chapters in this book are not printed lectures. They are designed to assist you to learn on your own. In the quiet of your home, prayerfully and diligently work through each chapter, including reading, looking up Bible passages, and writing down answers in your notebook. Think of questions you would like to bring to the group. Pray for your leader and the group during the week.

Group Meetings

While this course may be undertaken individually, it is designed for groups. At each meeting, groups will study the main themes of each lesson in a creative way, discussing questions and sharing personal truths and applications in greater depth. Group meetings should be interesting and enjoyable, so if you have any ideas or suggestions, please share them with the group.

Groups may take the form of adult Christian education classes on Sunday mornings or weekday evenings, home fellowship groups, small groups, or other configurations. The decision about group structure or when group meetings are to be held will ultimately be made between your facilitator and group. However, we suggest that you follow something close to the following pattern:

1. Group opens in prayer.
2. 10-15 minutes—leader summarizes main teaching points based on the chapter and additional readings.
3. 45 minutes—group discusses *For Thought and Application* questions from the end of the chapter.
4. Group closes in prayer.

Leadership

Group meetings should be led by a group facilitator who plans the logistics of session times and content, but this person need not have a theological degree in order for the group to be successful.

Textbooks

A study Bible and this book are your chief texts. For your Bible, we recommend using a more recent translation. We suggest either the *ESV Study Bible* (Crossway, 2008) or the *NIV Study Bible* (Zondervan, 2011).

Further Reading

Additional reading assignments are listed at the end of each chapter. While these readings are not required, they are highly recommended. However, group facilitators are expected to read and be familiar with these additional resources. The additional readings assigned for this course are from the following books:

J.R.H. Moorman, *A History of the Church in England, Third Edition* (Harrisburg, Pennsylvania: Morehouse Publishing, 1980).

Robert W. Prichard, *A History of the Episcopal Church, Third Revised Edition* (Harrisburg, Pennsylvania: Morehouse Publishing, 2014).

Chapter 1

The Anglican Way

A Creative Mixture

Late in the Middle Ages, in the city of Oxford, there was a magnificent shrine dedicated to St. Frydeswyde, an eighth-century prioress of a monastery there. Over the centuries pious donors had given gold and jewels to adorn her casket. Thousands of people came to pray at the shrine and ask St. Frydeswyde to intercede for their welfare.

At the time of the Reformation in the 1550s, however, prayers to the saints became unfashionable, or politically incorrect. The mayor and aldermen of Oxford decided it would be best to remove St. Frydeswyde's bones from the shrine, lest people continue to pray to her (which the Reformation discouraged). So her bones were moved to an attic in Christ Church College.

Shortly thereafter the wife of Peter Vermigli, a distinguished Italian Protestant theologian, died in Oxford. To show honor to Mrs. Vermigli, the mayor and aldermen ruled that her remains should be placed in St. Frydeswyde's erstwhile shrine. So it was done.

All was well until Mary Tudor came to the English throne in the summer of 1553. Mary was the half-Spanish daughter of Henry VIII and Catherine of Aragon. A passionate Catholic, she was determined to purify England from all its Protestant abominations. Sensitive to the new direction in the wind, the mayor and aldermen ruled that Mrs. Vermigli be moved to the attic, and St. Frydeswyde be replaced in her tomb. So it was done.

Mary Tudor ("Bloody Mary") died in November 1558, and her younger sister Elizabeth succeeded her. Elizabeth was blonde, graceful, and poised, and she had her father's political genius. No one knew for sure which way she would turn, whether Catholic or Protestant. So the mayor and aldermen of Oxford wrote to her and said (more or less), "Frydeswyde is in, Vermigli is out. Please advise."

Elizabeth and her council pondered this request for twenty-four hours. Then the queen dictated a terse response. She said, "Mix them."

I have often offered this story as a model of the Anglican way, and not wholly in jest. For the Anglican story tells of three different strands, or traditions, that have emerged in the Church of England (and its offspring throughout the world) in the past five hundred years. First, there has been the Evangelical tradition, heirs of the Reformation and emphasizing the Bible, preaching, and conversion. Second, there has been the Anglo-Catholic strand, briefly revived in the early 1600s and then coming back full strength in the 1830s. Anglo-Catholicism has stressed the sacraments, the authority of the priesthood, and gradual growth in grace. And third, there has been the Charismatic tradition, with its emphasis on renewal in the Holy Spirit, on healing, and on signs and wonders. These three strands in the Anglican story have often rubbed against one another uncomfortably, and caused considerable "vigorous fellowship." But each has pointed to valid biblical themes, to which their "opponents" had been arguably blind. So I present the Anglican story as a creative mixture of biblical truths, which other Christian traditions have sometimes emphasized in isolation, ignoring the others. The Anglican way (so far) has managed to hold them together in creative tension.

Historic Anglican theology, worship, and piety are consistent with the "faith once delivered to the saints," and they are valuable gifts the Anglican Church can offer to the universal Church. This overview makes no claims to clinical, value-free "objectivity" (as if the latter were even possible), but rather is written from within the orthodox Anglican tradition and for that tradition.

Three other introductory comments: First, here and there in the following chapters brief stories appear in italics. In every case they are based on factual data but have been imaginatively presented.

Second, though some attention is given to the Global South near the end, the book's focus is primarily on England and the United States. As the book is intended primarily for Anglicans in the United States, we trust our faithful Anglican sisters and brothers in Canada, Australia, and other westernized provinces of the Communion will forgive us for not giving them their due.

Finally, about the word *Anglican* and its derivatives: The Latin phrase *Ecclesia Anglicana* appeared in the Magna Carta in 1215 and in Henry VIII's Act of Supremacy (declaring him Supreme Head of that church) in 1534. The English form *Anglican* began to appear infrequently in the mid-1600s to distinguish the Church of England from Roman Catholics and Continental Protestants. But not until after 1800 did it become a common adjective to describe the Church of England, or a noun to denote an individual member of that church. *Anglicanism* is an even later term, evidently not appearing until 1846. Except in descriptions of the Anglican tradition in this chapter—where it will be employed copiously—we will avoid the terms *Anglican* and *Anglicanism* until we come to the nineteenth century, when the words first entered common use.

The Heart of the Anglican Way

The binding force that has held together the three orthodox strands in Anglicanism can be seen in a brief list of essential beliefs that has come to be known as the "Lambeth Quadrilateral." Let's first look at the background.

In the 1860s and the 1870s, Christians in the United States and Britain were conscious of the enormous changes that the Industrial Revolution was effecting in their societies. Steam power, huge factories, new sources of coal and iron, and rapidly expanding railway lines all offered huge opportunities for energetic and industrious people. At the same time, however, dangerous and toxic work sites, closely packed urban slums, cholera epidemics, and violent labor disputes all posed great dangers. Britain and the United States (and soon parts of Continental Europe as well) were experiencing the greatest revolution in human society since the discovery of agriculture some twelve thousand years earlier. Many Christians believed, therefore, that only a united national church could minister effectively in this new environment. How could Christians preach the gospel effectively if churches were squabbling among themselves over minor points of doctrine?

In 1870 an Episcopal clergyman named William Reed Huntington published a book called *The Church Idea,* in which he addressed the urgent problem of national Christian unity. He argued that as the Episcopal Church discussed cooperation and possible unity with other denominations, they should simply insist on four key features at the heart of Episcopal identity. Huntington cited the Bible, the Apostles' and Nicene Creeds, the sacraments of Baptism and the Lord's Supper, and the historic apostolic succession of bishops.

Sixteen years later, in 1886, the Episcopal House of Bishops took up Huntington's proposal and identified the same four nonnegotiables as the heart of Christianity according to this church's understanding. Finally, two years later, in 1888, the Lambeth Conference of worldwide Anglican bishops accepted the four-point scheme as well: hence the "Lambeth Quadrilateral."

The Lambeth Conference enumerated the four points as follows:

- "The Holy Scriptures of the Old and New Testaments as 'containing all things necessary to salvation,' and as being the rule and ultimate standard of faith."
- "The Apostles' Creed as the Baptismal Symbol; and the Nicene Creed as the sufficient statement of the Christian faith."
- "The two Sacraments ordained by Christ himself—Baptism and the Supper of the Lord ministered with unfailing use of Christ's words of Institution, and of the elements ordained by Him."
- "The Historic Episcopate, locally adapted in the methods of its administration to the varying needs of the nations and peoples called of God into the Unity of the Church."

The proceedings of the Lambeth Conference, which happens every ten years, are purely advisory to the churches to which the bishops return. Nothing that the Lambeth Conference had done in 1888 could bind the Episcopal Church back in the United States. To regularize matters, in 1895 the General Convention of the Episcopal Church took up the issue of Anglican essentials once more. Both Houses of Convention (bishops and deputies) passed the 1888 Lambeth version, committing the Episcopal Church to this summary of the faith.

After 1895, General Convention repeatedly reaffirmed the Lambeth Quadrilateral as the basis of unity with other churches. Nothing has come so far of the quadrilateral's original purpose. One fortunate by-product, however, was that the Episcopal Church did articulate repeatedly its core identity—the nonnegotiable elements that Anglicans have believed to be central to the Christian tradition.

In the struggle over modernist revisions of theology and belief in the early twenty-first-century Anglican world, the Lambeth Quadrilateral, with its brevity, was insufficient by itself to ward off unbelief. For this reason a group of Anglican leaders (mostly from Africa and Asia) issued the "Jerusalem Declaration," which we will consider in chapter 12. For the present, the Lambeth Quadrilateral may stand symbolically for all the other Anglican statements of faith, which elaborate and apply the four basic principles that the Lambeth Quadrilateral enumerates.

The Four Elements of the Lambeth Quadrilateral

Let's look at each of the four principles in turn, and see what the Anglican tradition means when it affirms them.

The Holy Scriptures

First of all, we believe in the "Holy Scriptures of the Old and New Testaments as 'containing all things necessary to salvation,' and as being the rule and ultimate standard of faith." The Scriptures are God's Word written. They are inspired, or "God-breathed," as 2 Timothy 3:16 puts it. They tell the story in the way that God wants us to hear it, and they contain "all things necessary to salvation" (a quotation from the Thirty-Nine Articles in 1571). There is no secret lore, no arcane wisdom passed down from guru to guru, inaccessible to ordinary Christians. The Scriptures tell the whole story, the entire truth about God's love for us, and about Jesus Christ saving us from sin and death. Therefore, the Scriptures are the authoritative standard for our faith and conduct. The Scriptures do not intend to pronounce on other matters, such as quantum mechanics or Chinese calligraphy. But in terms of their intended purpose, to bring us back to God, the Scriptures are utterly reliable, comprehensive, and effective. As Anglicans we are committed to teach only such doctrine and morality as can be proved from the Bible by reasonable demonstration.

The Two Creeds

Second, the Lambeth Quadrilateral states that we believe in the "Apostles' Creed as the Baptismal Symbol; and the Nicene Creed as the sufficient statement of the Christian faith." ("Symbol" is an ancient synonym for "creed.")

Why do we need the creeds if we have the Bible? Why have Anglicans listed those two ancient confessions of faith as nonnegotiable? There are at least two reasons why we need the creeds.

One is that we need a creed when we are baptized. In Holy Baptism we (or our sponsors in the case of infant baptism) promise to turn to Jesus Christ, to trust him, and to follow and obey him. But who is this Jesus? And why should we follow him? It would be very cumbersome to rehearse the entire Christian story while the congregation watches and waits. Even in the early church, there were limits to the patience of mothers and fathers and little children! So the Apostles' Creed emerged very early as the "Baptismal Symbol," the outline of the story for which people were prepared to risk their lives.

Another reason why we need the creeds is that the Bible is a huge library of books, full of history, law, prophecy, poetry, and personal letters. From very early in the Church's life, pastors and teachers recognized that Christians needed a guide to help them sort through all this wealth of material. Otherwise they might easily misinterpret it, or emphasize one passage out of proportion to the teaching of the Bible as a whole. (Without the creeds, for instance, we might go around baptizing people on behalf of the dead, which 1 Corinthians 15:29 says that some folks were doing in the 50s AD.)

Also there were many people in the early church who read Scripture through the lenses of pagan society, and conceived ideas that (as Christian leaders eventually had to declare) were contrary to the central story in Scripture. For example, one teacher in the early 300s named Arius taught that Jesus Christ was a lesser god, not equal to God the Father. The ensuing controversy caused the Council of Nicaea (AD 325) to sketch out a "Nicene Creed" that a later council polished and finalized in 381. The Nicene Creed helped the Christian movement focus on the true meaning of Scripture, and to rule out ideas (like those of Arius) that denied the full divinity of Christ.

Obviously the creeds are as necessary today as they were in the 300s. Neopagan North America is as religiously pluralistic as the Roman Empire, and people are just as hostile to the divinity and the authority of Christ today as they were then.

Baptism and the Lord's Supper

Third, the Lambeth Quadrilateral asserts the centrality of the "two Sacraments ordained by Christ Himself, Baptism and the Supper of the Lord, ministered with unfailing use of Christ's words of institution, and of the elements ordained by Him." Why are these two sacraments central to the Anglican way?

Most importantly, Jesus commanded us to do them. In the Great Commission he told his disciples to "make disciples of all nations, baptizing them in the name of the Father and of the Son and of the Holy Spirit" (Matthew 28:19). Likewise at the Last Supper he said, "Do this in remembrance of me" (Luke 22:19).

Furthermore, since the very earliest times Christians have recognized the sacraments as "visible words." The water and the bread and wine guarantee Jesus' promises. Unlike words, which are intangible, these physical objects and actions speak Jesus' love to our whole bodies. They remind us, too, that at the last day he will raise our bodies, not merely some ghostly holograph of our souls. God created the physical universe and called it good—and hence eligible to be reformed and transformed. All creation will awaken in glorious beauty at the end of the story.

Many people in the early church misunderstood this part of God's plan, and thought that salvation meant escape from their physical bodies. Despising the created universe, they also despised the earthly elements of water and bread and wine. They wanted "spiritual" sacraments (words and ideas) instead, against which the leaders of the churches had to warn people. Amazing as it may seem in materialistic North American today, many people are tempted by "purely spiritual" religions of this kind.

So the "sacraments of the gospel" not only seal and guarantee Jesus' promises to us; they also anchor us in the created universe, and warn us against trying to escape it, as in various Eastern religions. The Lambeth Quadrilateral insists that we must not only rehearse our Lord's "words of institution," but also unfailingly use the identical elements of water, bread, and wine that he employed. No "purely spiritual" sacraments! (No trendy coffee and doughnuts either).

The Historic Episcopate

Finally, according to the Lambeth Quadrilateral, we believe in the "Historic Episcopate, locally adapted in the methods of its administration to the varying needs of the nations and peoples called of God into the unity of His Church." Why do we need bishops? Are bishops really in the same league with the Bible, the creeds, and the sacraments? Why does the Quadrilateral make them non-negotiable? This question requires a rather longer explanation than the first three elements.

To understand the centrality of bishops we need to think back to the Church's situation in the late second century AD. Christians all around the Mediterranean were beginning to recognize the four Gospels and some of the Epistles as the "New Testament," building on and fulfilling God's revelation to us in the Hebrew Scriptures of the Old Testament. These Christians acknowledged that the Gospels and the Epistles represented the permanent written form of the good news that they had heard with their ears. The New Testament was beginning to give the Christian story a consistent shape, allowing believers to distinguish the true story from all the counterfeit versions in the Roman marketplace. Likewise, early forms of the Apostles' Creed were beginning to circulate, offering to new believers a thumbnail sketch of the gospel that they could memorize—and to which they pledged their lives at Baptism. But in the late second century there was still one necessary element missing. Who could legitimately expound the Scriptures? There were lots of self-professed teachers in the Roman cities, who claimed to have secret information that gave them the key to the Bible. Some of that secret lore was pretty bizarre. (We think of it now as "gnostic" from the Greek word *gnosis,* "knowledge"). So by the 190s or so, Christians were aware that they needed some way to distinguish the true Christian teachers from their gnostic rivals. Who had the true mind of Christ?

Irenaeus of Lyons was the bishop of a Christian community in southern France. He popularized the idea in the 190s that if you wanted to find the true Christian teachers—who exposited the biblical story as summarized in the creed—you should look to the bishops. In particular, you should listen to those bishops who led networks of house churches founded by the apostles, where the same story had been told and explained for five generations. These bishops were the true teachers, who had the mind of Christ. Their message was the one to which all Christians had access—not some secret lore taught by a storefront gnostic guru. So if you wanted to hear the pure apostolic teaching and its application, you should go to the bishop of Antioch, or the bishop of Ephesus, or the bishop of Rome. This teaching was the crucial third strand in the threefold cord of authority in the Christian communities: first the Bible, then the creed, and now the authorized teachers. When these three strands worked together, the early Christian movement was able to hold fast to the true story and to reject all the attempts by the Roman world to distort the gospel.

Therefore the "Historic Episcopate" was all about true teaching. The bishop is the symbol and steward of the apostles' teaching (Acts 2:42). The bishops' chief task was to pass on that teaching faithfully, while interpreting and applying the story to new cultures, in new languages. Today the historic episcopate is all about staying connected with the early Christian movement, all about continuity with the "faith that was once for all delivered to the saints" (Jude 3). From this connection flow all the Church's ministries. By the grace of the Holy Spirit, the bishop is the chief guardian of the story on earth.

You will be thinking of all sorts of questions by this time. What if the bishop tells a different story from the one that the apostles told? This problem has troubled the Church since the third century. Many bishops rejected the Council of Nicaea after 325, for example, and took the Arian position that Jesus is inferior to the Father. Many years of theological discussion had to ensue before the majority of bishops came back around to the Nicene Creed. When we say that we believe in the historic episcopate, we are not saying that we trust every bishop to get the story straight! Rather, we are stating our belief that in the long run, through the work of the Holy Spirit in the Church, councils of bishops will maintain the apostolic faith. Councils too have erred, to be sure. But those councils can be held accountable by other councils to the gospel story. What happened in Jerusalem in 2008 is a good example!

This process of mutual accountability is messy, and it takes time. Nevertheless, the Anglican tradition is committed to the principle that over time, by the work of the Spirit, the bishops of the Church will maintain the historic faith once for all entrusted to the apostles.

But what about churches that do not have bishops? Does the Lambeth Quadrilateral claim that because they lack this crucial component, they are not true churches in the fullest sense? This is a point on which Anglicans still disagree. Evangelicals, on the one hand, tend to argue that while bishops are good for the Church, maintenance of the apostles' teaching is the crucial element—and it doesn't matter so much what you call the people who symbolize and guard it. Therefore presbytery pastors and area ministers, for example, can perform the function of bishops without the name. Anglo-Catholics, on the other hand, insist strongly that the actual office of bishop is essential to the Church. There must be continuity in that office through an actual chain of consecrations back to St. Peter in the first century. Whatever view we hold, it's important to note what the Lambeth Quadrilateral actually says, namely, that the historic episcopate will be "locally adapted in the methods of its administration to the varying needs of the nations and peoples called by God into the Unity of the Church."

This wording seems to permit some negotiation about the specific structure of the office, and to allow the possibility that a denomination may be connected with the apostolic teaching without looking exactly like the Anglican Communion in its leadership.

Let's Pause and Reflect

1. Do you believe that all of the four elements of the Lambeth Quadrilateral are necessary to the life of the Church? Why or why not?

_____

_____

_____

_____

_____

2. Are there any other elements that you would add to the list, as necessary to the life of the Church? Why?

_____

_____

_____

_____

_____

_____

A Model of the Anglican Way

You may be wondering now whether the four essentials in the Lambeth Quadrilateral really make the Anglican way unique. The Roman Catholic Church affirms them all. So do the Orthodox churches. What makes Anglicans different?

For historical reasons (that we will study) the Anglican way has allowed the emergence of three distinct strands within the overall tradition: Evangelical, Anglo-Catholic, and Holiness/Charismatic. Each of these strands has emphasized certain features of biblical Christianity that are contained in the elements of the Lambeth Quadrilateral. But each strand has extrapolated from that center in different ways. I believe that the genius of the Anglican way has been its ability (so far) to hold those three strands together in creative tension. The Roman and Orthodox traditions have muted these differences. On the other hand, many Protestant denominations since the Reformation have emphasized one of the strands in isolation, and separated from their parent bodies on that basis. The Anglican way has held them together.

The model on the following page (Figure 1) will hopefully clarify the point. Notice that the Lambeth Quadrilateral stands in the center, symbolizing all the common and essential elements of the faith that all three strands profess. The two axes—vertical and horizontal—represent important issues in Anglican history on which the three strands have differed.

The _vertical axis_ represents different perspectives about revelation—about how God communicates with us. The top of the axis stands for an emphasis on God's otherness, God's transcendence, and the objective truth of the reve-

Figure 1. Model of the Lambeth Quadrilateral

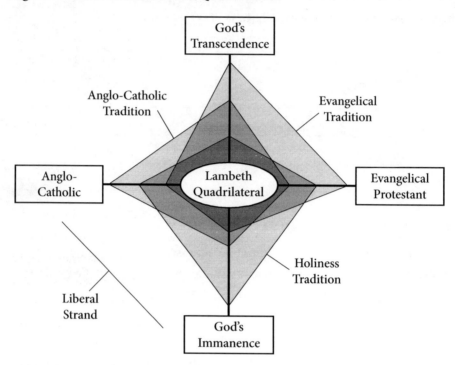

lation that God speaks and acts into creation. "For my thoughts are not your thoughts, neither are your ways my ways, says the LORD" (Isaiah 55:8). But the Lord goes on to say that "my word . . . shall not return to me empty, but it shall accomplish that which I purpose, and shall succeed in the thing for which I sent it" (Isaiah 55:11). God speaks and acts into creation. That revelation is true and effective, no matter how human beings feel about it. Scripture is objectively reliable, whether or not I feel particularly convinced by it this morning.

The bottom of the axis stands for an emphasis on God's nearness, God's immanence, and on our subjective experience of his Word. The Holy Spirit moved over the face of the waters on the first day of creation (Genesis 1:2). This same Spirit is the Counselor whom Jesus promised he would ask the Father to send, and who is now closer to Christians than our own heartbeats. Here, the stress is not so much on the objective truth of God's Word (though that remains very much the case) as on our inner experience of the Spirit and our response to the Spirit's work in our lives. God cares about how I feel. The Spirit convinces my heart that Scripture is true. And the Spirit softens my heart and strengthens my will so that I can walk in obedience to God's revelation.

Both God's transcendence and his immanence are absolutely true. But we will see that Anglican Evangelicals tend to put more weight on the former, and Anglican Holiness/Charismatics on the latter. Each one may supply a useful corrective to an overemphasis by the other.

The *horizontal axis* stands for different emphases on the way in which Christians respond to God's revelation.

The left-hand pole stands for what might be thought of as the Catholic response. This viewpoint sees the Church as a people gathered around an altar, at which a priest (ordained by a bishop in apostolic succession) celebrates the Eucharist. Christians do many other things, but around the altar they are closest to their deepest identity. Anglo-Catholic piety tends to be sacramental, to locate the Word in the midst of the Eucharist, to value multisensory worship, to stress community, and to expect that Christians will grow gradually in faith from Baptism onward, without the necessity of any "revolutionary" conversion experience.

The right-hand pole stands for what might be thought of as the Protestant response. This perspective sees the Church as a mission society, carrying the Word to the ends of the earth. Christians do many other things, but in the task of evangelism they are closest to their deepest identity. Anglican Protestant piety tends to be verbal, to view the sacraments as "visual words," to value preaching for conversion, to stress mission, and to expect that in response to the Word preached and read, Christians will undergo a radical conversion experience at some point in their lives.

Both the Catholic and the Protestant responses are faithful to the essentials of the faith. Each type encounters its own particular temptations. Catholics may fall in love with ritual and lose sight of the reality toward which it points. Protestants may become lone-ranger individualists, in love with their own private version of the Word. In neither case does the abuse invalidate the right use. Each one needs the other.

I have drawn kite-shaped figures on the model to represent each of the three orthodox Anglican traditions—the Evangelical, the Anglo-Catholic, and the Holiness/Charismatic. Each figure is centered on the Lambeth Quadrilateral. But each strand extrapolates from that center in different ways, with different emphases along the two axes. The exact accuracy of any of the kite figures, or the precise point at which each strand should be located on the two axes, is not the point. Rather, the point is to show commonality and diversity. That paradox and that creative tension are the key to the Anglican way.

The "liberal," or modernist, movement (on the bottom left), while often retaining Anglo-Catholic symbolism, ritual, and vestments, does not tend to appeal to the elements of the Lambeth Quadrilateral for its first principles. What's more, it introduces human experience as one of its basic assumptions. This point will be elaborated in some detail in chapters 10–12.

Let's Pause and Reflect

>   3. Think about this model. What would you add? What would you take out? Why?

_____

_____

_____

_____

_____

_____

The Three Anglican Traditions

Let's conclude this first chapter with a brief look at the Evangelical, Anglo-Catholic, and Holiness/Charismatic strands in the Anglican story. They are listed in this order because that's the sequence in which they appeared in history, following Henry VIII's break with Rome at the time of the Reformation. In later chapters their stories will be told in much greater detail, including how the three strands have interacted with one another.

Anglican Evangelicals

Archbishop Thomas Cranmer (1489–1556) symbolized the beginning of the Evangelical strand. With the grudging support of King Henry VIII and the enthusiastic backing of the young King Edward VI, Cranmer gave the Church of England an incomparably beautiful liturgy in his *Book of Common Prayer,* a draft confession of faith in his Articles, and an example of supernatural courage in his martyrdom at the stake in Oxford under Queen Mary.

The Puritan movement under Queen Elizabeth I (1533–1603) gave coherent shape to the Evangelical tradition, gradually looking more and more to Geneva for inspiration. Far from being an alien minority in the Church of England, by the end of Elizabeth's reign the Puritan movement represented the broad mainstream among the clergy.

The Elizabethan Puritans embodied all the characteristics of Anglican Evangelicalism, which would appear in various forms right down to the present day. First, they were Bible people. The Scriptures are God's Word written, and they contain, as we have seen, "all things necessary to salvation." While human traditions are always necessary to guide a Christian's daily life (Should I have my quiet time early in the morning or at night? And so on), nevertheless no practice should be commended as necessary to salvation, unless the Bible specifically commands it. Second, the Puritans emphasized not only the Word written, but especially the Word preached. "Faith comes by hearing," St. Paul said in Romans 10:17, and the Reformers insisted likewise. Puritans believed that the sermon was the key moment in worship, not the sacraments. The latter were meant to guarantee the promises of God, written and preached, but were not the primary means of grace. Third, the Puritans preached the cross. Later on in Anglican history, the Anglo-Catholics would stress the incarnation. Charismatics would emphasize the day of Pentecost. But for the Puritans—and for Evangelicals down to the present—the cross was the precise moment when God's work through Jesus Christ was fully accomplished. Finally, the Puritans believed in transformation. Preaching was meant to provoke conversion. Individuals should anticipate a "Great Change," a moment when they surrender fully to God (and when the promises made to the infant in Baptism come true). Individual conversion should lead to the transformation of households. And finally (the Puritans hoped and prayed) the conversion of households and villages and towns would culminate in the transformation of the English nation into the "new Israel" and the return of Christ.

In the early 1600s, the Puritans clashed with an early Anglo-Catholic movement (more on this later) and the struggle finally degenerated into the Civil

War of the 1640s. The Anglo-Catholics had no interest in the Puritans' transformationist vision, and they resisted it violently, as the Civil War broke out in 1642. Puritan General Oliver Cromwell defeated the royalist Anglo-Catholics and established a Puritan Commonwealth in the 1650s, but the experiment failed after Cromwell's death in 1658. England had not become the new Israel, and the Lord had not returned. Soon Parliament drove the Evangelical strand out of the Church—they became Baptists, Congregationalists, and Presbyterians, while the Church of England sank into a Laodicean torpor for three generations.

An Evangelical movement exploded within the Church of England in the 1730s with the preaching of revivalists like George Whitefield (1714–1770) in the British Isles and America. The revival in due time produced social reformers like William Wilberforce (1759–1833) who led the campaign against slavery in the British Empire, quickening once more the evangelical vision of social transformation. Wilberforce's generation of evangelicals also promoted the great wave of missionary evangelism that began to take the gospel to Africa, Asia, Latin America, and the South Pacific in the nineteenth century. In the United States, Episcopal Evangelicals were also committed to abolition and to world missions in the period up until the Civil War.

Eventually this wave of revival began to recede, especially when Evangelical Anglicans in England and America fell to squabbling with Anglo-Catholics over ritual and over theological issues such as baptismal regeneration. The Evangelical strand in the Episcopal Church disappeared in the 1870s, while the same tradition in England retired to its parishes and gave up its commitment to social transformation (though it continued to support missions abroad). Only after World War II did the Evangelical tradition in Britain recover its confidence, notably under leaders such as John Stott and J. I. Packer. By this time Britain was rapidly growing more and more secular, indeed was a mission field itself. The former Anglican "mission churches" of the Global South were beginning to grow astronomically in number, and by the end of the century, they were beginning to send missionaries back into the Church of England.

The Anglican Evangelical Movement

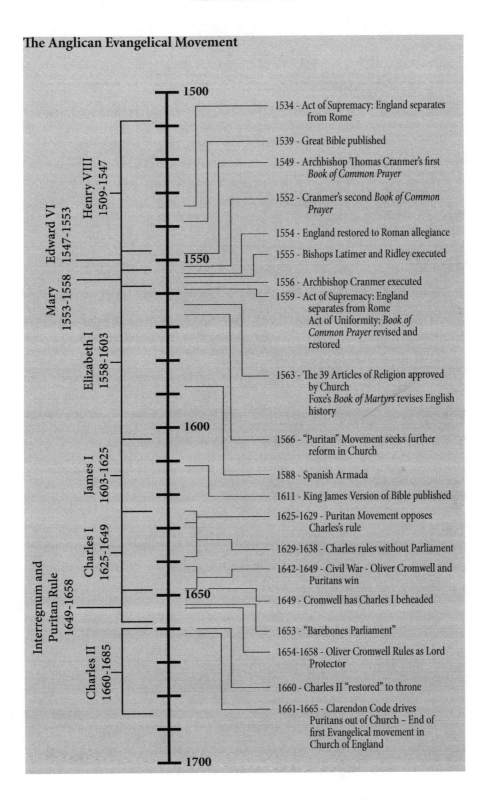

1534 - Act of Supremacy: England separates from Rome

1539 - Great Bible published

1549 - Archbishop Thomas Cranmer's first *Book of Common Prayer*

1552 - Cranmer's second *Book of Common Prayer*

1554 - England restored to Roman allegiance

1555 - Bishops Latimer and Ridley executed

1556 - Archbishop Cranmer executed

1559 - Act of Supremacy: England separates from Rome
Act of Uniformity: *Book of Common Prayer* revised and restored

1563 - The 39 Articles of Religion approved by Church
Foxe's *Book of Martyrs* revises English history

1566 - "Puritan" Movement seeks further reform in Church

1588 - Spanish Armada

1611 - King James Version of Bible published

1625-1629 - Puritan Movement opposes Charles's rule

1629-1638 - Charles rules without Parliament

1642-1649 - Civil War - Oliver Cromwell and Puritans win

1649 - Cromwell has Charles I beheaded

1653 - "Barebones Parliament"

1654-1658 - Oliver Cromwell Rules as Lord Protector

1660 - Charles II "restored" to throne

1661-1665 - Clarendon Code drives Puritans out of Church – End of first Evangelical movement in Church of England

Henry VIII 1509-1547

Edward VI 1547-1553

Mary 1553-1558

Elizabeth I 1558-1603

James I 1603-1625

Charles I 1625-1649

Interregnum and Puritan Rule 1649-1658

Charles II 1660-1685

1500
1550
1600
1650
1700

The Anglican Evangelical Movement (continued)

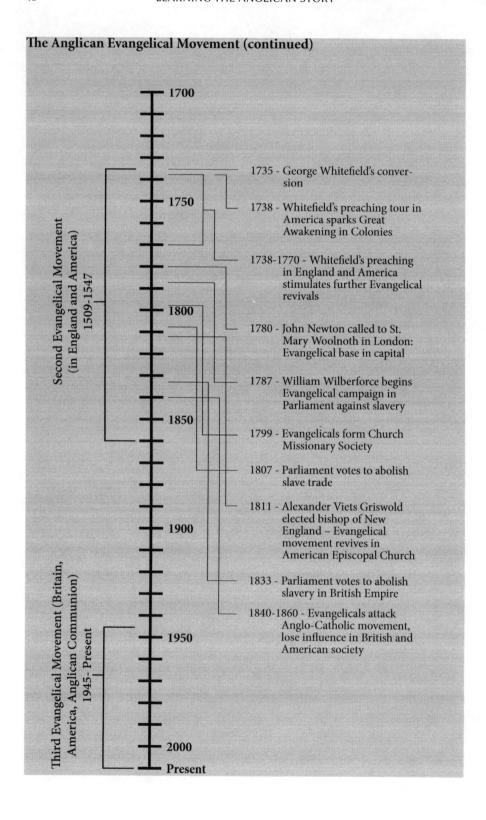

1700

1735 - George Whitefield's conversion

1750

1738 - Whitefield's preaching tour in America sparks Great Awakening in Colonies

1738-1770 - Whitefield's preaching in England and America stimulates further Evangelical revivals

1800

1780 - John Newton called to St. Mary Woolnoth in London: Evangelical base in capital

1787 - William Wilberforce begins Evangelical campaign in Parliament against slavery

1850

1799 - Evangelicals form Church Missionary Society

1807 - Parliament votes to abolish slave trade

1811 - Alexander Viets Griswold elected bishop of New England – Evangelical movement revives in American Episcopal Church

1900

1833 - Parliament votes to abolish slavery in British Empire

1840-1860 - Evangelicals attack Anglo-Catholic movement, lose influence in British and American society

1950

2000

Present

Second Evangelical Movement (in England and America) 1509-1547

Third Evangelical Movement (Britain, America, Anglican Communion) 1945- Present

Let's Pause and Reflect

> 4. Summarize the four major themes in Anglican Evangelicalism. Are there any emphases that you would add? Why?

_____

_____

_____

_____

_____

_____

_____

_____

_____

The Anglo-Catholic Tradition

An early Catholic movement in the Church of England emerged in the 1590s when some Cambridge scholars began to question the Puritans' emphasis on eternal predestination to heaven and to hell. What about texts like 1 Timothy 2:3-4, they asked, which speak of "God our Savior, who desires all people to be saved and to come to the knowledge of the truth"? Doesn't St. Paul also say in Romans 10:9 that "if you confess with your mouth that Jesus is Lord and believe in your heart that God raised Him from the dead, you will be saved"? So those who accept Jesus' good news will enjoy eternal life, and those who do not, will not. This line of thinking affirmed that we have a certain capacity to respond to God's grace, and that God's eternal decree is not the only perspective on salvation. The Dutch scholar Jacobus Arminius (1560–1609) was saying much the same thing on the Continent, and the nascent English anti-Calvinist movement took encouragement from his works.

The early Anglo-Catholics nevertheless differed from their Continental friends by adding liturgical and ceremonial interests to their theological concerns. They wondered if ugliness really was next to godliness, as the Puritan disdain for "the beauty of holiness" suggested to them. They believed that the Puritans' emphasis on the Word had gone too far, and that Word and Sacrament needed to be more intimately linked. In this regard they tried to repair the damage to English churches that Puritan iconoclasts had done, to replace Elizabethan Communion tables in the chancel with altars attached to the east wall, and to reintroduce fine silver Communion ware.

All these Catholic impulses offended most of the English population, whose anti-Roman paranoia still dwelt on the Catholic reign of "Bloody" Queen Mary (1553–1558), the Spanish Armada of 1558, and the Jesuit plot to blow up the Houses of Parliament in 1604. However, the new Stuart dynasty (James I, 1603–1625, and Charles I, 1625–1649) decided to favor the small Anglo-Catholic movement and to promote its members to high office in the Church. Archbishop William Laud (1573–1645) was the most visible and most unpopular of these prelates. His persecution of Puritan activists helped lead to the "Great Rebellion," the English Civil War of 1642–1649. But the early Catholic revival also included scholars like Bishop Lancelot Andrewes and poets like John Donne and George Herbert—collectively known as the Caroline divines since they flourished under Charles I (*Carolus I* in Latin). Despite their eminence, the Caroline divines suffered from their ties to the Stuart dynasty. When the latter lost the Civil War and Charles I lost his head in 1649, the Catholic revival went down with them.

A brief renewal of Archbishop Laud's program followed on the restoration of the Stuart dynasty in 1660. But the English aristocracy was disgusted with religious zeal in all its forms (particularly violent ones) and deeply craved a spirit of religious apathy. They turned against all "enthusiasm" (we would say fanaticism) and let the English church lapse into a slough of despond for three generations. In the mid-1700s the Evangelical movement seized the initiative, as we saw. A small minority of clergy (the "Old High Church" party) kept the Catholic vision barely alive through the eighteenth century, but its true revival would happen only in the 1830s with the Oxford and Cambridge movements.

On July 14, 1833, John Keble, the young professor of poetry at the University of Oxford, preached a sermon called "National Apostasy." Keble called into question the union of church and state that had existed for three hundred years, since Henry VIII had Parliament declare him "Supreme Head" of the

English Church. Keble recognized that Parliament was now an undeniably secular body, and he feared what a hostile Parliament might do to the admittedly corrupt and unpopular Church of England in the 1830s. Keble's proposal was that the Church rediscover its true Head in Jesus Christ, and its true authority in the apostolic succession of bishops. Other Oxford scholars like John Henry Newman and Henry Pusey joined Keble in publishing a series of ninety tracts that revived the Anglo-Catholic program of the Caroline divines (minus their devotion to the Stuart dynasty). Newman's departure for the Roman Church in 1845 effectively ended the Oxford phase of the revival.

Meanwhile in the University of Cambridge, a related movement was gathering force. An undergraduate named John Mason Neale had founded a journal called *The Ecclesiologist,* which aimed to revive the medieval glories of church architecture and ceremonial in England. Amid the "dark Satanic Mills," as the poet William Blake put it, of the early Industrial Revolution, many people yearned nostalgically for an imaginary Merrie Olde England of Robin Hood, Maypole dancing, and Yorkshire pudding. Sir Walter Scott's *Waverley* novels typified this romantic sentiment. So Neale's dream of reviving Gothic architecture appealed to a wider audience than one might have expected, given the perennial anti-Roman paranoia of English people in general. The interests of the Oxford movement had been mainly theological; the Cambridge movement presupposed these interests, but put its energy into the re-Catholicizing of worship.

The confluence of the two university movements produced modern Anglo-Catholicism. It quickly sparked bitter controversy in the Church, in Parliament, in the press, and in the country at large. Evangelicals often grew apoplectic at the specter of an international papal conspiracy that would undermine England's identity as a Protestant nation. While popular opinion did not approve of altars, bells, chasubles, holy water, and incense, nevertheless the Evangelicals behaved so badly—and the persecuted Anglo-Catholics relatively well—that by the late 1860s the Anglo-Catholic revival had vindicated its right to exist in the Church of England. The Episcopal Church in America saw a similar victory for the "Ritualists." All the features of worship that seemed "traditionally Anglican" by the mid-twentieth century (candles, colors, copes, and the like) had in fact been restored in the late 1800s after an absence of three centuries.

Let's Pause and Reflect

    5. Do you agree or disagree with the assertion that the Anglo-Catholic tradition offered a valuable compensation to an Evangelical overemphasis on *words*? Why or why not?

_____

_____

_____

_____

_____

The Holiness/Charismatic Strand

John Wesley had originally been George Whitefield's mentor in their years at Oxford, but after their conversions in the 1730s their paths began to diverge. Whitefield became an ardent Calvinist and helped revive the Evangelical tradition in England and America. Wesley's movement grew into "Methodism" in the 1740s and featured some distinct ideas that soon represented a third strand within the Anglican way. Three ideas in particular defined this new "Holiness" tradition.

First, Wesley believed that Jesus had died intentionally for the whole world, not merely for the elect. Second, Wesley noted a radical sense of joy in many of the miners and farm workers who responded to his preaching. Wesley came to identify this sense of "Christian assurance" as an important part of the Spirit's work in the Methodist movement. And third, Wesley came to believe in subsequent works of the Spirit throughout the believer's life. These further "blessings" subsequent to justification became very controversial, and Wesley struggled to define and explain them. Especially in America, though, the "second blessing" (or "blessings") defined the Wesleyan movement in the nineteenth century. We will look more closely at these three Methodist distinctives in Chapter 5.

The Holiness tradition, then, arose alongside the Church of England in the 1740s, marked by a vivid anticipation that the Holy Spirit could and would work miracles in peoples' lives. In the late 1760s, the first Methodist lay evangelists came to America as well, intending to promote Holiness teaching and experience in the colonial Church of England there. The War of Independence intervened in the 1770s. The Church of England was often on the wrong side in America, and it effectively died before the Peace of Paris ended the war in 1783. There were only twelve thousand or so communicants left in the thirteen colonies. By 1789 the new "Protestant Episcopal Church" in the United States had pulled itself together. But in the meantime, its Methodist members had watched the covered wagons trundling westward over the Appalachians, and believed that they needed to send "circuit riders" to evangelize the pioneers immediately. So in Baltimore, Maryland, at Christmas in 1784 the Methodists became a separate denomination. In England, the movement remained ambiguously alongside the Church of England until Wesley's death in 1791. His successors failed to inherit Wesley's deep loyalty to an institution that despised them, and Methodism quickly became an independent denomination in Britain as well.

During the nineteenth century in America in particular, the Wesleyan Holiness tradition grew and flourished. On the frontier, the summertime "camp meetings" offered ample opportunity for the gifts of the Holy Spirit to appear. (The upscale Episcopalians were not convinced that revivalist phenomena like the "barking exercise" really exhibited the *fruits* of the Spirit.) As the Methodist denomination grew and attracted more middle-class members in the late nineteenth century, its leaders began to forbid their pastors' participation in the exuberant Holiness revivals.

In response, after 1880 some two dozen different denominations emerged from American Methodism. Some were relatively sedate, like the Church of the Nazarene (1908). Others, like the Fire Baptized Holiness Church (1898), burned with the zeal of the old camp meeting tradition. These new churches generally believed firmly in a specific "second blessing," in which the Spirit would cleanse the believer from addiction to sin. Some leaders even taught a "third blessing" that would empower the believer for mission. (The nineteenth-century missionary wave of global church-planting was cresting at this moment.)

The crucial moment for the Holiness tradition, however, occurred on December 31, 1900, in Topeka, Kansas. At a small Bible college in that city, the revivalist preacher Charles Fox Parham had instructed his students to study the New Testament and discover whether any specific outward sign always accompanied what he assumed to be the third blessing. His students reported that in the book of Acts, the gift of tongues seemed to be that invariable and indispensable sign. Just before midnight on December 31, 1900, Miss Agnes Ozman spoke in "Chinese," which convinced Parham that she had indeed received the third blessing. The Pentecostal movement of the twentieth century was born.

The gift of tongues had appeared sporadically in modern revivals before. But now it was specifically linked to an experience that some Holiness leaders thought was the goal of Christian growth. The sign of tongues was empirical. People could tell whether you spoke in tongues or not. This sign gave the new Pentecostal revival a clear boundary, a specific membership criterion. That clarity helped the movement to spread across the globe in the twentieth century and become the fastest-growing dimension of worldwide Christianity.

After all these permutations, the Holiness/Pentecostal movement came back into the Anglican way in 1960. The Rev. Dennis Bennett of Van Nuys, California, received the baptism in the Holy Spirit and soon became a leading advocate of this piety within the Episcopal Church. About the same time, the Rev. Michael Harper in London did likewise within the Church of England. Anglicans tended to use the term *charismatic* to distinguish this revival from the nineteenth-century Holiness and the twentieth-century Pentecostal movements. Anglican Charismatics gradually moved away from the idea of separate baptisms, and saw the gifts of the Holy Spirit as a fulfillment of God's promises in the one baptismal covenant. Likewise the centrality of tongues gave way to an appreciation of the Spirit's diverse charisms. The Anglican Charismatic movement after 1960 owed much to classical Pentecostalism, but in many ways it had come back around to resemble its origins in the eighteenth-century Methodist tradition.

In the meantime the Spirit had been doing a new work in the Anglican churches in East Africa. The East African Revival broke out in Rwanda in the 1930s, and energized the rapid growth of the Anglican churches in Uganda, Kenya, and Tanganyika (Tanzania after 1961) as well. We'll look more closely at the East African Revival in Chapter 12. Suffice it to say that by the early twenty-first century, the Charismatic strand in Anglicanism had taken its place as a distinct tradition alongside the Evangelical and Anglo-Catholic strands in the worldwide Anglican Communion.

Let's Pause and Reflect

6. Do you think that the emphasis of the gifts of the Holy Spirit in the Charismatic movement is an important contribution to Anglicanism? Why or why not?

_____

_____

_____

_____

_____

_____

All three movements have remained faithful to the four essentials of the Lambeth Quadrilateral: Scripture, creeds, sacraments, and the historic episcopate. This binding force has kept the three Anglican strands together so far: not easily, not always charitably, but effectively enough. This remarkable diversity-in-unity gives the Anglican way its distinctive shape and its varied richness.

Before we study the three traditions in more detail, however, we must contemplate the first millennium of Christianity in the British Isles up until the Reformation of the sixteenth century. That period will be our focus in the next chapter.

Review

A. Summarize briefly the four nonnegotiables in our Anglican way, as expressed by the Lambeth Quadrilateral in 1888.

_____

_____

_____

_____

_____

_____

_____

_____

B. Briefly describe the essentials of the three orthodox Anglican traditions (Evangelical, Anglo-Catholic, and Charismatic).

_____

_____

_____

_____

_____

_____

_____

_____

For Thought and Application

C. Some Anglicans object to the threefold model presented in this chapter on the grounds that it presents Anglicanism as a confused muddle. These critics would often prefer to specify *one* of the three traditions as "true Anglicanism" (although they differ passionately over which one this is!). Argue for or against the idea of a valid threefold Anglicanism.

_____

_____

_____

_____

_____

_____

_____

_____

_____

_____

_____

D. How does the threefold model reflect your experience of Anglican or Episcopal parishes and dioceses?

_____

_____

_____

_____

_____

_____

_____

_____

_____

_____

_____

_____

For Further Reading

J.R.H. Moorman, *A History of the Church in England, Third Edition.*

- Chapters 1-5

Chapter 2

Christianity in the British Isles

(314–1525)

Before Christianity in England became the Church *of* England in the 1530s, the Faith had flourished in the British Isles for more than a millennium. We take time here to look at three brief pictures from this long history. I've chosen these episodes because they speak to issues that still interest us today.

Celtic and Roman Christianities

A pyramid of rock rises seven hundred feet above the dark blue waters of the Atlantic, off the southwestern coast of Ireland. The sheer-sided mountain of stone is called Skellig Michael ("St. Michael's Rock"), and the long Atlantic swells crash against its sides, shooting spray a hundred feet into the air. There are no smooth beaches, no inlets or bays, in this great rock. If you want to come ashore, you must leap from your pitching boat straight onto the cliffs themselves.

Just below the sharp summit of Skellig Michael there are dry-stone bee-hive huts where Christian monks lived for hundreds of years after the fall of the Roman Empire. Living on fish, birds' eggs, and a few vegetables grown in beds of kelp, these Irish monks worked and prayed and copied books by hand. They kept the lamps of Christian scholarship burning during a violent era when the lights were going out all over Europe. From Skellig Michael and hundreds of other tiny communities of monks and nuns, Celtic Christianity later spread throughout the British Isles and even planted outposts in the barbarian West as far away as Switzerland and Italy.

How did Christians settle in such remote and inhospitable sites as Skellig Michael, and thereby help lay the foundations of the Anglican way? The story begins with the earliest Christians in Roman Britain.

Roman legions conquered what is now England in the first century AD. Soon Roman administrators, army officers, and merchants were building comfortable villas in the rolling countryside among the native Celtic population. We don't know when the first Christians came to the island, or who they were. The tale of Joseph of Arimathea's trip to England in AD 63—carrying the Holy Grail—makes a great story but is almost surely legendary. We do know that three Christian bishops from Britain attended a Church council in southern France in 314, so there must have been house churches on the island for some decades before that. After the emperor Constantine legalized the Christian faith around this time, communities of believers could begin to meet publicly without fear of persecution. Wealthy Christians began to decorate their villas with symbols of the faith. Some of these mosaics from the fourth century still exist today.

The Romans withdrew their legions from the British Isles in the early fifth century, to plug gaps in the long frontier elsewhere. Southern Britain lay open to attacks by barbarians from across the North Sea—the Saxons and the Angles (who eventually gave that area the name Angle-land, or England). During the fifth century these invaders gradually pushed the Roman-Celtic population westward toward Cornwall and Wales, and northward into the Lowlands of Scotland.

Celtic Christianity in Ireland and Scotland

Somewhere in this beleaguered Roman-Celtic world of the early fifth century, a boy named Patricius grew up in a Christian family. His father was a deacon, but Patrick (as we know him) never showed any great interest in the faith while he was a child. One night, however, a boatload of Irish pirates swooped down on the little coastal town and carried Patrick off into slavery. For six years he shivered and starved, keeping sheep on the mountains of northwestern Ireland. But now he prayed to God, and the gospel story gave him hope. Somehow he made his way down to the southeastern coast near Waterford, probably skulking by night and hiding by day. He took passage on a boat carrying Irish wolfhounds, and made his way home to Britain. Now Patrick was on fire for the Lord, and despite his meager education, around 432 the British bishops sent him back as a missionary to the fierce pagan tribes across the Irish Sea.

The Celts in Ireland lived in small tribes at that time, more than two hundred "kingdoms" scattered throughout the swamps and forests of the rainy island. Although they traded with Roman Britain, they were wholly outside the empire. They worshiped the gods and powers of nature, whose beauty they loved and whose cruelty they feared. We don't know how Patrick told the gospel story in a way that the Irish could hear it. We do know that he valued their delight in the beauties of sky and sea and forest. Perhaps Patrick began by introducing them to the Creator, whose steadfast love lay behind the fascinating, shape-shifting, and frightening surface of the fallen world. We do know that Patrick won the allegiance of strong-willed men and women who embraced Christianity with an exuberance that was totally Irish. The story goes that Patrick baptized a young girl named Brigid. She was already a headstrong and imperious character, like the legendary Queen Maeve, and she went on to found convents that recruited hundreds of women. Another early Christian leader was Enda, who founded a monastery and a school on Inishmore, the largest of the cold and foggy Aran Islands off the west coast. Soon after this, as early as the sixth century, some enterprising monks leapt onto the rocks at the foot of Skellig Michael and clambered up to build their beehive huts under its rocky summit.

Celtic Christianity in Ireland was verbal, extravagant, and risky, like the faith of the brothers who settled Skellig Michael on the very edge of the world. They loved God, they loved the gospel story, and they loved words. Somehow they obtained copies of the Bible, the early church fathers, and even the Greek and Roman classics. There were traders who sailed out the Straits of Gibraltar into the Atlantic and linked Ireland tenuously with the Mediterranean world. The monks copied these manuscripts carefully, and also wrote down the oral histories and the poetry of the pagan Celtic past. Ireland had received Christianity freely and willingly, not under the heel of any Roman legions. Therefore, the Celtic monks felt confident enough in their new faith not to fear the old pagan religion they had left behind.

In their enthusiasm, Irish Christians often sought out those remote islands and mountains where they felt the barrier between this world and the next dissolve into gossamer mist. Going into exile, looking for places where they could almost see through to heaven, Celtic brothers and sisters often left the protection of their tribes and set out into the vast wider world. Sometimes they pushed off the shore in tiny leather boats called curraghs and let the wind and tide take them wherever the Spirit blew. Wanderers like Brendan the Navigator (d. 575) may well have crossed the Atlantic and landed in the New World. Certainly there were hundreds of Irish monks in Iceland by the tenth century.

Columba (d. 597) was another famous sea wanderer. He was a prince-priest who might have become high king had he not turned to the rugged life of a monk. Before he achieved complete sanctification, however, Columba took part in a tribal war and may actually have killed some of his enemies. He decided to go into exile with a small band of his disciples, to do penance and to calm the other tribe down a bit. The exiles rowed off in their curragh, and determined not to settle on dry land until they had lost sight of their beloved homeland. They found a suitable refuge on Iona, a tiny island off the towering purple mountains of Mull. Columba and his monks built their stone huts and

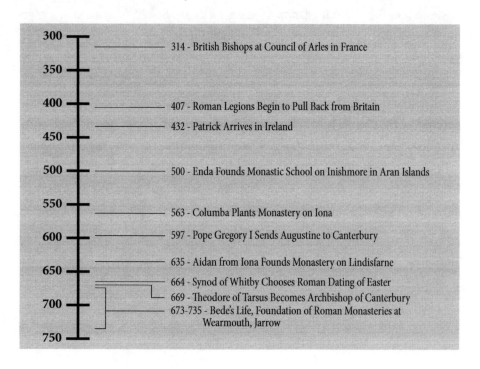

300	314 - British Bishops at Council of Arles in France
350	
400	407 - Roman Legions Begin to Pull Back from Britain
450	432 - Patrick Arrives in Ireland
500	500 - Enda Founds Monastic School on Inishmore in Aran Islands
550	563 - Columba Plants Monastery on Iona
600	597 - Pope Gregory I Sends Augustine to Canterbury
650	635 - Aidan from Iona Founds Monastery on Lindisfarne
	664 - Synod of Whitby Chooses Roman Dating of Easter
700	669 - Theodore of Tarsus Becomes Archbishop of Canterbury
	673-735 - Bede's Life, Foundation of Roman Monasteries at Wearmouth, Jarrow
750	

their chapel. But still the urge to wander stirred them to go island-hopping north and east. Columba preached the gospel to the pagan Picts at Inverness (probably not preaching to the Loch Ness monster en route, despite persistent legends to the contrary). "Christ is my druid!" Columba cried, beating the local priesthood in power encounters and miracle contests. Soon Iona became the base for a wave of evangelism all over Scotland.

On June 9, 597, Columba died on Iona, aged and deeply respected both in Scotland and even back home in Ireland. At almost the same moment, a different wave of missionary monks landed on the south coast of England near Canterbury.

The Roman Mission

A monk named Augustine (not the North African theologian) led a band of monks from Rome to evangelize the kingdom of Kent. Augustine embodied a very different Christian tradition than the Celtic missionaries in the north. For almost two centuries the church in Rome had been threatened by waves of violent barbarians who poured southward through the Alps. In the 590s Pope Gregory I concluded that the Latin church in the western Mediterranean could no longer expect help from Constantinople, where the Eastern Roman Empire continued to survive. Gregory knew that he needed to turn his attention northward, away from the Mediterranean basin, and try to find allies among the barbarian kings of Europe. An appeal from Queen Bertha of Kent offered Gregory the opening he had prayed for. Bertha was a Frankish Christian princess from the Continent, married to the fierce pagan King Ethelbert of Kent. Bertha wrote to Gregory and asked him to send missionaries to evangelize her husband (could this marriage be saved?).

Gregory chose a monk named Augustine to lead the risky mission. Augustine belonged to a community in Rome that led a very different sort of life from the brothers on faraway Iona. The monastery of St. Andrew in Rome—probably influenced by St. Benedict of Monte Cassino—lived a very orderly and regular common life. They were accustomed to authority and obedience to their "father" the abbot. They had all promised to stay put in the community that they joined, and not go wandering where the Spirit blew them (unless the abbot specifically ordered them to go). Augustine's brothers represented a

Roman model of Christianity, committed to rules and to law. It was not a bad thing in a violent world of battle-axes and barbarian blood feuds. The church in Rome had inherited the empire's genius for administration and wide-area government. This was the brand of Christianity that Augustine and his brothers carried across the English Channel to the shores of Kent in 597.

Ethelbert unexpectedly agreed to hear Augustine preach, and even more miraculously responded by giving his allegiance to Christ (whether he ever internalized the Sermon on the Mount is another matter). From their new mission base in Canterbury, Roman evangelists began to move out north and west. By the 660s Roman Christianity had planted outposts as far north as Yorkshire. But the missionaries discovered that the Celtic monks had gotten there first.

Back in the 630s a northern prince named Oswald had fled to Iona for refuge when his enemies temporarily drove him into exile. Later when he reclaimed his throne, Oswald asked the brothers on Iona to come and tell the Christian story to the peasants in his kingdom of Northumbria. A young monk named Aidan responded. Traveling southwest, Aidan planted a missionary base on the island of Lindisfarne, off the coast of northern England. From Lindisfarne the Celtic monks roved all over northern England. Oswald often went along to protect them. A wave of Celtic evangelism was pushing southward.

The Synod of Whitby

Oswald's successor Oswy continued to support the missionaries from Lindisfarne. But Oswy had married a southern princess who had grown up as a Roman Christian. In 663 the two traditions collided in Oswy's court. Celtic and Roman Christianity differed in their laws and customs, in their basic temperament, and even in their haircuts. They also followed different calendars for the Christian year. So it happened in 663 that Oswy was feasting at Easter while his wife was still fasting in Lent. This was not a recipe for domestic harmony.

Oswy decided to settle the issue between the two traditions. He called the leaders of each party to a conference in 664 at a community of monks and nuns at Whitby on the coast of Yorkshire, where they enjoyed the hospitality of the abbess Hilda. Oswy asked both sides to present their case. The Roman spokesman stood on the authority of St. Peter, who evidently kept the keys to the gate of heaven. "Is this true?" Oswy asked the Celtic monks. They could not deny it. So Oswy decided that he had better sign on with Rome, for fear of meeting an irate St. Peter at a later date. The Celtic monks gave way with (mostly) good grace and retired to Lindisfarne. They had plenty of work to do up north.

Nevertheless the English church embraced much of Celtic culture after 664. English Christianity saw a happy marriage between the two very different styles of Christianity. On the Roman side, the pope sent one Theodore of Tarsus (the city's second most distinguished son) to be Archbishop of Canterbury in 669 after the bubonic plague had killed off most of the southern leaders. Theodore imposed Roman order on the church, organizing dioceses and holding meetings and passing laws, giving the English church a national identity for the first time.

But at the same time, scholars and artists were working in the Celtic spirit—decorating exquisite books like the Lindisfarne Gospels and preserving pagan literature just as the Irish monks had done before. Some unknown poet gave the tale of Beowulf its final shape about this time. In the early eighth century, the most learned scholar in all of Europe was a monk named Bede, in a faraway village called Jarrow on the North Sea coast of England. Likewise in the early eighth century the English church began to send its own evangelists back to the Continent, where the Frankish church was violent and corrupt, and where many pagan tribes had never heard the gospel. The English church had riches to spare.

The point of the story is that very early on, in its formative centuries, Christianity in Britain showed that it could accommodate two very different strands of Christianity, to the mutual enrichment of both and to the strengthening of the whole.

Let's Pause and Reflect

1. Describe briefly the two Christian traditions (Irish and Roman) that came together in England in the late seventh century.

_____

_____

_____

_____

_____

_____

_____

King Henry II and Archbishop Thomas Becket

Let's pick up the story of English Christianity nearly five hundred years later. The golden age of the eighth century had given way to the Viking world of the ninth. Terrifying raiders from Scandinavia sailed their longships across the North Sea and around the British Isles, burning and killing and looting wherever they landed. The Vikings sacked Lindisfarne in 793. Then they sailed to Ireland and destroyed hundreds of Christian communities there. Even the hermits on remote Skellig Michael felt the sharp edge of the Viking swords. Christianity in the British Isles almost died in the Viking holocaust of the ninth century.

Eventually the Vikings stopped burning and killing. King Alfred of Wessex in southern England led his tiny army out of a swamp and defeated the Danish king, Guthrum, in 878. Alfred served as Guthrum's godfather when the surly Dane submitted to Baptism shortly thereafter (an offer he couldn't refuse). The Danes settled down in northern and eastern England and over the next three generations gradually converted to Christianity. Christian kings and warlords began to build parish churches, bequeathing them lands to support their priests. And they endowed religious communities, whose monks and nuns were to pray for their patron's soul in purgatory (more about that later). In the tenth century, the Church in England began to flourish again. Deeply rooted

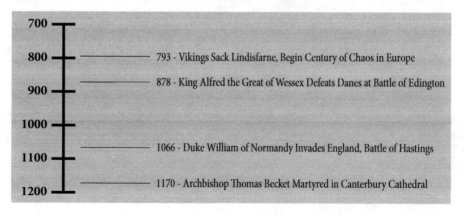

700

800 — 793 - Vikings Sack Lindisfarne, Begin Century of Chaos in Europe

900 — 878 - King Alfred the Great of Wessex Defeats Danes at Battle of Edington

1000

1100 — 1066 - Duke William of Normandy Invades England, Battle of Hastings

1200 — 1170 - Archbishop Thomas Becket Martyred in Canterbury Cathedral in the culture of the Celts, Saxons, and Danes, English Christianity was still a frontier phenomenon. English bishops acknowledged the distant authority of the pope in Rome, but otherwise had little to do with the Continent.

All this changed in 1066, when Duke William of Normandy sailed his army across the English Channel and claimed the English throne. At Hastings near the south coast he met King Harold and narrowly defeated his English army. William had invaded under the bishop of Rome's authority, flying the papal flag, and William thought of his conquest as a crusade. He intended to reform the Church in England and bring it more into communication with Christianity on the Continent.

Unknown to William in 1066, however, Christianity in Europe was about to experience one of the most violent revolutions in its history. The late eleventh century would see open warfare between popes and kings across Europe over which should rule the Church. The Norman Conquest brought England into these disputes. A hundred years later the struggle came to a head on the dark winter afternoon of December 29, 1170, in Canterbury Cathedral.

> By a stone pillar in the north transept of the cathedral stands a man in the robes of an archbishop, grasping his staff of office in his right hand. The towering cathedral is dark, for the sun has set early on this winter afternoon. Torches gutter in their brackets on the stone walls of the interior. Monks are chanting Vespers in the choir. But the service is interrupted by four drunken, roaring men in chain-mail armor. "Where is the traitor?" they shout.
>
> The thugs recoil for a moment when they see a man in robes standing by a pillar. "Here I am, no traitor, but archbishop and priest of God," replies Thomas Becket calmly. The warlords recover, and in a rush they seize him and try to drag him outside. But the crowd is too dense. So they hack at the archbishop with their broadswords where he stands. They beat him to the stone floor and split his skull. Satisfied at last, they sheathe their weapons and stalk out of the cathedral. One of them boasts, "This fellow shall rise no more." The archbishop's bloody corpse lies crumpled by the pillar.

Other than the obvious, what on earth was going on here?

Papal Sovereigns vs. Divine-Right Kings

In order to understand why King Henry II's thugs assassinated Archbishop Becket, we need to go back some four hundred years to the mid-eighth century. At this time the bishops of Rome were riding on a wave of confidence, and began to elaborate the ideology of the Church's supremacy over European society, for which Thomas Becket would give his life.

The papacy had just formed an alliance with the powerful Frankish king, Pepin. The latter had brought his armies down over the Alps, defeated the barbarian Lombards, and given a large swath of territory in central Italy to the pope as a buffer zone. King Pepin had even led the pope's horse through the city of Rome, symbolically proclaiming that even the great Frankish king was subservient to his Holiness. No wonder the popes were feeling optimistic.

In the mid-750s some enterprising clerk in the Roman hierarchy composed the famous document known as the *Donation of Constantine.* It was a forgery, but most likely the author thought that it recreated a real document that had been unfortunately mislaid. According to the *Donation of Constantine,* back in the 320s, Sylvester, the bishop of Rome, had cured the emperor Constantine of leprosy. Grateful for this miracle, Constantine had allegedly given the whole Western Roman Empire to the bishop of Rome and his successors—effectively making them emperors of the West. The bishops of Rome might delegate civil authority and military leadership to laymen if they chose. But those powers were theirs to delegate.

It wasn't totally ridiculous for the bishop of Rome to make these claims in the 750s. The old Western Roman Empire had collapsed in the fifth century, and the bishops of Rome were the only potential statesmen left in that entire area. The Germanic chieftains who carved up the West were bloodthirsty ax-wielding killers. They felt no more responsibility to their victims than a jackal would. If anyone were to resurrect civil order in the West, it would not be these brawny thugs. For instance, in the 590s Pope Gregory the Great (who sent Augustine to Canterbury) fortified and defended the city of Rome against the Lombards, another warlike Scandinavian tribe that had erupted through the Alps in the 560s. During emergencies like this, the bishops of Rome had assumed a temporary political leadership in the West. There were no other adults on the playground.

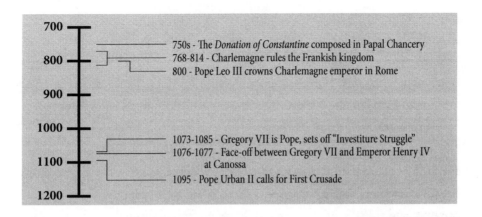

700

800 — 750s - The *Donation of Constantine* composed in Papal Chancery
768-814 - Charlemagne rules the Frankish kingdom
800 - Pope Leo III crowns Charlemagne emperor in Rome

900

1000 — 1073-1085 - Gregory VII is Pope, sets off "Investiture Struggle"
1076-1077 - Face-off between Gregory VII and Emperor Henry IV
at Canossa
1100 — 1095 - Pope Urban II calls for First Crusade

1200

However, the *Donation of Constantine* did not go unchallenged for long. In 768 the Frankish kingdom passed to Pepin's son Charles, who became the greatest monarch in the West since the fall of Rome. Charles the Great, or "Charlemagne" (768–814), was the greatest of all the Germanic warlords. He stood six feet three inches tall when other men of his time seldom topped five feet seven inches (scholars have measured his skeleton). He was a terrifying warrior. He personally led thirty military campaigns, and delegated many others. At his death his territory stretched from the English Channel southward to the plains of northern Italy, and from the high Pyrenees eastward into the forests of Germany. Charlemagne's kingdom could claim to have revived an empire in the West.

Now Charlemagne took a very different approach to the Church than his father Pepin. He proclaimed an ideology of divine-right kingship that bluntly contradicted the *Donation of Constantine*. Charlemagne claimed that God had anointed him to rule over his people's bodies and their souls as well. He did not claim to be a priest, to say Mass, or to ordain clergy. But he did assert that God had appointed him to rule over the entire outward life of the Western church. That job included appointing bishops of dioceses and abbots of monasteries. It also meant calling Church councils and defining what Christians believed. The emperor's job was to rule; the clergy's job was to pray and obey.

So it was, by the year 814, that two rival ideologies of Church leadership were at odds with each other in Europe. For the next two hundred years or so, divine-right monarchy had more success. The bishops of Rome (we'll call them "popes" for now—why is another story) fell into a long depression. They were often reduced to serving as chaplains to this or that warlord family in the city of Rome. A new dynasty of German kings in the tenth century was able to wrap itself in the magnificent robes of divine-right kingship. They appointed bishops and abbots. They oversaw the administration of the Church's lands. They commanded the knights whom the Church's lands supported. In general, they called themselves vicars of Christ.

The upstart dukes of Normandy copied the policy of the German kings toward the Church in northern France. When Duke William sailed across the English Channel in 1066, he was sporting a papal banner, but he was hoping to conquer and rule the English church in divine-right fashion.

The Investiture Struggle

In 1075, however, one of the most powerful popes in history attacked divine-right kingship head on. Pope Gregory VII (1073–1085) aimed to reassert the *Donation of Constantine* and to vindicate the pope's authority over Christendom. His plan was to snatch the Church and its lands away from their subservience to kings and dukes, and to make the papacy the true sovereign of the West. Many people suspected Gregory's motives and indeed his sanity (one saintly churchman called him "Holy Satan"), but no one denied his ability, his passion, or his determination. Gregory's revolution was one of the key turning points in Western history.

Gregory opened his campaign by attacking the cornerstone of the European rulers' control over the Church, namely, the right they claimed to invest a new bishop or abbot with the ring and staff of his office. Rulers could also withhold those symbols if they chose, and thus veto any candidate who would not loyally bring his knights to the royal army each year. Gregory attacked "lay investiture" so as to deny the lay rulers this power base in the Church. At first he scored a big victory. Emperor Henry IV of Germany (1056–1106) actually had to stand barefoot in the snow outside the castle of Canossa, where Gregory was warming himself in the winter of 1076–1077. Gregory had excommunicated Henry for hanging on to "lay investiture," and the emperor had to come and beg forgiveness. But soon Henry rallied more support, invaded Italy, and drove Gregory out of Rome into southern Italy, where the pope died, a broken man.

But the struggle went on. Ten years later, in 1095, Pope Urban II summoned what became the First Crusade. Urban's call signaled that the bishops of Rome had the power to summon great armies for purposes that they specified. Likewise in the early 1100s, the popes began to expand and develop their judicial administration in Rome. Hundreds of appellants from all over Europe were bringing their disputes over lands and titles to the pope's court for decision. Rivers of gold (in legal fees) began to flow into the papal treasury. Now the popes had the money to support their claims to sovereignty over Europe— against the titanic resistance of the kings and dukes.

Soon this struggle involved England. William the Conqueror (1066– 1085) was lucky to have had an Archbishop of Canterbury who believed in divine-right kingship. Archbishop Lanfranc backed William faithfully when the new king reorganized the English church to his own specifications. For example, William gave the Church its own judicial system, parallel to the royal courts, because the king thought that he could control the Church more easily this way. With Lanfranc's help, this plan worked more or less well. But in the early twelfth century the independent church courts became notoriously lax in their punishment of felonious clergy. Later monarchs regretted William's plan and sought to reverse it.

This brings us to King Henry II and Archbishop Thomas Becket. Over his long reign (1154–1189), Henry was determined to bring the English church under royal control. But now its leaders were inspired by Roman ideals of ecclesiastical independence, and they bluntly refused to surrender their separate judiciary. Henry's chancellor, Thomas Becket (though a deacon), had always supported his master, and Henry assumed that if Becket were archbishop, he would continue to promote the royal policy. Becket begged Henry not to proceed, and warned him that as archbishop he would certainly oppose the king and support the papal vision. But Henry shrugged off Becket's protests and the appointment went forward. Becket was ordained priest and then consecrated archbishop in 1162.

Instantly Becket switched roles. Having been the king's obedient servant, he now became the pope's forceful advocate. He utterly refused Henry's demands that "criminous" clerks be punished under the royal laws of the land.

The king grew more and more frustrated. Finally in late 1170 he cried out, "Will no one rid me of this troublesome priest?"

Four of Henry's knights heard his outburst, and decided to act on it. They traveled to Canterbury, and on December 29, 1170, they butchered Becket in his cathedral. True to his latest role, Becket died as a martyr for the independence of the Church, and for the pope's vision of its sovereignty over Europe.

What *should* the Church's relationship to civil society actually be? We will watch this issue come up again and again as the Anglican story unfolds.

Let's Pause and Reflect

    2. Describe briefly the two rival ideologies of sovereignty in the early medieval Western world, "papal primacy" and the "divine right of kings."

_____

_____

_____

_____

_____

_____

_____

Peasants and Purgatory

Now three centuries have passed since the murder of Thomas Becket in Canterbury Cathedral. It's the year 1470. The kings of England and the popes have long since reached a profitable compromise. The kings have agreed to allow the popes to appoint two English bishops (out of sixteen) and a long list of minor church officials. The lucky winners draw salaries from these posts, but never travel from Italy to England to serve their flocks. In return the popes concede that the kings may appoint their own officials to the other bishoprics, and to the many minor posts under royal patronage. The English church still retains its own courts. But the kings are satisfied, because they can staff their own administration with churchmen whom they don't have to pay. Almost all of these bishops, archdeacons, deans, and so forth are trained in law, not in theology or (heaven forbid) pastoral care. They delegate their "cure of souls" to poorly paid substitutes. Often these royal churchmen accumulate half a dozen church posts or "livings" and siphon off most of their endowed income. Absentee pastors at the top set a poor example for the under-shepherds of Christ's flock. Midway down the ladder of promotion in the Church, ambitious would-be prelates also pile up as many plural "livings" as they can. The leadership of the English church is not focused on the pastoral needs of the lower 95 percent of the population.

Nor do the leaders recognize the spiritual problems that the peasants and artisans are suffering, due to the actual teaching of the Church at the grassroots level. Let's take a look at a peasant family in East Anglia (say a hundred miles northeast of London) in the year 1470. What sort of gospel are they hearing from their poorly paid and scarcely trained local priest?

There is a tiny village on a ridge over the flat green marshes of the fen country near Norwich. The hamlet of Burnaby stands on a rise of land some twenty feet higher than the marsh. There are sixteen thatched cottages, their walls made of mud spread over a latticework of sticks and branches. Smoke pours through the roof holes as the farmwives prepare the meager evening meal for their families. The men of the village are still at work fishing or setting traps for birds. As the sun touches the western horizon, a light breeze from the southwest carries the faint sound of church bells in Norwich, ringing the Angelus. At the sound the weather-beaten peasants straighten up, cross themselves, and begin to trudge home to supper.

In her one-room hovel, Martha stirs the gruel and swats a scrawny dog away from the iron pot over the fire. Martha's latest baby tugs at the hem of her mother's filthy gown. Martha is thirty-two years old. She is nearly toothless, and bent over from her nine exhausting pregnancies. Of the nine babies, only four survive—a boy of twelve, two girls (nine and five), and the youngest, another boy. Martha has never had enough milk to nurse her infants for long. Her diet consists mostly of gruel, with the occasional fish or bird. So Martha's babies have never had much to eat, and five of them have died be-

fore the age of two, about average for Burnaby village. The surviving children have bellies distended from hunger, and sores on their dirty limbs. There are doctors in Norwich, but who can afford them?

Martha's life is empty with hunger, and also haunted by fear. There are rumors of plague again in Norwich, carried (though Martha does not know it) by fleas on the same kind of rats that scrabble in the wet straw of her hovel. Martha thinks that the plague is caused by evil spirits that infest the marshes, and occasionally attack the village at the instigation of some witch. Martha feels defenseless, harried, and hopeless. Her eyes are hollow above her sunken cheeks. She stirs the gruel listlessly, waiting for her husband Will to come crouching through the low doorway.

On Sundays and saints' days, Will, Martha, and the children sometimes trudge seven miles into Norwich. Their parish church is St. Margaret's by the marketplace, with its tall Gothic spire and its pointed stained glass windows. On the stone walls inside, in the dim smoky interior, there are gruesome paintings, many of the last judgment. Will and Martha shudder as they look at the terrible demons that drag everyone (rich and poor, merchant, noble-man, and peasant) down into the fiery mouth of hell. The prospect of torment for all eternity stares them in the face every time they go to church.

They go to Mass to escape that horrible future. Every Sunday the parish priest explains to his flock that Mother Church offers a way out of hell. You need not look forward to an eternity of agonizing torture. To be sure, the Great Bookkeeper in the sky is constantly recording your deeds, good and bad. Ninety-nine people in a hundred will die with a large excess of sins on their record. But as long as you do not die with an unconfessed mortal sin on your conscience, you will not go straight to hell. Rather you will spend a long time—maybe thousands of years—in "purgatory." There the cleansing (but very hot) flames will burn away all your impurities, and at last you should be clean enough to approach the gates of heaven in some hope.

Purgatory is no picnic. The parish priest stokes its flames to hellish tem-peratures. But again Mother Church has a remedy. You can escape purgatory as well. You may burn a candle to St. Margaret by a side altar, asking her to pray for you, and maybe she will have your sentence reduced. Or you can pay for a Mass to be said for your benefit. Better still, you can make a pilgrimage to the shrine of Our Lady in Walsingham, west of Norwich. If you pray at the altar there, perhaps the Virgin may persuade the Great Bookkeeper to let you off purgatory altogether. Finally, if all else fails to reassure you, you can buy an indulgence, a piece of paper that reduces your sentence by so many years, depending on the size of the indulgence that you can afford to buy.

The Church offers many ways out of purgatory, says Master Woodman. It all depends on what you can afford to pay. No wonder that Martha and Will trudge home, backs bent and faces still hopeless. They can't afford even a single candle.

By 1470 the Roman Church had been teaching the existence of purgatory for almost a thousand years. The argument was that most people die with more sins than good deeds on their record, and that God must have foreseen this problem and provided a solution. In the late Middle Ages, the teachers of the Church expounded the doctrine of purgatory like this: They argued that Christ and the saints had done more good works than they strictly needed to get into heaven themselves. These extra merits accumulated in a treasury in heaven. Since our Lord had given Peter the keys to heaven, his successors the popes could unlock that treasury and dispense those merits at their discretion. If you needed some extra credits on your record, or if someone you designated (say, a loved one) needed help, you could appeal to his Holiness and have some merits transferred. The normal device for this transaction was an "indulgence." At the village level, people thought of indulgences simply as "pardons," which you could even purchase in advance of a sin that you planned to commit. Chaucer's *Canterbury Tales* in the late fourteenth century described an indulgence sales-man (a "pardoner") with a satchel full of pardons "all hot from Rome." You can imagine the amount of superstition and corruption that this trade afforded.

Another depressing feature of late medieval theology was the burden it placed on you to do your very best before God would help you. Medieval theo-logians anticipated Ben Franklin's travesty of the gospel, "God helps those who help themselves." The Church taught that the sacraments (and especially the Mass) offered "grace" in the form of power to do good works. The more power you had, the more good works you could do, the less time you would spend in purgatory, and the fewer indulgences you needed to buy. Sounds great. The catch was that unless you came to the Mass fully prepared, having done your absolute best to live a good life, the Mass would not help you. No grace would come to you. One English theologian in the late fourteenth century said, "God will not deny grace to those who do their best." But how could you do your best all the time? Indeed, how could you know whether you had done your best at any time at all?

One way of guaranteeing your place in heaven was to leave behind some visible monument of your piety, like a stained glass window, an additional chapel attached to your parish church, or if you were exceedingly wealthy, a whole new church building. And you could leave behind you endowments that would provide for priests (ideally in your new chapel or church) to say Masses for the speedy exit of your soul from the fires of purgatory. East Anglia (the counties of Norfolk, Suffolk, and Essex northeast of London) is dotted with "wool churches" that prosperous wool merchants built especially in the fifteenth century. Many of these are gems of late medieval "perpendicular" Gothic architecture, such as the parish churches at Lavenham and Long Melford in Suffolk. The "do it yourself" theology of salvation was not wholly repressive and deadly, but could produce great works of architectural beauty.

Likewise, people who hungered for teaching and guidance could occasionally take matters into their own hands, and produce their own "education materials." Think of the wonderful "mystery plays" that groups of merchants in some larger towns wrote and performed for the edification of the whole populace (or even the passion play still being performed once per decade at Oberammergau, Germany). The city of York currently puts on a cycle of about eighteen twenty-minute pageants, each produced by a different civic group (merchants, parishes, drama students, and so on), and performed in a public park. Each pageant uses medieval costumes and medieval music on authentic instruments, but with three narrators telling the stories in modern English. Altogether the eighteen plays survey the whole biblical story from creation to the Lord's future return. In sufficiently wealthy towns like York in the fifteenth century, these "mystery plays" ensured that people had at least a general familiarity with the Bible.

But what about the 95 percent of the population that lived in rural villages, or who walked to church in a nearby village or small town? What was their mental picture of Jesus, or of the future that awaited them after death? What did they see painted on the walls of their church? The Church's teaching at this grassroots level was less than comforting to ordinary rural peasants like Will and Martha. It certainly generated revenue for the Church's coffers. Indulgences built cathedrals. But it was also setting the Church up for the Reformation that would come in the early sixteenth century.

Let's Pause and Reflect

3. What was the Western church's teaching about salvation in the fifteenth century? How did this teaching support the sale of indulgences?

_____

_____

_____

_____

_____

_____

_____

_____

_____

Review

A. In the long twelve-hundred-plus years of Christianity in England before the Reformation, from roughly 300 to 1500, what kinds of relationship do we see between kings and the Church? Say a few words especially about the following monarchs: Oswy of Northumbria, Alfred of Wessex, Henry II, and the kings of England after 1300 or so.

_____

_____

_____

_____

_____

_____

_____

_____

_____

_____

B. Think about pastoral care at the parish level in the fourteenth and fifteenth century. What were its strengths and weaknesses?

_____

_____

_____

_____

_____

_____

_____

For Thought and Application

C. The late medieval church taught that "works" were necessary to salvation. You had to "do your best" in order that the sacraments of penance and the Mass would give you "grace" to do more good works. The higher your good works score at the end of your life, the less time you would need to spend in purgatory, and the sooner you would get to heaven. Do you believe this teaching—or some form of it? If not, what do you think is the place of "works" in the process of salvation? Why?

_____

_____

_____

_____

_____

_____

_____

_____

_____

_____

_____

_____

D. In the Middle Ages, everyone thought that Christian society was—and ought to be—structured hierarchically. Society was like a pyramid, with the lower 95 percent or so made up of peasant farmers and rural clergy, another 3 percent above them made up of merchants and town clergy, and then 2 percent noble warlords and higher clergy (deans, abbots, and bishops) led by a few dozen super-warrior nobles. At the very top was the monarch—either the king or the pope, depending on the balance of power at any given time. Do you think that society ought to be structured hierarchically? Why or why not? Why do you suppose people thought this way in the Middle Ages?

_____

_____

_____

_____

_____

_____

_____

_____

For Further Reading

J.R.H. Moorman, *A History of the Church in England, Third Edition.*

- Chapters 6-10

Chapter 3
The English Reformation
(1525–1603)

Everyone agreed that the medieval church in England was corrupt and needed reform. Even successful careerists called for institutional repentance—for example, the famous scholar John Colet, Dean of St. Paul's Cathedral in London. But religious institutions are very resistant to change. In any event, Reformation came to the English church in a very messy way, through a combination of pressures from the (reluctant) king himself and from his Protestant subjects.

Reformations from Above and Below

We are standing in the marketplace of a small town near Brussels, Belgium, on October 6, 1536. On all four sides of the cobblestoned square you can see tall brown and white, half-timbered houses where the wealthy merchants live. The morning sunshine is bright, with only a few fleecy clouds in the blue sky. The merchants' stalls in the marketplace offer goods from all over Europe. You can smell the pleasant odor of bread baking and chestnuts roasting, along with earthy hints of animal dung and unwashed bodies. The market is crowded with peasants in dirty smocks, soldiers in leather jerkins, and merchants in dark cloaks with their wives in gray homespun and white aprons.

But amid the noise and bustle of an ordinary market day, an ominous hush falls in the center of the square. A blackened stake rises from a pile of logs and bracken. Four soldiers are tying a man to the stake, while the crowd grows silent. The prisoner is a gaunt, black-bearded man of forty, wearing only a loincloth. His white body shivers as the soldiers chain him to the stake. When the guards finish tying him and step back, the man turns his eyes upward and cries, "O Lord, open the king of England's eyes!" Then an executioner in a black hood reaches around the stake and strangles the prisoner with a knotted rope, while the guards light the fire.

The prisoner at the stake that October day was an Englishman named William Tyndale. The local Catholic authorities were executing him for translating the New Testament into English. Why was that a crime? And why did Tyndale cry with his last breath, "Open the king of England's eyes"?

You probably know about King Henry VIII and his six wives ("divorced, beheaded, died, divorced, beheaded, survived"). And you will recall that Henry broke with the Roman Church so that he could marry number two, Anne Boleyn. What's not so well known is that Henry's marital woes allowed the Evangelical strand in the Anglican way to emerge, and that the English Bible was the centerpiece of that tradition. Without Henry, the English church may not have become a distinct branch of Western Christianity. But without heroes and martyrs like William Tyndale, that church would not have embraced the Reformation or appealed to the Bible as the standard for its faith and life. Let's take a look at both Henry VIII and William Tyndale, and see what each of them contributed to the English Reformation.

The Reformation from Above

As a teenager, Henry had married Catherine of Aragon, the widow of his deceased elder brother Arthur. Their father, Henry VII, had wanted to hang on to his alliance with Spain, which the marriage cemented. It was technically contrary to church law for a brother to marry his sister-in-law like this. It was also customary for popes to sell waivers to the European nobility to do so when they needed to—as now. So Pope Julius II had granted a "dispensation," and Henry and Catherine got married. For a while their marriage was a happy one, and Catherine gave him a baby daughter in 1516. But Henry needed a legitimate male heir. He knew that without an acceptable heir to the throne, England would collapse back into the Wars of the Roses that Henry VII had ended in

1485. When Catherine failed to produce the much-desired son, and when she passed beyond the age of childbearing in the 1520s, Henry began to worry. He asked the present pope to annul the marriage on biblical grounds, claiming that Pope Julius should never have granted the dispensation in the first place. Unfortunately the pope at the time, Clement VII, was a prisoner of the German emperor Charles V. And Charles was Catherine's nephew. At Catherine's urgent plea, the pope stalled and stalled. Meanwhile Henry fell in love with a pert young lady named Anne Boleyn. In January 1533 Anne conceived a child. Now Henry needed an annulment fast.

Even if Clement VII had agreed, Henry would probably have still thrown off his allegiance to Rome. Henry had been reading about Charlemagne and about divine-right kingship. He had begun to think of himself as the earthly head of the church in England, with the same responsibility for his subjects' souls that Charlemagne had claimed in the late eighth century. Henry wanted to end the compromise that his forebears had struck with the papacy in the thirteenth century—the deal by which the king and the pope had split the revenues from the English church. Henry wanted the whole pie. And now the example of Charlemagne convinced him that the whole pie was rightly his.

Because Anne Boleyn was pregnant and Henry had cast himself in the role of Charlemagne, the church *in* England threw off its allegiance to Rome and became the Church *of* England. Henry's new Archbishop of Canterbury, Thomas Cranmer, annulled Henry's marriage to Catherine of Aragon and blessed the king's marriage to his (temporarily) beloved Anne. At this point, Henry had no desire to become a Protestant. He was a conservative, late medieval Catholic who believed in purgatory, Masses for the dead, indulgences, and the lot.

But Henry needed political support among the English aristocracy for his radical break with Rome. And some of them were Protestants. In particular, he needed the help of his chief minister Thomas Cromwell. Cromwell was a master politician. He had engineered the laws in Parliament that had made Henry the Supreme Head of the English church. But Cromwell was also a Protestant. So Henry had to allow Cromwell and his ally Thomas Cranmer to push the Church of England in a Protestant direction for a time, in the 1530s. This was where Tyndale came in.

The Reformation from Below

Tyndale was an Oxford graduate, a priest, and a scholar who had begun to read forbidden Lutheran books soon after the German Reformer wrote his famous Ninety-five Theses in 1517. Tyndale discovered the great Reformation truth of justification by grace through faith. As Paul wrote in Romans 1:17, those who are right with God ("the just") receive the favor of his love "by grace" and by trusting in that love "by faith." There is no need to try and climb a ladder to heaven by good works. There is no need to "do your very best" to win God's favor. The moment you put your trust in Jesus, you are as completely beloved by God as you will ever be. Of course, the Holy Spirit will help you to clean up your life. But your relationship with God depends totally on his initiative and not on your obsessive striving to please him.

This great biblical truth changed Tyndale's life. He was determined that everyone in England should hear it too. There was no need for people like Will and Martha of Burnaby to go on suffering. The trouble was that over a hundred years earlier, the English church had outlawed Bibles in English. The bishops had been frightened by the Oxford reformer John Wyclif in the 1370s, whose followers had produced an early English Bible. The bishops were anxious lest the lower classes in England contrast the rich and arrogant institutional church with the early Christian communities in the book of Acts. Tyndale's chances of getting permission for a new English translation were vanishingly slim.

Tyndale fled to Germany as a result. Secretly, and in great danger to himself, he managed to publish an English New Testament in 1525. He smuggled the copies back into England in bales of imported woolen cloth. The bishops at home burned the books as fast as they could find them. Finally the Roman Catholic authorities caught up with Tyndale in Belgium, where Bibles in the local tongue were also illegal. So it was that Tyndale's last cry was, "O Lord, open the king of England's eyes!" The English people could not read the gospel in their native language until Henry VIII changed his mind.

Three years later Henry gave in to Thomas Cromwell and Archbishop Cranmer and authorized a "Great Bible" in English. He commanded that copies be placed on the lecterns in all the nine thousand parish churches, where any literate person could come and read the gospel out loud to anyone who might listen.

In a couple of ways, then, Henry VIII did found the Church of England. His need for a male heir provoked the break with Rome. He did permit the initial steps that introduced the Church to Protestant Christianity. But without the Reformation from below, without heroes like Tyndale and brave Crown servants like Cromwell and Cranmer, the Protestant option would never have had a voice.

The Early Evangelical Tradition

Tyndale's faith helps us grasp the spirit of the Anglican Evangelical tradition that he helped to found. First, Tyndale was wholly committed to the authority of the Bible. The gospel had given him liberty, and without the Bible he would never have heard the gospel. He believed that the Bible is God's message to us, and tells us everything that we need to know about his love. Obviously the Bible does not teach on subjects extraneous to this message, like modern astrophysics or the engineering that built the Egyptian pyramids. Its purpose is to tell us the story of God's love. It does this comprehensively, teaching us "all things necessary to salvation." As God's word to us, it is objectively true no matter how I may feel about it today.

Second, Tyndale believed that the heart of the Christian story is the cross. He wrote, "We believe the promises of God without wavering, how that God is true, and will fulfill all his good promises to us, for Christ's blood's sake." Jesus' death on the cross has covered all of our guilt, and reconciled us to God effectively and completely.

Third, Tyndale's New Testament provided the basis for another great Evangelical conviction—that preaching the gospel must be central to Christian ministry, and preaching must aim for conversion. Tyndale's Protestant generation did not undervalue the sacraments of Baptism and the Lord's Supper. But, like Bishop Hugh Latimer, they knew that only the Word of God could reach the heart, and open closed hearts to the love of God. Only a revolutionary conversion could turn us from apathy or fearful striving to a confident faith in Jesus. The sovereign Word in the mouth of the preacher—forcefully applying the Word written—was God's anointed instrument for the work of conversion in the heart of the believer.

Finally, Tyndale's faith expressed the Evangelical emphasis on God's sovereignty and on his power to transform the world. The Lord *could* open the king of England's eyes, and turn the Bible loose. Later we will notice how Anglican Evangelicals have persisted in expecting God to transform society. Not that Tyndale was a radical social reformer. He believed in the medieval ideal of a hierarchical society, with a divine-right monarch at the top. In fact, Tyndale wrote the book that persuaded Henry VIII that he was Charlemagne! Two principles of authority were at odds in Tyndale's thought—Holy Bible and holy king. We'll see how those two principles went on colliding in the centuries to come. Eventually the Evangelical tradition would jettison Tyndale's loyalty to the holy king. But in the meantime there would be much wrangling over these issues.

Let's Pause and Reflect

1. Describe briefly the reasons why King Henry VIII cut England off from the pope's jurisdiction in 1533–1534.

_____

_____

_____

_____

_____

2. What were the chief characteristics of the early Evangelical movement, the backbone of the "Reformation from below," in the 1520s and 1530s?

_____

_____

_____

_____

_____

Elizabeth I and the Middle Way

On Saturday morning, January 14, 1559, the twenty-five-year-old Eliz-abeth Tudor rode in a chariot through the city of London to Westminster, where she would be crowned queen the next day. The streets had been newly graveled to make them less treacherous than usual. The half-timbered build-ings along the way were hung with banners. Elizabeth's triumphal procession stretched for several hundred yards. Before the princess rode the nobles of the realm and the bishops of the Church. Behind her were the ladies-in-waiting, dressed gorgeously in velvet with sleeves lined with gold.

The crowds of Londoners in the streets were eager above all to see the princess. She wore a mantle fashioned from twenty-three yards of gold and silver cloth trimmed with fur. Elizabeth was tall and stately, with red-gold hair, an oval face, and clear skin. Her hands were lovely—long, slender, and graceful, and constantly in motion as she smiled and acknowledged the cheers of the crowd. Her poise and her graciousness in public reminded older people of her father as a youth. Elizabeth smiled especially warmly when she heard one old man cry, "Remember good King Henry the Eighth!"

Along the way to Westminster there were many displays and tableaux, and the princess stopped her chariot often to hear speeches by allegorical fig-ures. At one street corner, a tableau featured Deborah, the judge of Israel sitting under an artificial palm tree. The speaker emphasized Deborah as a worthy model for a princess to emulate. A special round of applause went up when a child representing Truth gave Elizabeth an English Bible. With an astute sense of drama, the princess kissed the book and held it to her bosom, and in a clear voice promised always "to be a diligent reader thereof."

Scarcely two months had passed since Queen Mary Tudor had died of can-cer, the "Bloody Mary" of later legend who had taken England back to Roman Catholicism. Mary's marriage to King Philip of Spain, their commitment of England's poor resources to Spain's European wars, and Mary's execution by fire of nearly three hundred Protestants had soured public opinion toward the queen. The English people were still by no means Protestant in the 1550s, but the courageous death of the martyrs made them jaded toward Spanish Catholicism. On January 14, 1559, the nation was still technically subject to the pope. But the tableaux lining the streets of London implied a Protestant shift in the religious winds.

The princess who became Elizabeth I was a serious Protestant, who nearly died for her faith under her sister Mary's harsh rule. But Elizabeth was also a politician to her fingertips. She recognized acutely her weakness as a ruler in 1559. She had no standing army, her treasury was empty, she was at war with France (thanks to Mary) and dependent on Spain for defense, and she was the wrong sex.

Europe expected rulers to be male. Mary Tudor had married Philip of Spain, and everyone looked for Elizabeth to choose a mate who would rule. Elizabeth had all her father's imperious personality, and despite flirtations, she had no intention whatsoever of sharing her reign. But she had to move cautiously and catlike.

A Protestant by conviction, she could not afford to offend arch-Catholic Spain. The majority of her subjects were still traditionalists, not very enthusiastic about Rome but still skeptical about Protestantism. The Bible had been loose in England for twenty years, but it had a long way to go before it took root in people's hearts. Most English people were still more comfortable with Latin Masses than they were with Protestant sermons. Elizabeth needed to give the traditionalist majority some leeway, so as not to split the nation into warring religious factions and invite a Spanish invasion.

The Elizabethan Settlement

Beginning in 1559 Elizabeth worked out a solution that made the Church of England solidly Protestant in its teaching, but left its medieval Catholic structure largely intact and provided a reassuring continuity with the ceremonies of the late Middle Ages. In 1559 Parliament passed an Act of Supremacy that made Elizabeth "Supreme Governor" of the Church, reviving her father's authority while avoiding his questionable adoption of Christ's headship. Meanwhile, an Act of Uniformity mandated the use of the English Prayer Book that Archbishop Cranmer had published in 1552. The latter had been a very Protestant book, and Elizabeth made only a few concessions to Catholic sensibilities in her 1559 revision (praying against "the bishop of Rome and his detestable

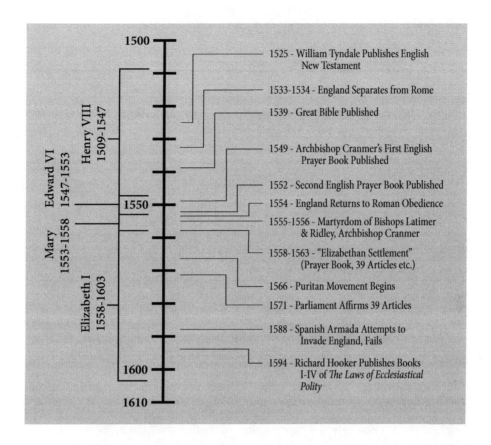

Henry VIII 1509-1547
Edward VI 1547-1553
Mary 1553-1558
Elizabeth I 1558-1603

- 1500
- 1525 - William Tyndale Publishes English New Testament
- 1533-1534 - England Separates from Rome
- 1539 - Great Bible Published
- 1549 - Archbishop Cranmer's First English Prayer Book Published
- 1550
- 1552 - Second English Prayer Book Published
- 1554 - England Returns to Roman Obedience
- 1555-1556 - Martyrdom of Bishops Latimer & Ridley, Archbishop Cranmer
- 1558-1563 - "Elizabethan Settlement" (Prayer Book, 39 Articles etc.)
- 1566 - Puritan Movement Begins
- 1571 - Parliament Affirms 39 Articles
- 1588 - Spanish Armada Attempts to Invade England, Fails
- 1600
- 1594 - Richard Hooker Publishes Books I-IV of *The Laws of Ecclesiastical Polity*
- 1610

enormities" had been a bit much). At the same time, nothing in 1559 changed the structure of the English church, with its bishops and dioceses, priests and parish churches. Elizabeth took care that her new archbishop, Matthew Parker, be consecrated by the standard three bishops in apostolic succession. She prescribed (with characteristic lack of specificity) that clergy should wear at least some of the traditional vestments. Her aim overall was to provide a Church in which traditionalist Catholics could worship more or less comfortably, until such time as Protestant preaching would convert their minds and hearts to the truth of the gospel.

Elizabeth's subsequent policy made it clear that the theology of the English church would be explicitly Protestant. In 1563 the Church's legislative assembly approved a statement of belief called the Thirty-Nine Articles of Religion. Originally drafted by Archbishop Cranmer in 1553, the Articles express a firm commitment to the authority of Scripture. Article 6 says:

> *Holy Scripture containeth all things necessary to salvation: so that what-soever is not read therein, nor may be proved thereby, is not to be re-quired of any man, that it should be believed as an article of Faith, or be thought requisite or necessary to salvation.*

Likewise, the Articles teach very plainly the Protestant confidence in Christ alone for our salvation.

> *We are accounted righteous before God, only for the merit of our Lord and Saviour Jesus Christ by faith, and not for our own works or deserv-ings. (Article 11)*

There is nothing that we can do, there is nothing that we need to do, in order to enjoy God's love. Jesus has done everything that was necessary on the cross. All we have to do is to trust him.

The *Via Media:* A Causeway, Not a Bridge

It is important to understand that the Elizabethan Settlement was a *via media* (middle way) but not in the sense of a wishy-washy compromise between two equally valid alternatives. (This was a late nineteenth-century myth about the Anglican way.) Nor did the *via media* mean simply "whatever" (a late twenti-eth-century myth about the Anglican way). Rather, Elizabeth intended that the English church embody the central biblical truths of Christianity that are the heart of the gospel. She was seriously in earnest when she kissed the English Bible as she rode to Westminster for her coronation. So the *via media* was not a "bridge" between (say) nineteenth-century Roman Catholicism and (say) nine-teenth-century American Methodism—let alone a license for New Age subjec-tivism. A better metaphor for Elizabeth's intentions would be a causeway across a marsh, with treacherous swamps on either side. Elizabeth feared both the murky superstition of late medieval piety on the one hand and the subjective individualism of many radical reformers on the other ("me, my Bible, and the Holy Ghost"). She meant her Church to be a rock-solid causeway for the King's Highway, leading her subjects safely across the swamps of error toward the City of God. We do well to remember Elizabeth's intentions when we hear modern-ist Anglicans claim that the Anglican way has "no core doctrine," and that *via media* means dialogue is a substitute for truth. Still less should we pay attention to revisionist bishops who allege that "since the Church wrote the Bible, the

Church can rewrite it." Nothing could have been further from Elizabeth's mind when she kissed the English Bible on that January day in 1559.

Let's Pause and Reflect

3. What were the main features of the Elizabethan Settlement?

_____

_____

_____

_____

_____

4. Why is it more accurate to describe Elizabeth's *via media* as a causeway rather than a bridge?

_____

_____

_____

_____

_____

The Elizabethan Puritans

Not all of Elizabeth's subjects were content to wait patiently with her while Protestant preaching converted the traditionalist majority. Many "hot Protestants" believed that the biblical theology of the Thirty-Nine Articles was good but was not enough. They wondered what was the use of godly theology on paper, while the clergy's attire (for example) told the laity that nothing had really changed? How could Her Majesty require that the clergy wear the white surplice as if they were still priests saying Masses? Wasn't the Church sending mixed signals and actually inhibiting the Bible's work in people's hearts? In the 1560s a small group of zealous "Puritans" emerged within the Church of England. They loved and needed Elizabeth as the "new Deborah," and they realized acutely that the alternative was Philip II of Spain. Yet the queen frustrated the Puritans terribly. They wanted a pure and zealous Church, and they wanted it *now*. It's no wonder that the queen and the Puritans drove each other to distraction.

The little town of Maldon lies some forty miles northeast of London on the River Blackwater. In the year 1585 it is a typical market town, crowded with animals whose lowing and bleating competes with the cries of vendors selling oysters, pies, and cheese. Maldon is an ancient town, ringed with Saxon earthworks that remind the citizens of the famous battle there against the Vikings in 991. The famous Beeleigh Abbey stands a mile outside the town, its early English chapter house a jewel of the countryside, rising from the marshes. The Church is deeply rooted in the life of Maldon. Every citizen is a member of the parish.

There is not much life in that parish church, however, at least in the opinion of some. Master Robert Palmer is the vicar, and some of his flock claim that he spends most of his time in the bowling alley in his orchard "daily and weekly . . . with a great sort or swarm of men." When it rains he allegedly plays backgammon in the New Inn. Hot Protestants are not happy with Master Palmer's commitment to the Reformation.

It is evening now. Mist is rising from the fens outside the town as the sun sets red in the gathering dusk. Across the marsh there is a sturdy thatched farmhouse, with smoke rising from its chimney in the still evening air. Friendly candlelight flickers through the diamond-paned windows into the farmyard before the door. Singly and in little groups, caped and hatted against the evening chill, people are strolling along the path through the fen toward the farmhouse.

Inside, in front of a bright fireplace in the front room, a gentle-featured man sits waiting with a Bible open on his lap. This is Master George Gifford, the former vicar of Maldon. The Archbishop of Canterbury has removed him for his bold preaching against the lukewarm Church of England. A group of Maldon merchants have supported him since his suspension, and each night of the week he holds prayer meetings like this one (while Master Palmer plays backgammon in the pub).

When all the guests have arrived, Gifford leads them in singing a metrical psalm. A boy in a leather jerkin reads from the English Bible that the pastor hands him. Gifford then expounds the text briefly. He urges the people to keep a daily quiet time, to hold regular family prayers in their households, to worship at All Saints' Maldon every Sunday, and to intercede with the

Lord for Master Palmer. Then the little group turns to prayer. A middle-aged housewife prays eloquently for the queen and for Maldon's two members of Parliament (both hot Protestants). An old man asks God's blessing on the English troops fighting the Spanish army in the Netherlands. Finally Master Gifford leads the group in saying Evening Prayer according to the 1559 Book of Common Prayer. Then rising from their knees they all embrace one another cordially, and don their hats and capes.

Groups like this were gathering in different parts of England in the 1580s. Elizabeth probably feared them more than she needed to. But observing the Wars of Religion between Protestants and Roman Catholics on the Continent, and painfully aware that public order was very fragile in England, Elizabeth chose to repress Puritans like Gifford. She was anxious lest religious fanaticism break out into civil war in her realm. Of course, her policy only stiffened the Puritans' determination. While Elizabeth lived, however, the Puritans' loyalty to their new Deborah restrained them from open rebellion.

The Elizabethan Puritans stood for the same beliefs that Reformers like Tyndale and Cranmer had espoused a generation or two earlier. They held the Bible to be God's love letter to the human heart. They believed in frequent sermons, and that preaching should aim for conversion. The center of their message was the cross. Jesus' blood paid for our guilt completely, and all we need to do is to open our hearts to his gracious forgiveness. The Puritans anticipated that this message would transform human lives and cumulatively transform the nation.

The Elizabethan Puritans evinced one characteristic that their Evangelical descendants in later centuries would not all affirm, namely, a high Calvinist theology. In the generation after the great Reformer John Calvin's death in 1564, his followers were concerned to tidy up his theology, to express it in strict logical terms, to dot every *i* and to cross every *t* in his system. This zeal for precision led them to locate the doctrine of predestination closer to the center of Christianity than Calvin himself had done. Calvin had argued that predestination was chiefly a message of comfort, an assurance that nothing could separate us from the love of God. But Calvin's successors made it the centerpiece of a logical system. If God knows everything, they argued, and if nothing happens apart from his will, then he must have chosen the elect from all eternity and condemned the rest to hell. This system made logical sense, and the Elizabethan Puritans embraced it. As we will see, later Anglican Evangelicals would back away from the doctrine of "double" predestination (to heaven and to hell) and accept more readily the mystery of God's saving activity and the paradoxical teaching of the Bible on the scope of human freedom.

The Elizabethan Puritans remained within the Church of England, even as they tried to push it in the direction of a more Protestant piety (Bible study, sermons, plain worship). Only a few radicals left the church wholly in Elizabeth's reign, like the little groups of dissenters who went to Holland and eventually to Plymouth, Massachusetts, in 1620. The Puritans who remained in England had a difficult time promoting their cause for "purifying" the Church of England and for speeding up the queen's glacial pace (as they saw it) in completing the Reformation. They never found a spokesman who could make an effective case for their sense of urgency for a couple of reasons.

First, the queen had a huge advantage in that everyone in England still believed in a hierarchical society with a monarch at the top. And Elizabeth was the monarch. The Puritans shared this prevailing world picture, however much they chafed at the apparent delay tactics of this particular monarch. Likewise the Puritans knew full well that only a heartbeat separated England from Roman Catholic rule—either in the person of Mary Queen of Scots until 1587 or Philip II of Spain in the years following. So the Puritans faced a dilemma. They opposed the queen's religious policy, and took to publishing pamphlets against her, but they still loved and needed her. On one occasion, a Puritan printer was sentenced to have his right hand chopped off for publishing inflammatory tracts. The printer (ironically named Stubbs) laid his hand on the block, and as the ax fell he swept off his hat and cried, "Long live the queen!"

Second, as mentioned above, many of the Puritans' grievances had to do with matters like vestments, which were not specified either in Scripture or in the creeds. They were "things indifferent" (adiaphora in Greek) that were important, but not at the same level as the incarnation or the resurrection. Elizabeth argued that since wearing a surplice was a "thing indifferent," the Puritans had no right to protest when she told them to do it. The Puritans retorted that since surplices were "indifferent," the queen had no right to force them to wear the offending garments against their consciences. The Puritans had a point. The Roman clergy who had burned their Protestant friends under Bloody Mary had worn surplices. The latter were a deeply offensive symbol of everything the Puritans rejected. Likewise the surplice suggested to local congregations that nothing had changed, that late medieval piety was still acceptable (no matter what the Puritans said from the pulpit). The Puritans believed that the queen was forcing them to send mixed signals, and was subverting their work of evangelism in the parishes. But the Puritans could not say this too loudly for the reasons cited above. They needed Elizabeth.

What authority could someone in the 1570s cite in a pamphlet (however timidly) against the authority of a monarch who was the "Supreme Governor" of the Church? One could resort to Scripture, of course, but unfortunately Scripture didn't explicitly say, "Thou shalt not wear a surplice." Elizabeth's third Archbishop of Canterbury, John Whitgift (in office 1583–1604), took on the Puritans in controversy and pointed out this lamentable deficiency in the Bible. Not so, the Puritans retorted. Paul said in 1 Corinthians 14:20, "Let all things be done for edification." Whitgift naturally inquired what in the world that text had to do with surplices. The Puritans naturally responded that everyone *knew* that surplices weren't edifying. Not so, said Whitgift. The queen says that surplices *are* edifying, so wear them. The Puritans and the archbishop were talking past one another, and getting nowhere.

Let's Pause and Reflect

5. What were the main concerns of the Elizabethan Puritan movement in England?

_____

_____

_____

_____

_____

_____

Richard Hooker

This unedifying pamphlet warfare produced a champion for Elizabeth's *via media* in the person of Richard Hooker (1554–1600), one of the greatest minds in the Anglican tradition. Scarcely noticed in his own lifetime, Hooker's reputation for judicious wisdom has continued to grow—even though modern Anglicans do not share his Elizabethan worldview. Hooker made the definitive case against the Puritans, though, as we will see, the latter were not thereby dissuaded from going to war with the Crown in the 1640s. Hooker is often mentioned today in Anglican debates, so his thought merits a brief (if wholly inadequate) summary here.

Hooker's life was not exciting. An Oxford graduate, he served in the 1580s as chaplain to the nation's school of common law, the Inns of Court in London. Here he ran afoul of his assistant, a hot Protestant named Walter Travers. Hooker preached in support of the queen on Sunday mornings, and Travers in favor of the Puritans in the afternoon. Hooker was a soporific preacher. Travers was incendiary. Finally the queen transferred Hooker to a country parish in Kent, where he spent the rest of his days peacefully composing his great eight-volume tome *The Laws of Ecclesiastical Polity.*

Hooker's Great Work

Hooker's book is a fount of wisdom on many topics, but what concerns us here is his response to the Puritans. Instead of answering them line by line as Archbishop Whitgift had done, Hooker described an elaborate model of the universe to show (in a wide context) why the Puritans were being irrational, especially in their interpretation of Scripture. God is fundamentally orderly, Hooker argued, and God proclaims his order to humankind in three ways. First, God created the universe in an orderly fashion according to the blueprint of his natural law. Second, God imprinted a moral law on the human heart. But, after the fall we cannot obey this moral law. Third, God gave us a divine law, according to which we may be saved through faith in Christ. To apply these laws in changing historical situations, God left humans (with the help of the Spirit) to frame human laws, which were valid if they were consistent with God's natural, moral, and divine laws.

How could we humans perceive these laws of God and frame our actions accordingly? Hooker insisted that fallen humanity has always needed the help and guidance of the Holy Spirit. That is clear. But with the Spirit's assistance, human reason is the God-given faculty that is designed to perceive and put into practice God's laws. The fall has weakened reason's reliability, but with the Spirit's help it can still do the job. Now the laws of God are not all alike in their content. Natural law governs the physical universe. Moral law gives us ethical guidelines. Divine law speaks about matters of faith, specifically God's plan of salvation. The New Testament isn't intended to teach us astronomy and physics. Natural law isn't meant to teach us about the Trinity. Reason's job is to figure out which kind of divine law applies to what topics, and to ascertain those matters that God has left to human judgment (the sphere of human laws). And then reason should make logical decisions with all the former in mind. Hooker therefore thought the Puritans were acting irrationally in appealing to Scripture for laws of church polity and liturgical haberdashery. Those were "things indifferent" that God had left to human discretion, and in a monarchial society, specifically to the queen's discretion. So 1 Corinthians 14:26 did *not* mean no surplices. Hooker exhorted the Puritans to stop thinking irrationally, and to use their reason in a judicious and competent fashion.

Modern Misconceptions

For Hooker, reason is the faculty that God has given us to discern and follow his will. In the century after Hooker's death in 1600, however, European intellectuals gradually began to reject the Christian worldview and to redefine reason as the tool of the sovereign self for ruling the universe. Recent Anglicans seeking to incorporate a more modernist outlook into the Church have sometimes tried to enlist Hooker as an ally, viewing him as a precursor to the modern worldview. But Hooker was not a modern rationalist. He did not believe in a closed, atheistic universe or in autonomous human reason, and it is anachronistic to picture him as an Elizabethan forerunner of modernist Anglican trends.

Nor did Hooker promote the idea that Anglicans appeal to three separate authorities—Scripture, tradition, and reason—and that this triad represents a "three-legged stool." The "stool" metaphor had its origin in the late nineteenth century, when some observers wrongly supposed that Evangelical Anglicans looked to Scripture, Anglo-Catholics appealed to tradition, and modernist Anglicans relied on reason. In fact the case was much more complicated, even at that time. Anglo-Catholics had a high view of Scripture, for example. In the twentieth century, the stool model mostly served modernists in their efforts to marginalize Scripture. If Scripture, tradition, and reason are all "legs," then, according to modernists, they are all equally important principles among which we may choose to emphasize whichever we prefer. But in fact, the legs are not identical, and the analogy of a stool falsely attributed to Hooker is itself suspect. Scripture is God's Word written, and takes priority in whatever areas it chooses to address (e.g., salvation but not astronomy or fluid mechanics). Tradition is a lens through which we read Scripture, and it depends on conformity to Scripture for its validity. Reason is a God-given human faculty for figuring out what God is saying. These are apples, oranges, and bananas. Tradition is not on a par with Scripture, nor does reason stand in judgment over Scripture. The stool metaphor does not reflect reality, and it impedes our understanding of the Anglican way.

On one occasion (in book 5, chapter 8, section 2) Hooker briefly addresses the relationship of Scripture, tradition, and reason (in its sixteenth-century sense). He says that where Scripture speaks plainly on matters of faith and behavior, it has preemptive authority. When Scripture is not plain in reference to these matters, then human reason can legitimately try and figure out what Scripture is saying. If reason cannot sort out the truth, then we had best continue with tradition on the subject until further intelligence comes down. This throwaway line oversimplifies Hooker's position as a whole. For example, it does not address the everyday role of reason in interpreting Scripture judiciously and accurately. But this brief text certainly makes it eminently plain that Hooker was no advocate of a three-legged stool that leaves modern secular human reason at liberty to select which leg to emphasize.

Hooker reminds us that the Elizabethan Puritans were not the only major voice in late sixteenth-century England. In fact, at the very end of Elizabeth's reign a tentative Catholic revival was also beginning to take shape, as we shall see in the next chapter.

Let's Pause and Reflect

6. What did Richard Hooker mean by "reason," and what was its role in our search for truth?

_____

_____

_____

_____

_____

_____

7. Why isn't the three-legged stool an accurate metaphor for the relations between Scripture, tradition, and reason in Christian thought?

_____

_____

_____

_____

_____

_____

Review

A. In the course of the English Reformation in the sixteenth century, we have seen that William Tyndale, Queen Elizabeth I, the Puritans, and Richard Hooker were all Protestants. But they were very different kinds of Protestant! List what major concerns they had in common and the peculiarities of each that set them apart.

_____

_____

_____

_____

_____

_____

_____

_____

_____

_____

For Thought and Application

B. From what you have read in this chapter, how would you differenti-
ate between the sixteenth-century Christian worldview and the worldview of modern secular society around us today?

_____

_____

_____

_____

_____

_____

_____

_____

_____

_____

_____

_____

_____

_____

_____

C. Queen Elizabeth I and the Puritans fought over clerical vestments. The queen wanted the Church of England clergy to wear the old pre-Reformation vestments, so that traditionalist parishioners would come to church peacefully (she hoped). The Puritans argued that Elizabeth was sending mixed signals to the parishioners, implying that the Reformation really hadn't changed anything—and that English people could go on earning their salvation through good works. Which view would you have supported? Why?

_____

_____

_____

_____

_____

_____

_____

_____

_____

_____

_____

_____

_____

_____

_____

_____

For Further Reading

J.R.H. Moorman, *A History of the Church in England, Third Edition.*

- Chapters 11-13

Chapter 4

The English Civil War and the Scientific Revolution

(1603–1736)

The Caroline Divines: An Early Anglo-Catholic Movement

At the end of Elizabeth's reign, a small but influential Catholic revival began to flourish. Its leaders wanted to revive certain medieval beliefs and practices they thought the Puritans had unnecessarily discarded, such as the idea of human cooperation with God in salvation, or the use of beautiful vessels in Holy Communion. This movement was briefly influential from the 1590s through the 1630s and produced a generation of distinguished theologians, pastors, and poets. After Elizabeth's death in 1603, the Stuart monarchs James I (1603–1625) and Charles I (1625–1649) patronized this group and promoted some of them to high office in the Church. Since the group's moment of greatest influence came under King Charles I (*Carolus Primus* in Latin), they have been known as the Caroline divines. Unfortunately the Stuart dynasty was rapidly growing unpopular, wasting all the accumulated goodwill that "Good Queen Bess" had carefully accumulated over forty-four years. The Catholic revival thus suffered from its identification with the incompetent Stuarts. What's more, the continuing anti-Roman paranoia prevailing in much of the country meant that the Catholic movement sparked much controversy, especially in the south and east of England.

The parish church of Hockley in Suffolk, built in the fourteenth century, is a small stone Gothic building. The nave is about forty feet long and twenty-five feet wide. The chancel stands three steps higher than the nave, and extends fifteen feet further to the east. This Sunday morning in 1635, a loud argument is disturbing Morning Prayer. Master Edward Smith, the vicar, is standing at the east end inside a wooden railing that he has recently had installed. He intends to create a sanctuary here for a stone altar. There is no altar at present. Down in the nave an oaken Communion table stands lengthwise in the aisle. Ever since the Act of Uniformity in 1559, English law has forbidden stone altars attached to the east wall. Rather, tables are to be placed in the chancel or the nave for Holy Communion. The point of the exercise is to emphasize that the Holy Communion is a communal meal, and not a representation on an altar of Christ's sacrifice on the cross. So for three generations now the people of Hockley parish church have been used to seeing the vicar celebrate Holy Communion at the table, and to receiving the elements as they stand around it.

But today Master Smith has announced a change. The congregation is roaring its displeasure, and Smith is trying to shout them down. Archbishop William Laud of Canterbury has determined to undo the Elizabethan practice of Holy Communion. He wants the wooden tables to be removed, and stone altars rebuilt at the east end. He intends that the celebrant face away from the congregation, symbolically representing the people to God and suggesting that he is performing a sacrifice on their behalf. Laud wants to rail in the altar, emphasizing its holiness and its inaccessibility to the laity. Master Smith is trying to comply with the archbishop's orders. The irate congregation is having none of it. Standing on the Communion table in the nave, Wat Underwood is waving his hat and shouting, "Little Laud to the devil!"

Archbishop Laud was not the most winsome advocate for a more Catholic style of worship. He was tiny and stout, red-faced with a mustache and a goatee, often swinging his arms and shouting, always in a hurry, and never willing to suffer fools gladly. Laud was impatient to set the world to rights. Friends who knew him well appreciated his administrative ability and his vision of an orderly kingdom. He was a devout Christian, and he thought (with good reason) that the Puritans were insufficiently concerned for order and dignity in worship.

But Laud seemed like a dangerous threat to much of the English nation. He was publicly identified with King Charles I, whose policies were evoking strenuous resistance among the Puritan merchants and gentry and among the influential lawyers in London. Charles was a shy, intense man who closeted himself with a few trusted advisers, and had no sense at all for English public opinion. He imposed taxes and customs duties without consulting Parliament. He required that the justices of the king's courts render verdicts that he dictated himself. He tolerated the Roman Catholic Masses that his French queen heard daily at court—with no idea of the paranoia he was whipping up in a populace that vividly remembered the Spanish Armada. Charles seemed to be opening the door for an international Roman Catholic conspiracy that plotted to bring in the Inquisition and destroy England's Protestant identity. Charles himself was in fact a conscientious Anglican, but his support for Archbishop Laud and the Catholic revival naturally provoked misunderstanding, and sparked a firestorm of protest.

A distinguished group of saints and scholars shared Laud's desire to revive the beauty of holiness in worship. Not all the Caroline divines shared Laud's vigorous impatience or his impulse to crush his opponents. But they all favored a piety that included dignity, beauty, and order. George Herbert was a poet whose brief pastoral ministry (he died of tuberculosis at thirty-nine) set a lasting standard for sensitivity and commitment. John Donne, dean of St. Paul's Cathedral in London, wrote vivid poems and sermons from the depths of an intense and struggling heart. Bishop Lancelot Andrewes of Winchester composed some of the most eloquent private prayers ever written in England. The Caroline divines adorned the universal Church by their lives and their godly learning. They maintained the Protestant faith of the Thirty-Nine Articles of Religion, but they also aspired to be both "Catholic" and "Reformed" at the same time. Specifically they wanted to recover certain features of medieval Catholicism that they believed the Reformers had needlessly discarded.

First, they wanted to restore the sacraments of Baptism and Holy Communion to their central place in Anglican piety. They believed that the Puritan majority had gone too far in their emphasis on the sermon. They aspired to a balance of Word and Sacrament that they thought the Reformation had upset. God speaks to us not only in words, they believed, but also through symbols and actions. What we do with our bodies reinforces what we think with our minds and believe in our hearts. Cannot beautiful silver Communion vessels stir up piety and reverence? So the Caroline divines sought to restore the sacraments to prominence, to celebrate them with beauty and dignity—and to discourage such irreverent behavior as Wat Underwood's use of the Communion table as a political platform.

Second, the Caroline divines took a more gradualist view of the Christian life than the Puritans did, and they questioned the latter group's narrow emphasis on conversion. Rather than anticipating a single revolutionary moment, the Caroline divines tended to expect that Christians should grow in grace slowly and over time, through daily prayer and weekly attendance at worship. They hoped that more and more English people would be able to say, "I've never known a time when I didn't trust in Jesus." This gradualist approach to Christian life also had implications for their political views. They believed firmly in a hierarchical society under their divine-right monarch, and they deeply feared the impulse to violent transformation that they sensed in the Puritan spirit.

A third quarrel with the Puritans had to do with predestination. Archbishop Laud in particular believed that Christ died for the whole human race, and offered salvation to all those who responded to the gospel. Didn't Jesus' call for repentance imply that people had some ability to respond? Puritans attacked these ideas as Arminian (after the Dutch theologian Jakob Arminius) and saw them as a slippery slope back into popish works righteousness.

Finally, the Caroline divines adopted a "high church" position, in that they stoutly maintained the Church of England's unique authority grounded in the apostolic succession of bishops. The Laudians were not "high church" in the sense that they used bells and incense and holy water. Those practices would have seemed impossibly Romish in early seventeenth-century England, and would have caused an immediate political meltdown. ("Ritualism" in that sense would return only in the 1830s.) Rather, the Laudians took a high view of episcopacy and therefore of the English church, which had maintained the order of bishops. They thought the Puritans were too soft on apostolic succession and too friendly to Calvinists in Europe who had rejected episcopacy. Indeed, a few

Puritans harbored Presbyterian (and even Congregational) ideas about church government. The Caroline divines wanted to ensure the survival of episcopacy as the visual link between the seventeenth century and the apostolic age, and as the token of a true church.

As we'll see, the Laudians' fatal alliance with the Stuart dynasty meant that they enjoyed only a brief moment of sunshine in the 1620s and 1630s. They did, however, model a moderate Catholic revival in the Anglican way (both "Catholic and Reformed") to which their Anglo-Catholic successors in the 1830s would look for inspiration.

Let's Pause and Reflect

1. What values did the Caroline divines hold in common?

_____

_____

_____

_____

_____

The Wars of Religion

On January 30, 1649, we are standing across the street from the royal banqueting hall in Westminster, just down the River Thames from the city of London. On either side of us, stretching up and down the street, a huge crowd waits in silence. Facing us on the far side of the street, mounted soldiers keep the crowd from approaching a wooden platform draped in black cloth. In the midst of the platform stands a block of wood ten inches high. The facade of the banqueting hall rises behind the stage, its seven tall windows partly boarded up. Craning our necks, we can see that the scaffold is not empty. A masked man stands at the back, gripping the handle of a large ax whose head rests by his right foot. There are also five soldiers and an officer on the platform, and two secretaries holding quill pens and inkwells. They all wait silently.

Suddenly through one of the broken windows three men step out onto the scaffold. One of them is an army officer, one a bishop in episcopal robes. The third man is the king. He is a short, slight man, looking weary but holding himself proudly erect. His face is pale. He has a long nose, a mustache, and a pointed beard. Deep pouches beneath his eyes betray his fatigue, but his voice is clear as he begins to make a few prepared remarks.

The king is prepared to die for the laws of England, he says. He utterly rejects the authority of the court that has condemned him to death. It has no standing or jurisdiction according to the ancient laws of the realm. Furthermore, he says that he dies "a Christian according to the profession of the Church of England. . . . I have a good cause and I have a gracious God. I will say no more." The king removes his cloak, stands praying for a moment with his eyes turned to heaven, then kneels down and puts his head on the block. A few seconds later he stretches out his hands. At this sign the executioner swings his ax and cuts off the king's head with a single stroke.

A seventeen-year-old boy at the back of the crowd sees the ax fall. Later he writes in his diary that at that moment, the crowd gave such a groan as he had never heard before, and hopes fervently never to hear again.

King Charles died because he had started and lost a civil war, and because his subsequent plotting and scheming had convinced his opponents that no final peace would come until this "man of blood" was dead. Charles was never good at understanding what others were thinking and feeling. He was a shy man, as we have seen, and he relied on a few close advisers like Archbishop Laud. Convinced that he ruled by divine right, Charles never felt obligated to consult his subjects on matters of government or religion, and did so only when he had to. He tried to rule without Parliament as much as possible. He did not consider himself bound by any agreements he made with his enemies while under duress. Charles was difficult.

Charles's ignorance of public opinion led him to support Archbishop Laud's foolish plan to impose the English Prayer Book on the Scots in 1638. Scotland had been Presbyterian for three generations. Now the entire nation rose up unanimously to oppose this "popish" enormity. The Scots invaded England and camped on the northern border. Charles had no army to resist them, so he had to summon Parliament and ask for money to raise one. Parliament refused to grant him money until he should redress a long list of grievances. Charles balked, Parliament dug in their collective heels, and a stalemate en-

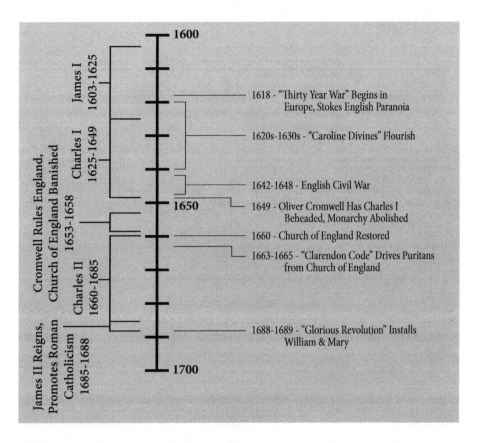

sued. In 1642 Charles finally abandoned London and went north to raise an army on his own. Parliament formed its own army. War broke out in the fall of 1642.

The royal army won some early battles. Parliament made a treaty with the Scots, and they agreed to fight the king together. But the Scots' price for their support was a big one. The Church of England would become Presbyterian! And it did, for a brief time in the mid-1640s, in those parts of England that Parliament controlled, mostly in the south and east.

But a new force was rising in the Parliamentary army, a new religious movement that was more radical and more democratic than the elitist Presbyterian church favored by the aristocrats in Parliament. The new movement in the army was Congregationalist. They believed that each body of gathered believers should be autonomous. Their leader was Oliver Cromwell, who emerged by 1645 as the great general on the Parliamentary side. Cromwell was an East Anglian gentleman with no formal military training. He raised a troop of "Ironsides" cavalry at his own expense when the war broke out. Cromwell led his troopers into battle chanting metrical psalms. These zealous warriors cut through the royalist armies like a hot knife through butter.

Despite Cromwell's overwhelming military success, Parliament soon came to fear him and his radical ideas. Cromwell promoted officers in his army on the basis of merit, not of family or wealth. Butchers and farmers and shepherds could rise from the ranks, provided they were staunch Puritans and showed their worth as leaders. Cromwell was threatening the historic hierarchical structure of English society to which Parliament was committed (provided they could have a king with whom they could work). In an amazing about face, the Parliamentary leaders reluctantly decided that King Charles was the lesser evil, and they joined forces with him and the Scots against Cromwell and the Congregationalists.

Cromwell's army beat everyone. By 1649 he had mopped up all the opposition. But Charles continued to plot, and Cromwell concluded that peace could not come while the "man of blood" still lived. But Cromwell did not intend merely to kill Charles Stuart the man. He resolved to cut the king's head off with the crown still on it. Cromwell believed that once he had abolished the apostate English monarchy, Christ the true king would return in glory. So he set up a court to try Charles and to condemn him to death. There was no provision for such a court in English common law, and Charles had a point when he claimed on the scaffold that he was dying for the laws of England. Cromwell was going too far. Hence the groan from the crowd when the ax fell.

In 1649 it seemed as though the Puritans' dreams had come true. They had chafed under Elizabeth I when she restrained their desire to purify the English church from its remaining Romish traditions. When Charles had declared war on Parliament in 1642, the Puritans eagerly took up the sword as well. But as the war went on, they split into conservative and radical factions, Presbyterians versus Congregationalists. And when it was all over, and the Lord did not return, Oliver Cromwell had no plan B. The Puritans knew what they didn't want, but they could not agree on what they wanted in its place (absent the second coming).

Cromwell refused the obvious solution, namely, to become king. He didn't believe in human kingship. Finally he reluctantly agreed to style himself "Lord Protector." He divided the nation into thirteen military districts, each ruled by a major general who ruled by martial law. A number of the major generals were zealous and repressive Puritans. They tried to close alehouses and to outlaw horse racing (not popular). The English aristocracy—now thoroughly alienated from Cromwell—gritted their teeth and bided their time.

Let's Pause and Reflect

2. What were the issues between King Charles I and Oliver Cromwell, and why was Cromwell convinced that only the king's death would settle them?

_____

_____

_____

_____

_____

_____

_____

The Stuart Restoration

Oliver Cromwell died in September 1658 in the midst of a hurricane in England. Neither his son Richard nor any of his major generals had the stature or the ability to replace him as Lord Protector. Even some of the generals decided that the only way to restore political stability was to bring back a king. So in 1660, a hastily convened Parliament invited Charles II to come back from exile in Holland. The son of the "martyred" Charles I, the new king brought back with him many clergy who were determined to restore the Church of England as they had known it before 1640. For a few years they had some success. They drove all the Puritan ministers out of the church. Presbyterians, Congregationalists, and various lower-class leaders (from the Quakers, Ranters, Muggletonians, and the like) seceded, becoming "Dissenters," and suffered grievous legal penalties. The Church of England remained legally established, but it lost its claim to represent the entire nation at prayer.

But religious passions continued to simmer beneath the surface. Rumors of "popish plots" caused hysteria in London. King Charles' brother, James, succeeded him in 1685, and openly declared his Roman Catholic faith. What was England's religion actually to be? In the past three generations it had been successively Church of England, then Presbyterian in the south and east, then the Cromwellian mixed bag of Congregationalists and lower-class sects like the Ranters and Muggletonians, then Church of England again in 1660—and now Roman Catholic? The English aristocracy still associated the latter option with Bloody Mary, the Armada, and the Spanish Inquisition. They would have none of it. They rose up almost unanimously, and Parliament threw James out, along with his wife and the baby boy who would have made a Catholic succession to the English throne permanent. Parliament invited the impeccably Protestant William and Mary to come over from Holland in 1689. This "Glorious Revolution" settled the religious issue in favor of the Protestant Episcopalian option that Queen Elizabeth I had established in 1559.

But by 1689 the English aristocracy were tired of religious passion. The long shadow of King Charles' execution in 1649 reminded them that Christian fanaticism (or "enthusiasm" as they put it) led to bloodshed and political chaos. The Wars of Religion that Elizabeth had managed to avoid had finally wreaked their bloody havoc in England. It seemed as if Christianity itself presented an insoluble problem. How could England ensure that violent Christianity would never explode again and destroy civil society?

Science and the Age of Reason

On a farm in Lincolnshire in 1666 there is an orchard that slopes down to a little stream. Fleecy clouds overhead drift slowly eastward in the blue sky. The sunshine is warm, though the autumn air is still crisp this morning. Under an apple tree a tall young man is lying on the ground. His eyes are unfocused and far away. Now and then he crosses and uncrosses his legs and leans back on one elbow or the other. He is clearly preoccupied with some mental exercise. Suddenly the thump of a falling apple jogs his attention. The young man sits up abruptly. Under his breath he mutters, "Aha." He stands up and begins to stride around the orchard, fists clenched as he grapples with the significance of a new insight.

Isaac Newton (1642–1727) was in his mid-twenties when he had this "Aha" moment in his mother's orchard in Lincolnshire. He had been studying at Cambridge, but an outbreak of bubonic plague had closed the university. Sometime during Newton's enforced holiday, he seems to have had an intellectual breakthrough, an intuition that suggested a solution to a problem that had puzzled European scientists for several generations. (It did take Newton twenty more years to work out all the math.) Newton's achievement, and others like it, would suggest to certain British intellectuals that science might offer a solution to religious violence.

As to Newton and the apple—ever since the early sixteenth century astronomers and physicists had been revising European "cosmology," their mental map of the universe. In the Middle Ages, most Europeans assumed that the earth lay at the center of the cosmos, surrounded by crystalline spheres that carried the moon, the sun, the five known planets, and the fixed stars in their paths around the earth. But this world picture had become very complicated by the early sixteenth century, because astronomers had to posit a great many squiggles (called "epicycles") in the planetary orbits to explain and predict their actual motion. The old model was growing ugly and cumbersome.

Finally a Polish clergyman and astronomer called Nikolaus Copernicus (1473–1543) suggested that a model with the sun at the center would eliminate many of the squiggles, and produce a cleaner and simpler picture of the cosmos. Wisely he decided to postpone publication of this radical idea until he

1500	
1550	1543 - Nikolaus Copernicus' *De Revolutionibus* Published
1600	1609 - Johannes Kepler Publishes First Two Laws of Planetary Motion
1650	1632 - Galileo Publishes *Two World Systems*
1700	1687 - Isaac Newton Publishes *Principia Mathematica*

was on his deathbed. In 1543 Copernicus' *On the Revolution of the Heavenly Orbs* touched off a heated scholarly debate.

Most people just laughed at Copernicus' crazy idea. Anyone could watch the sunrise in the morning and realize that the sun obviously goes around the earth, and not vice versa. Martin Luther erupted in a seismic guffaw. But gradually a few scholars distanced themselves (with great difficulty) from their sense perceptions, and began to play with Copernicus' new model and to improve it. A German astronomer named Johannes Kepler (1571–1630) discovered that the planetary orbits were elliptical and not circular, as Copernicus had supposed. Kepler produced a simple and elegant equation to describe the planets' actual paths. The Italian scientist Galileo Galilei (1564–1642) then established that the same patterns in physics apply both on Earth and in the heavens—contrary to the old model, which said they were different. Galileo used his new telescope to look deeper into the heavens than humans had ever done before. Many Catholic intellectuals in Rome came to agree with Galileo's ideas. But Galileo got tangled in a faction fight within the Vatican. The persecution he suffered was not a matter of ignorant Christians beating up a pioneering scientist. Some clergy were for the new model, some against it. Meanwhile his ideas appealed to more and more scientists in Europe.

One problem remained unsolved, however. What kept the planets in their elliptical orbits? Why didn't they just fly off in a straight line like a stone from a slingshot? Kepler and Galileo had discarded the old notion of crystalline spheres that held the planets in place. But what was the force holding them in orbit?

Enter Isaac Newton. In a flash of insight the young genius in the orchard realized that the force pulling the apple to the ground was the same as the force pulling the Moon toward the Earth, and the Earth toward the Sun. He would call that force gravity. Newton never said exactly what gravity was, but he worked out a simple and elegant equation that described its operation. Newton's laws of gravitational attraction put the final piece of the puzzle in place. They were a brilliant achievement of scientific reason. They will still get you to the Moon and back (though now we know that Newton's model doesn't work for very, very big things or very, very little ones). In praise of Newton's achievement, the English poet Alexander Pope wrote:

Nature and nature's laws lay hid in night:
God said, Let Newton be! And all was light.

When Newton finally published his great synthetic work in 1687, *The Mathematical Principles of Natural Philosophy*, it seemed as if scientific reason had banished medieval tradition and ancient authority and staked a claim to supremacy in describing the universe. Not surprisingly, scholars began to wonder whether science might go a step further. Could scientific reason find a solution to the Wars of Religion?

Let's Pause and Reflect

3. Summarize briefly the contributions to the new astronomy made by Copernicus, Kepler, Galileo, and Newton.

_____

_____

_____

_____

_____

_____

_____

_____

John Locke and the Age of Reason

Newton's contemporary John Locke (1632–1704) took this step in the 1690s. Filled with confidence by Newton's great scientific achievement, Locke offered one of the most momentous suggestions in the English-speaking world for containing and minimizing religious fanaticism. Instead of the historic Christian story that began "In the beginning God . . ." Locke suggested an alternative story that began "In the beginning Man . . ." Europe had utterly failed to agree on the great question of authority, namely: Who has the right to interpret God's will? Holy pope? Holy monarch? Holy reformer? Holy peasant alone in the loft with his candle and his Bible? Who could say? Now after more than a century of religious bloodshed, some intellectuals in Europe were open to a new perspective, which Locke offered.

Locke suggested that we set aside all the old authorities (pope, monarch, reformer, peasant) and begin with human reason. Why not decide to believe nothing unless human reason could verify it? Then surely all reasonable people of goodwill could agree on a simple basic Christianity, and stop the passion, the fanaticism, and the carnage. Locke's proposal sounded very attractive in the 1690s.

Locke theorized that each human baby comes into the world as a "blank slate" *(tabula rasa* in Latin) on which "sense experience" proceeds to write. Then each of us can reflect rationally on what we learn through our senses.

If we follow the right scientific procedures (Newton's, for instance), we can know the truth about the world around us. Then we can make valid inferences from our knowledge of the universe—again following logical, reasonable, step-by-step procedures. For example, we can infer that Newton's orderly universe implies a Creator God who so ordered it. Locke thought that this "argument from design" approached mathematical certainty. So why shouldn't we all come together around this basic simple Christian faith that we can prove by human reason? Then we can agree to disagree about the things that we can't prove, like predestination versus free will, infant baptism versus adult baptism, congregational versus episcopal church government, and so on. We can stop fighting.

When we read Locke's *The Reasonableness of Christianity* (1695) it sounds pretty orthodox. Locke even thought that he could make a rational case for miracles and for Jesus' claims to be the Messiah. But looking back on Locke's momentous proposal with the benefit of three centuries' hindsight, we can see some problems.

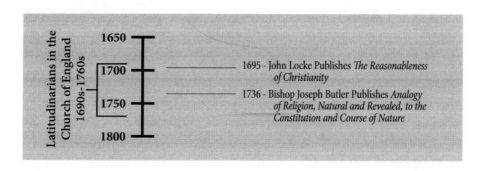

Latitudinarians in the Church of England 1690s–1760s

1650
1700
1750
1800

1695 - John Locke Publishes *The Reasonableness of Christianity*

1736 - Bishop Joseph Butler Publishes *Analogy of Religion, Natural and Revealed, to the Constitution and Course of Nature*

First, Locke's proposal was intellectually flawed. It didn't work even in terms of the human reason that he extolled. Locke thought that he could set aside all previous authorities like Christianity, affirm the reliability of reason as his first principle, think objectively about the data of sense experience, and so reach absolutely certain truth (i.e., "beginning with me"). He thought that there were foundational axioms (like the validity of sense experience) that every human being could affirm, quite apart from faith or religion. In retrospect, Locke was too optimistic about reason's ability to create its own axioms, and about the possibility of totally certain objective knowledge. We realize today that every system of thought—including modern science—depends on some unverifiable axiom that we have to accept on faith. Modern Western science rested on the Christian axiom that the universe is orderly, rational, and knowable because God made it so. This axiom would not be self-evident at all to a Buddhist or a Hindu, let alone an Aztec. Confidence in human reason and the order of the universe is a gift we receive from the Bible. Reason alone cannot verify it. So when Locke stepped outside the Christian story and began with reason, he was cutting off the branch he was sitting on.

Second, we now realize that there is no such thing as wholly "objective" knowledge that gives science an edge over religious knowing. We all see the world from a particular standpoint and through specific lenses. This fact is no excuse for sloppy thinking. We do the best we can to correct for our own biases, but absolute objective certainty doesn't exist. Locke's confidence in science was understandable for his time, but excessive.

Third, when Locke claimed that he was trying to rescue Christianity from its propensity to violence, he was trying to end the Wars of Religion—which was a very good thing to do. But in fact he was abolishing religion. From the earliest days, the ancient Hebrews had believed in a God who took the initiative in revealing himself to the human race. God announced that, "I AM WHO I AM" (Exodus 3:14). God was the first principle, the basic assumption, the ultimate beginning point for understanding reality. That's why the Bible begins with an assertion, not an argument. "In the beginning God . . ." doesn't argue for God's reality, or offer a rational proof. The Bible simply announces the axiom and proceeds to tell the story. When Locke proposed human reason as providing axiomatic truth—the new standard, the new criterion, the new authority—he was stepping outside the Christian story. If the entire Christian story is to be subjected to the test of scientific reason, if we are to believe only what scientific reason can verify, then we have made reason our god. However much Locke wanted to support a minimal Christianity, however much he desired to establish at least some of the faith on a "firm scientific foundation," he was in fact proposing faith in reason over faith in God.

Nor, finally, did Locke's move put "reasonable" Christianity on a firm scientific foundation as he intended. Rather, the result was to weaken Christian faith and throw it on the defensive. When Locke effectively demoted God from axiom to hypothesis, he made belief in God dependent on the strength of this or that proof. If I offer you one proof that God exists, someone else can come along with an even more convincing proof that God doesn't exist. C. S. Lewis used the metaphor of the prisoner's "dock" in a British courtroom to say that Locke and other Enlightenment philosophers had "put God in the dock." Instead of being the first principle on the basis of which the whole universe makes sense, God was now forced on the defensive, to plead his case before an increasingly skeptical modern jury.

Let's Pause and Reflect

4. Describe briefly Locke's strategy for ending the Wars of Religion.

_____

_____

_____

_____

_____

_____

5. What were the major intellectual problems with Locke's proposal?

_____

_____

_____

_____

Deists, Latitudinarians, and Atheists

Within a year of Locke's *The Reasonableness of Christianity,* other thinkers began to chip away at his "proof" of the faith. First, they limited the elements of Christianity that they thought scientific reason could verify. To begin with, they mocked the notion of miracles. If the universe were as orderly and as predictable as Newton had evidently shown, how could there be interruptions and reversals to the "ironclad laws of nature"? The most that we could infer from order in the universe, they thought, was the probability of an absentee-landlord deity who had set the cosmos in motion and then gone on permanent holiday. This "Deism" was basically watered down Christianity and did not find many adherents in England. (It would have some influential supporters in America later on, in the likes of Ben Franklin and Thomas Jefferson.)

Most leaders of the late seventeenth-century Church of England, like John Tillotson, Archbishop of Canterbury from 1691 to 1694, did not go as far as to preach radical Deism. Rather, they expressed a "Latitudinarian" perspective, which held matters of doctrine to be obscure, complicated, and potentially explosive, but matters of morality to be clear and socially useful. Speaking to the aristocracy, Tillotson and his generation said that belief in God was a good, inexpensive bet. It offered the reward of conscious self-righteousness in the present, with the prospect of rewards in the life to come. Speaking to the lower 95 percent of the population, the Latitudinarians' message was more succinct: "Obey." Shuddering at the memory of social chaos in the Civil War, the Church of England in 1700 stood foursquare behind the monarchy, the nobility, the rural squirearchy, and the wealthy London merchants. And against "enthusiasm." There was no good news for the starving peasants.

The Church of England did produce a brilliant critic of Locke's faith in science (or "scientism," if you will) in the person of Bishop Joseph Butler (1692–1752). Butler's *Analogy of Religion, Natural and Revealed, to the Constitution and Course of Nature* (1736) refuted Locke's distinction between allegedly objective and certain scientific knowledge on the one hand and allegedly subjective and uncertain religious faith on the other. Not so fast, said Butler. Both science and Christianity involve unknown mysteries, and both require faith. Science tells us that a small area of the cosmos—the part that we can observe—seems to be orderly. But it takes a leap of faith to extrapolate from this small quadrant of the universe to the cosmos as a complete whole. Likewise Christianity can point to evidence that prayers are answered, for example. But it takes a leap of faith to extrapolate from this experience to the existence of a God who raised Jesus Christ from the dead. Both science and Christianity entail evidence and uncertainty, reason and faith. So Locke was wrong to distinguish so absolutely between "objectively certain science" and "subjectively uncertain religion." In fact, he was being irrational in so doing.

Despite Bishop Butler's refutation of Deism, however, the prestige of science continued to grow as its searchlight shone on new and different aspects of the cosmos (geology, for example—more about this later). By the 1790s there were radical thinkers in Europe who supposed that somehow science had actually "disproved" the existence of God (not likely—can you imagine constructing a controlled experiment to test for the presence of God?). While this view had some currency among the less reflective intellectuals in Europe, for the more rigorous thinkers, God simply grew less and less relevant. Pierre-Simon de Laplace was a French scientist who wrote a book on the cosmos and sent it to the emperor Napoleon, who actually read it. Napoleon invited Laplace to his court and said, "Well, Laplace, what do you make of God?" Laplace replied, "Sire, I had no need for that hypothesis." God was in the prisoner's dock, on the defensive. By 1800 more and more scholars and intellectuals in Europe were thinking that his case was pretty weak and that they could safely ignore it.

Let's Pause and Reflect

6. Briefly define "Deism" and "Latitudinarianism" as they appeared in England around the year 1700.

Deism _____

_____

_____

Latitudinarianism_____

_____

_____

Review

A. Summarize the considerations that persuaded the English aristocracy to look for another "religion" in the late 1600s.

_____

_____

_____

_____

_____

_____

_____

_____

For Thought and Application

B. What do you think of Locke's idea that he could reconstruct Christianity from the ground up, starting with our sense experience, and using scientific reason to build a case for faith in God? Why?

_____

_____

_____

_____

_____

_____

_____

_____

_____

_____

_____

C. How do you respond to the assertion that modern science is based on the Bible, namely, on Scripture's teaching that the cosmos is orderly, good, and knowable by human beings? Do you think that human beings would have come up with those ideas independently, apart from the Bible? Why or why not?

_____

_____

_____

_____

_____

_____

_____

_____

_____

D. If the whole enterprise of modern science depends on axioms it borrows from the Bible, what do you think will happen to science if and when Western society rejects Christianity?

_____

_____

_____

_____

_____

_____

_____

_____

_____

For Further Reading

J.R.H. Moorman, *A History of the Church in England, Third Edition.*

- Chapters 14-16

Chapter 5

Holiness and Evangelical Revivals in England

(1735–1791)

The Early Methodist Movement

John Locke's "reasonable Christianity" and Archbishop John Tillotson's Latitudinarianism had spread a fog of spiritual torpor over the English aristocracy in the early eighteenth century. When the French philosopher Montesquieu visited England, he wrote that "there is no religion in England, and when the subject is raised in polite society, it excites only laughter." This upper-class religious apathy meant that the wealthy in England were not motivated to repair the parish churches for which they were responsible, or to care in any other way for the spiritual welfare of the lower 95 percent of the population. The early eighteenth century was a bleak time for Christianity in England. But renewal was just over the horizon.

It began with a small group of pious undergraduates at the University of Oxford. They were an unlikely lot. The two leaders were brothers, John and Charles Wesley. Shaped by the stiff piety of their father Samuel (a Lincolnshire vicar) and their intense mother Susannah, John and Charles gathered a small group of earnest Oxford students to encourage each other in rigorous Christian discipline. They fasted. They prayed all night on cold stone floors. They imitated the rigors of early North African Christianity. They visited prisoners in Oxford's filthy jails. Their enthusiastic Christianity attracted attention from debauched and rowdy undergraduates (the prevailing Oxford norm). Sneering enemies called them the "Holy Club," or (a mocking label that stuck) the "Methodists." Never more than about a dozen, the group's numbers shrank as crowds hooted them and pelted them with garbage. But persecution hardened the determination of the survivors. They trusted that their sufferings might somehow awaken the somnolent Church of England.

But first, an apparent diversion. After the Wesley brothers left Oxford in 1735, they answered a missionary call to America. Governor Oglethorpe was planting a new colony in Georgia. The settlers needed spiritual ministry (so the governor thought). The Society for the Propagation of the Gospel (the SPG) was willing to pay for mission clergy. Also there were Native Americans in Georgia who needed to hear the gospel. Full of hope and zeal, the Wesleys and two other Holy Club veterans set sail in the fall of 1735.

In the midst of the Atlantic voyage, the little ship met a great hurricane. The winds and waves tore the mainsail apart, and water poured down the hatchways. John Wesley was petrified, sure that he would die immediately. But down in the hold, he saw a little group of families praying and singing hymns peacefully. He was amazed. Later he asked one of the men, "Weren't you afraid?" The man replied, "I thank God, No." Who were these brave people?

The ship survived the hurricane and sailed on, and Wesley came to know these people. They were a group of Germans known as Moravians (from their origin in what is now the Czech Republic). Fleeing from persecution, they had settled in 1722 on the lands of Count Nikolaus von Zinzendorf in eastern Germany. Von Zinzendorf was a devout Lutheran in the Pietist tradition. He and the Moravians quickly bonded in fellowship. Together they felt the power of the Holy Spirit in a watch-night service. Then almost at once, the Spirit sent them out—as whole families, in groups—to take the gospel to Greenland, to the Caribbean, and now to Georgia.

John Wesley knew at once that these humble Christians had a depth of faith that he completely lacked—for all his anxious striving to be perfect. But for the moment, Wesley resolved to carry on in his own strength.

His ministry in Savannah was a disaster. In little more than two years, he fled the colony in disgrace.

On a little brig bound out of Charleston, South Carolina, in January of 1738, a small man stands at the aft rail looking back over the ship's wake. He is huddled in a dark cloak and wears a broad-brimmed black hat. His eyes are pale, and they match the gray waste of the Atlantic in winter. The skies are leaden, and from horizon to horizon you can see nothing but gray waves and whitecaps. The small man leans on the rail hopelessly, memories sit leaden in the pit of his mind. Two years earlier he had gone to Georgia as a missionary from the Church of England. Idealistic, tense, and anxious, he was convinced that if he could persuade both the settlers and the natives in Georgia to take up the harsh spiritual discipline that he embraced himself, he could advance the kingdom of God.

His ministry in Georgia had been a failure. The natives stared at him incredulously. The settlers mostly ignored him, except when they mocked him. Then the young missionary fell in love, but he was too shy to propose. The young lady sensibly married someone else. Then Wesley excommunicated her. A bad decision. Finally the poor young clergyman simply fled from Savannah to Charleston, his ministry and his reputation in ruins. His pale eyes stare hopelessly over the receding gray waves.

Now it is three months later, May 24, 1738. Off busy Aldersgate in London, a quiet courtyard sleeps in the peace of an English sunset. Rosebushes are blooming in profusion before the door of a three-story brick house at the far end of the cobblestoned courtyard. The front door stands ajar. In the parlor to the right, you can see two dozen people seated on straight-backed chairs in two concentric circles. One of them is reading from an English translation of Martin Luther's preface to Romans. Peace lies on the little assembly, at least on all but the small, tense man who sits gripping the seat of his chair, his knuckles white. He is thinking to himself, "I am still persuaded that by my own efforts I am able to keep God's whole law." Suddenly he feels a strange warmth spread through his body, as the reader's gentle voice continues to speak of God's grace. The small man's hands relax. He takes a deep breath and thinks, "I do trust in Christ, Christ alone, for my salvation." The frozen winter of his anxious spirit begins to thaw, as for the first time in thirty-seven years he really hears the good news of God's love.

John Wesley soon began to preach this gospel in such parishes as would receive his ministry, particularly in London, where he preached as many as four times a Sunday. But the response from his clergy colleagues turned cool. Wesley's message sounded too much like the "enthusiasm" of the Puritan sects back in the 1650s—the worst sin a preacher could commit. (An apocryphal gravestone in Devon reads, "Here lie the bones of the Rev. George Ponsonby, who for thirty-eight years preached the Gospel in this parish WITHOUT ENTHUSI-ASM.") So the London pulpits began to close. Wesley wondered if he had heard the Lord wrongly.

Then suddenly in January 1739 Wesley had a letter from his friend George Whitefield, one of his Oxford "Holy Club" friends from a few years earlier. Whitefield was born in Gloucester in the west of England in 1714. He was of a lower social class than the Wesleys and had grown up in poverty. George's father died while he was a baby, and his mother scraped together a living for her seven children by keeping the Bell Inn in Gloucester. She remarried badly and then divorced, and George had to work hard in the tavern. An attack of measles left his visual muscles impaired, so that he often looked cross-eyed. Despite his disadvantages, George was ambitious and longed to go to Oxford, but there was no money. Finally he was able to enter Pembroke College in the university, paying his way by waiting on the wealthier students and cleaning their rooms. He joined the Holy Club and shared in their rigorous self-discipline. But this harsh life plunged him into a deep depression. Finally at Eastertide in 1735, the sun broke through. He felt the love of God streaming through him, and new hope and energy quickening his spirit. The renewal of English Christianity had begun with a single young student.

Not long thereafter, Whitefield applied for ordination to the bishop of Gloucester, and was made deacon. His first sermon a week later caused a sen-sation. Many were thrilled at his oratory. Critics claimed that Whitefield had driven four people mad. Ever since he was a boy, Whitefield had yearned to be an actor. Not a suitable vocation for a future clergyman! But in the pulpit, Whitefield discovered a godly use for his gift. He would revolutionize preach-ing in the Western world. Instead of the dry and rational lectures the Latitu-dinarians favored, Whitefield acted out dramatic monologues. A blind man is

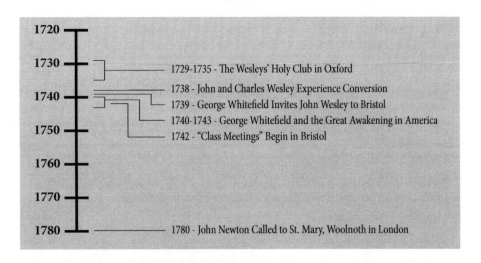

1720

1730 — 1729-1735 - The Wesleys' Holy Club in Oxford

1738 - John and Charles Wesley Experience Conversion

1740 — 1739 - George Whitefield Invites John Wesley to Bristol

1740-1743 - George Whitefield and the Great Awakening in America

1750 — 1742 - "Class Meetings" Begin in Bristol

1760

1770

1780 — 1780 - John Newton Called to St. Mary, Woolnoth in London

stumbling toward a cliff in the fog. Who will rescue him? Help! The congregations were transfixed.

But like his friends the Wesleys, Whitefield made a detour to America. In 1738 he went out as an SPG missionary to Georgia. Whitefield's experience was quite the opposite of Wesley's. His preaching was a brilliant success. But his heart was broken by the many orphans in Savannah, where the mortality rate was devastating. Whitefield decided that he must build them an orphanage, and go back to England to raise money for it. Yet the crucial result of his visit to Savannah was that he had discovered America. He would make six more trips to the colonies, where he would become the most famous public figure in the mid-eighteenth century. His preaching would spark the Great Awakening, the first event in American history that would draw all thirteen colonies together. More on this presently.

Back in England to raise money, Whitefield preached wherever he could. Predictably, the pulpits began to close against his "enthusiastic" oratory, so Whitefield began to experiment with preaching outdoors, wherever he could draw a crowd. Visiting the port city of Bristol one Sunday early in 1739, he walked out to the Kingswood. Here he discovered a hideous slum, where coal miners and their families lived in mud huts among the pits and slag heaps, where the fuel was dug to heat the wealthy merchants' homes in the city. In the Kingswood there was no school, no church, no hope. Whitefield stood up on a mound of rubble and began to preach to the miners about the love of God.

The news came as an immense surprise. Some two hundred filthy wretches gathered round to hear him. Whitefield came back day after day, and despite raw temperatures of early March, the crowds soon grew to twenty thousand. Pitching his voice perfectly, Whitefield found that he could speak audibly to listeners a hundred yards away.

But soon the question arose, What next? The Kingswood miners had no parish church. Who would teach them, help them overcome their addictions to gin and violence? Whitefield knew that he himself had no gift for organizing groups of converts. His job was to preach. And the institutional Church of England was in no position to care for starving miners and their families, in Bristol or anywhere else.

One cold and rainy April Sunday in 1739, we are in the sodden fields outside the tiny village of Winford, in the West Country of England. From a distance, through the mist, we can see the tall fifteenth-century tower of Winford parish church rising above a clump of mud-and-wattle, thatched-roof peasant hovels. Although the church tower looks graceful from afar, as we approach the village we can see that the church roof has lost many of its slates. The churchyard is a jungle. Weeds have grown knee high, even in winter. Gravestones lurch like drunken sailors. Here and there whitened bones protrude from the sodden earth.

Coming through the crumbling gate into the churchyard, approaching the west door, we shudder at a musty odor. The door is ajar, and its hinges creak as we tug it fully open. Inside, the smell of decay envelopes us. Black mold makes ugly patterns on the plastered walls. Cobwebs streak the dirty windowpanes. In the back pew, tumbled in a heap, are several decades of rat-eaten parish registers. This is not a parish church that welcomes visitors warmly.

Up in the bell tower, Dibble the parish clerk peers through the fog, scanning the wet fields for the curate. The latter is a young clergyman from Wells, hired at a pittance to read Morning Prayer in seven rural parishes a Sunday, including Winford. (The rector of Winford, a scholar in Oxford, has never visited this hopeless village, and merely sends a bailiff around annually to collect his tithe income.) At last Dibble spies the curate slumping across the fields on a scrawny nag. Dibble rings the bell, threatening to bring down the tower around him. Nine elderly peasants tramp through the muddy village square and into the church. The young curate slips off his horse at the gate. He stumbles through the west door, tosses off a tankard of ale that Dibble hands him, slips a grimy surplice over his shoulders, and rattles through Morning Prayer in eleven minutes. Then he takes off his surplice, receives his cloak back from Dibble, and is out the door and onto his horse, to exercise his ministry in five more parishes on this bleak Sunday.

This same picture was repeated in hundreds of villages up and down the length and breadth of England. The Church had no vision for ministry to the poor, either to evangelize them or to care for their spiritual needs. Hence George Whitefield's letter to John Wesley in March of 1739, saying in effect, "Come over to Bristol and help me."

When Wesley received the message, he was appalled. He was (he later admitted) so scrupulous about decency and order that he thought it would be almost sinful to save a person's soul unless it happened in a church! But he duly made his way to Bristol and saw the crowds in the Kingswood. And on April 2, 1739, as he later wrote in his journal, "At four in the afternoon, I submitted to be more vile, and proclaimed in the highways the glad tidings of salvation, speaking from a little eminence in a ground adjoining the city, to about three thousand people."

We are standing in the Kingswood, outside the city of Bristol, England's principal port on the Atlantic. A generation ago the Kingswood was a royal hunting park, uninhabited save for the gamekeepers. But since then coal has been discovered just beneath the surface, and mining operations have turned the greenwood into a hideous lunar landscape. Strip mining has torn great wounds in the earth, and huge piles of debris leach out streams of green and yellow poison when it rains. It's raining today. Mud-and-wattle hovels house the filthy, starving miners and their families. Living in such brutal squalor, the miners have no hope on earth.

But today a man in a black cloak is standing on a pile of rock and gravel. He is speaking to a crowd of some three thousand, telling them news that most of them have never heard before. He is preaching on the text of Jesus' inaugural sermon in Nazareth, "The Spirit of the Lord is upon me because he has anointed me to preach good news to the poor" (Isaiah 61:1). Tears make gutters down the grimy faces of the miners and their equally filthy families. By twos and threes, soon by dozens and scores, they fall to their knees in the mud as they hear the message of God's love.

John Wesley embarked that day on a career of evangelism and church planting that would take him more than 250,000 miles up and down England, on foot and on horseback, over the next fifty-one years. He preached more than 40,000 sermons at the rate of three or four a day. He had discovered the medium that matched the message God had given him in the Aldersgate Bible study, namely, outdoor preaching to the vast crowds of miners and peasants and artisans who had never heard of God's love before. Wesley's own conversion helped spark a revival in England and America—and the world—that has carried on to the present day.

Wesley's gifts as an evangelistic preacher were powerful (though exceeded by those of his friend George Whitefield). But it was Wesley's genius as an organizer that made "Methodism" a coherent movement with a profound social impact on eighteenth-century England. Wesley recognized that his working-class converts needed holistic ministry. What was the use of hearing the gospel if they continued to be slaves to gin or victims of hopeless disorder in their families? In 1742 one of Wesley's friends in Bristol hit on the key to building a movement that changed people's lives permanently. He recommended that Wesley organize his new converts into "classes" of twelve, meeting weekly for prayer and Bible study and mutual accountability. These small groups helped new Christians to take on whole new lives, breaking free from generations-old systems of addictive behavior—drunkenness, spouse abuse, recreational violence, and so on. At the same time the classes taught new members the basics of the Christian faith, serving the same purpose as the three years of pre-baptismal teaching (catechesis) for seekers in the early centuries of Christianity.

Wesley's teaching took note of the transformed lives that he observed among his followers. His theology understood the hearts of Christian believers, and spoke directly to those hearts. He had no use for the "reasonable Christianity" that Locke had prescribed in the 1690s. Indeed, the Holiness revival made sense as a divine "No" to the Age of Reason. The Methodist movement emphasized three issues of the heart in particular.

First, Wesley was an Arminian, and he believed that Jesus had died for the sins of the whole world. His parents, Samuel and Susannah, had maintained this High Church doctrine (though their own parents had been Puritan Dissenters—John Wesley had a complex heritage). This "unlimited atonement" meant that Wesley could preach the gospel with the firm expectation that anyone who surrendered to the Word and the Spirit could be saved. His friend George Whitefield became a predestinarian Calvinist, as we will see, and the two of them had some painful disagreements. Fortunately this theological difference did not mean that either of them preached with any less conviction or popular effect.

Second, Wesley noticed that many of his new converts exhibited a remarkable assurance of salvation. Hitherto in the Christian tradition this kind of assurance had been reckoned to be a rare gift, reserved by the Lord for faithful saints after a long life of obedience. But Wesley heard "baby Christians" testifying consistently to a powerful confidence in God's love for them. Concluding that the Holy Spirit was doing a new thing in these latter days, Wesley began to preach that "Christian assurance" was available to all those who sought it.

Third, Wesley also noted that many Methodists testified to powerful works of grace subsequent to justification. The Spirit anointed them powerfully at the moment they repented and fell on their knees before the Lord. But with the scaffolding of the class meetings surrounding them, they also experienced further touches of the Spirit's power. Often these subsequent blessings freed them from the addictive power of some particular sin. Again John Wesley concluded that the Spirit was doing a new work, and began to speak sometimes of a "second blessing." He infuriated his brother Charles with this language, which seemed to contradict the historic Anglican belief in "one baptism." John struggled throughout his life to find language to describe what he was observing. But the main point was that the Spirit continued to work in the believer's life after conversion, and that growth in "holiness" was possible for the ordinary believer.

The vital presence of the Spirit among the Methodists meant that the term "Holiness movement" came to be an apt descriptor. Not that the Evangelical or the Anglo-Catholic movements in Anglicanism failed to appreciate the third person of the Trinity. But the Methodists put special emphasis on the availability of the Spirit, on subjective experiences of the Spirit, on the transformational effects of the Spirit in the lives of believers, and on the importance of pressing further into deeper levels of surrender to the Spirit. In fact the Methodist movement proved so effective in personal transformation that it had a profound effect on British society. Although the actual number of class members was perhaps only 100,000 by Wesley's death in 1791, the wider impact of the movement (among members' families, and visitors to Methodist meetings) was much greater than those numbers alone would suggest. In the brutal days of the early Industrial Revolution and its "dark Satanic Mills," Methodism gave the British lower classes an energizing hope and the opportunity to better their lives through discipline, fellowship, and the Spirit's transforming power. The French historian Elie Halevy reckoned that the Holiness movement gave workers in Britain a ladder up out of despair, and spared the country the horrors of the mob violence and the guillotine that marred the French Revolution of the 1790s. As we will see, Methodism had a similar transformative effect in America in the early years of the new republic.

The Methodists' relationship to the Church of England was fraught from the very beginning. Wesley intended his followers to be a parachurch movement alongside the established church, and he remained an Anglican priest until his dying day. He urged his followers to attend their local parish churches on Sundays and to pray for their unsympathetic pastors. He instructed his assistants never to schedule Methodist meetings at times that conflicted with services in the local parish church. Wesley's personal authority held the movement barely within the Church of England until his death in 1791. But Methodism was a grievous offense to the port-sodden British aristocracy in the eighteenth century, who were content with a noninterfering, Deist spirituality. The Holiness movement represented the "enthusiasm" that the upper classes hated and feared when they recalled the Cromwellian chaos of the 1650s. Wesley was also raising up lower-class men and women into leadership, talented people who could never have found expression for their gifts in the established church. Under the care of these unconventional evangelists and pastors, the Methodist meetings soon became their members' true Christian communities. They felt no love for the Church of England, which despised them. So after Wesley's death in 1791, the British Methodist movement quickly seceded as a "dissenting" denomination (it happened seven years earlier in America, for reasons that we'll see) and moved outside the Anglican tradition. In 1960 the Holiness tradition came back to its Anglican roots. But that's another story.

Let's Pause and Reflect

1. How did the ethos of the eighteenth-century Church of England keep John Wesley away from what he was seeking during his Holy Club years?

_____

_____

_____

_____

_____

_____

2. What were the three major emphases of the Methodist movement, as it emerged in the 1740s?

_____

_____

_____

_____

_____

_____

The Early Evangelical Movement in the Church of England

George Whitefield continued to preach to thousands in the fields in America and all over the British Isles, parallel to Wesley's Methodist movement, which gradually diverged in theology and in organization. On a preaching trip to America in 1740, Whitefield met Jonathan Edwards, the Congregational pastor and brilliant theologian in Northampton, Massachusetts. Whitefield hadn't had much time to read theology at Oxford (he was too busy cleaning students' rooms). So Edwards gave him a crash course in Calvinism. This system of theology held that Christ had died only for the elect, whom God predestined to salvation from before the beginning of time. Whitefield's preaching didn't change after he became a Calvinist. But unfortunately his new beliefs alienated him from John Wesley. (As we saw, the latter believed that Christ had died for everyone who would receive him.) Whitefield and Wesley tried to stay in touch, and in fact they did reconcile by the time Whitefield died in 1770. But for a time, there was "vigorous fellowship" between the two groups. Wesley's movement grew organically. Whitefield thrilled crowds on both sides of the Atlantic, but he left behind no coherent movement. He lamented, "My people are a rope of sand."

At the same time, however, a tiny number of Church of England clergy resolved to preach the Evangelical message but (unlike Whitefield) to remain in their parishes. They generally persisted in the Calvinist theology of their Puritan forebears. But like Whitefield and the Wesleys, they preached to people's hearts. They encouraged their hearers to respond with a radical change of life. These early Evangelical pioneers suffered the contempt of their fellow clergy, who believed that such "enthusiasm" was repulsive and undignified and apt to provoke social disorder. Nevertheless the tiny band of Evangelical brothers held on through the mid-eighteenth century, and from the 1780s exploded into a movement that would transform English society.

One early pioneer was the Rev. William Grimshaw of Haworth in Yorkshire, a rude village on the moors whose rustic inhabitants responded only to forceful methods of evangelism. Grimshaw regularly required that his parishioners sing the 119th Psalm (all 176 verses) before his sermon, while he patrolled the village with a bullwhip. Grimshaw would drive any Sunday-morning sluggards out of their houses and into the church, where he would preach on the love of God for them in Christ Jesus. This was tough love, but effective. Gradually the villagers came to understand Grimshaw's rough affection for them. In 1757 they had to enlarge the parish church to accommodate all the worshipers. John Wesley visited Haworth in May of that year and reckoned that there were nearly a thousand in attendance.

Another early Evangelical pioneer was the Rev. William Romaine in London. In the late 1750s there was not a single Evangelical preacher in the city's nearly three hundred parishes. Romaine held only a part-time appointment as a supplementary afternoon preacher at St. Dunstan's, where the vicar and vestry hated him and despised his gospel sermons. For a number of years they refused to heat or light the church for him in the wintertime. Crowds of poor people had to grope their way in the cold darkness, while Romaine held a candle by which he read his sermon notes—the only light in the church. But he told them about Jesus.

The most famous Evangelical pioneer was the Rev. John Newton, the slave ship captain and later author of the hymn "Amazing Grace." Newton became a Christian gradually in his twenties, partly by reading books like Thomas à Kempis' *The Imitation of Christ*. He came ashore and read for ordination, a very unlikely and unaristocratic candidate in his blue pea jacket. The bishop of Lincoln finally consented to ordain him in his late thirties, and sent him to a depressing little village called Olney in Buckinghamshire. Unemployment was nearly total, and alcoholism ravaged almost every squalid cottage. Newton finally won the village to Christ (and mostly to sobriety) through his patient parish visits, his homely language and illustrations, and his transparent love. In 1780 he was called to St. Mary Woolnoth near the Bank of England, so that there was finally one Evangelical rector in the city of London. People visited him from all over England for pastoral care. Nothing could shock Newton, who had done it all as a young man, and remembered all the details. One such visitor was a young political superstar, a member of Parliament named William Wilberforce, in late 1785. We'll pick up this story again at the beginning of Chapter 7.

Before we move on, a few more words are in order about the Evangelical tradition in the Anglican story. Like their forebears the Puritans, the eighteenth-century Evangelicals maintained four central convictions. First, they believed that the Bible was God's message to the human race, "containing all things necessary to salvation," and the preemptive authority in all matters of the faith. Second, they held that the heart of the Bible was the cross. Jesus' sacrifice paid for our guilt completely, and that changed everything. This was the moment *par excellence* when God's mighty power burst into the world. Third, the Evangelicals believed in preaching specifically for conversion. Every human being needed to hear the Word of God, to receive it, and believe it. Evangelicals called this conversion experience "the Great Change," and it was essential for every person's salvation. Finally, the eighteenth-century Evangelicals trusted that these three essentials—Bible, cross, and evangelism—would transform individual lives, and cumulatively reform the entire English nation. In this they would not be disappointed, as we shall see.

In a couple of ways the eighteenth-century Evangelicals differed from the sixteenth- and seventeenth-century Puritans. First of all, they were not as insistent on "double predestination," as the Puritans had been. True, Whitefield imbibed this belief as part of the Calvinism that he learned from Jonathan Edwards in America. This did cause a rift with John Wesley and the Methodist leaders. But in the fields and in the marketplaces, in their preaching, both Whitefield and Wesley stressed the *accessibility* of grace. It was no use speculating on the hidden decrees of God, when people needed to hear the good news and be saved. The urgency of the mission field, in Britain and America, and the eagerness of the crowds to hear the gospel, meant that formal theology shrank in importance, compared with the all-important message, "Decide now!" Systematic Calvinism was therefore less central in this chapter of the Anglican Evangelical tradition than it had been a hundred years before.

We also hear in the eighteenth-century Evangelicals a new whisper of optimism about history. The Puritans before them—like virtually all Christians at the time—had believed that this world would get worse and worse, until Christ finally returned and put it to rights. It would be too much to say that the eighteenth-century revivalists (Methodist or Evangelical) believed in human progress. But in both groups there was a growing sense that the Holy Spirit was doing a new thing in their time. The Spirit was offering salvation wholesale. Some scholars have suggested that the scientific revolution spilled over into the revivals. If God was showing Isaac Newton how the universe worked in perfect detail, maybe God was doing a new thing in the hearts of the Kingswood miners as well. I don't think we can draw direct connections between the scientific revolution, the eighteenth-century revivals, and the new sense of possibility in history. But something new *was* happening.

And it was happening in America as well as in Britain. It's time to cross the Atlantic and see what was happening in the thirteen colonies, especially in the Church of England parishes in that new world.

Let's Pause and Reflect

1. Compare and contrast the eighteenth-century Evangelical revival with the Methodist movement in the same period (1740–1780 or so). How were the two similar and different in their beliefs and their ministries?

_____

_____

_____

_____

_____

_____

_____

_____

Review

A. The Puritan movement (1560–1660) and the early Evangelical revival (1735–1780) were both representatives of the Evangelical strand in Anglican history. Leaving aside the Methodists, how were the Puritans and the early Evangelicals similar and different in their beliefs and their ministries?

_____

_____

_____

_____

_____

_____

_____

_____

_____

_____

_____

_____

For Thought and Application

B. Considering the Church of England in the seventeenth and eighteenth centuries, do you think that the Puritans doomed their movement to failure for three generations when they went to war with the king in 1642? Why or why not?

_____

_____

_____

_____

_____

_____

_____

_____

_____

_____

_____

_____

C. Some historians have argued that ordinary Americans today have no more idea of the Christian story than did the Kingswood miners in the 1740s. Do you think that evangelism requires something like the Methodist class meetings today—that is, a process of catechesis, assuming that its new members are purely pagan? Why or why not?

_____

_____

_____

_____

_____

_____

_____

_____

_____

_____

_____

_____

_____

_____

_____

_____

_____

For Further Reading

J.R.H. Moorman, *A History of the Church in England, Third Edition.*

- Chapter 17

Chapter 6

The Church of England in Colonial America

(1607–1789)

The New World

We are ready to cross the Atlantic Ocean. In this chapter we will see how the Church of England planted offshoots in America, beginning in Virginia and then up and down the Atlantic Seaboard by the War of Independence in 1775. We will notice that all three orthodox strands of the Anglican way appeared in America by that time, as well as the Latitudinarian torpor and the post-Christian Deism that we observed in Chapter 4.

Though we have already been discussing the Evangelical Anglican tradition, it actually first appeared in America. The Jamestown settlement in Virginia (1607) represented the first successful and lasting English colony in the New World. In its early years Jamestown embodied the moderately Puritan and Prayer Book Christianity of the English aristocracy in the early seventeenth century. However, the spiritual life of the colony gradually declined, as conditions in Virginia made it hard to maintain regular worship and the settled disciplines of the faith. By the late seventeenth century, the Church of England in Virginia had become lukewarm, its parishes dominated by the aristocratic planters whose lifestyle was less than apostolic in its zeal.

The High Church tradition appeared next. In 1701 a clergyman in England named Thomas Bray founded a missionary movement called the Society for the Propagation of the Gospel in Foreign Parts (known as the SPG). Bray was an Old High Churchman (a descendent of the Caroline divines) who stressed the centrality of bishops to the Church's identity, and the importance of the sacraments. Over the next seventy-five years, the SPG sent some three hundred missionaries to America, all of whom commended a vision of the Church of England as the only really authentic form of Christianity. Many colonists found the SPG's viewpoint to be arrogant and imperialistic. Some were impressed by its commitment to the apostolic succession. The colonial Church of England grew substantially by recruiting Congregationalists and Presbyterians to the SPG's ecclesiastical vision.

Meanwhile the Latitudinarian impulse was affecting America, especially among Anglicans in the larger seaport towns like Boston and Philadelphia and on the plantations of the Chesapeake tidewater. The scientific achievements of Isaac Newton seemed as impressive to many American merchants and gentry as they had to English aristocrats back home. Some likewise felt the desire to subject Christian claims to rational scrutiny, and to "prove" scientifically a low-

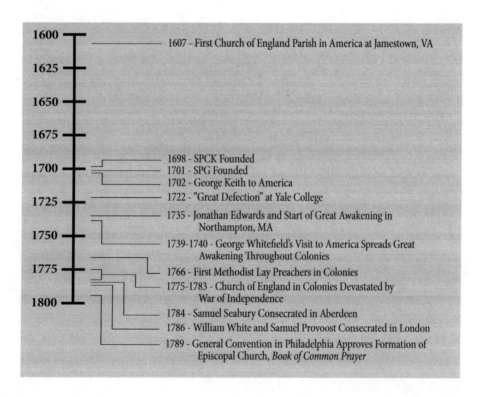

1600	1607 - First Church of England Parish in America at Jamestown, VA
1625	
1650	
1675	
1700	1698 - SPCK Founded
	1701 - SPG Founded
	1702 - George Keith to America
1725	1722 - "Great Defection" at Yale College
	1735 - Jonathan Edwards and Start of Great Awakening in Northampton, MA
1750	1739-1740 - George Whitefield's Visit to America Spreads Great Awakening Throughout Colonies
1775	1766 - First Methodist Lay Preachers in Colonies
	1775-1783 - Church of England in Colonies Devastated by War of Independence
1800	1784 - Samuel Seabury Consecrated in Aberdeen
	1786 - William White and Samuel Provoost Consecrated in London
	1789 - General Convention in Philadelphia Approves Formation of Episcopal Church, *Book of Common Prayer*

est-common-denominator version of the faith. We can see this spirit among upper-class Anglicans already in the early eighteenth century.

Both High Church Anglicans and Latitudinarians faced a strong challenge from the Anglican Evangelical tradition when George Whitefield landed in Savannah, Georgia in 1738. Whitefield had been profoundly converted in 1735, and was already a gifted preacher and had published ten volumes of sermons in England in 1737. The Great Awakening in the colonies had begun before he arrived. Jonathan Edwards's preaching in Northampton, Massachusetts, had occasioned a revival as early as 1735. But Whitefield's itinerant and extemporaneous preaching fanned the flames. In 1739 he began a preaching tour northward from Georgia, igniting a blaze of renewal and of controversy wherever he preached. Most of his Anglican colleagues reacted to Whitefield with shock and horror. For the next generation, the colonial Church of England would define itself largely over against the evangelistic ministry of its most famous clergyman.

Finally, on the eve of the War of Independence, the Wesleyan Holiness tradition appeared in America as well. Two lay evangelists landed in 1766, one in New York and the other in Maryland. Nine years later, there were already nineteen Methodist lay preachers traveling around the middle colonies. It was a small beginning, but the War of Independence failed to slow it down, and by 1783 there were already fifteen thousand Methodists in America. The following year, as we will see, they organized themselves as a separate denomination. More on this in due course.

The War of Independence nearly destroyed the Church of England in the colonies. By 1783 there were fewer communicants (some twelve thousand) than there were nascent Methodists. But over the next six years the remnants of the colonial church managed to pull themselves together, and in 1789 formed the Protestant Episcopal Church in the United States of America. The established Church of England had planted (however unintentionally) an independent daughter church in the New World. The Episcopal Church would be the prototype for thirty-seven additional Anglican provinces over the next two hundred years.

Let's Pause and Reflect

1. When and how did the three orthodox Anglican traditions appear in colonial America, as well as the theologically dubious Latitudinarian movement?

_____

_____

_____

_____

_____

_____

_____

_____

_____

_____

Evangelicalism and Decay in the Chesapeake Tidewater (1607–1775)

In a clearing in the forest near the banks of a broad river, men have tied a ship's sail to four trees, providing a little shade from the hot summer sun. At one edge of this sheltered space, there is a rough-sawn board nailed waist high between two saplings. Facing this crude pulpit, under the sail, planks laid across tree stumps supply four rows of seating. Three dozen men sprawl on the planks. Some are dozing in the heat, others are slapping the mosquitoes, while others try to listen to the clergyman behind the pulpit reading from the Book of Common Prayer. *The minister's face is thin and sallow with prominent cheekbones. Neither he nor his congregation have eaten heartily in the past few weeks. Yet the clergyman reads the service of Morning Prayer earnestly, and at least some of the congregation are paying attention. The sun beats down on the ragged sail, and the mosquitoes bite mercilessly.*

The Rev. Robert Hunt was the pastor of the ragged band of settlers who landed at Jamestown, Virginia, in 1607. Like so many of his fellow colonists, he was dead within a year of his arrival. The Chesapeake tidewater was not a healthy place for Englishmen. Just to the south, the Roanoke colony (founded in 1587) had vanished with hardly a trace. Yet merchants back in England remained optimistic about the commercial possibilities that the New World offered, and in 1606 King James I had granted a charter to plant a new venture. Three little ships carrying about a hundred colonists left London in December 1606 and sailed across the Atlantic by way of the Canary Islands and the Caribbean. They reached the Chesapeake after five months and landed their passengers some thirty miles up the James River. Here at "James Fort" (later Jamestown) the tiny band rigged their crude shelters and almost immediately began to hold Morning and Evening Prayer.

The early Jamestown settlers represented the moderate Puritanism of the English aristocracy in the early seventeenth century. The colonists relied on the Thirty-Nine Articles of Religion for their theology, and tended to read the Articles through Calvinist lenses. They believed in God's sovereign grace and in predestination. Human beings depended exclusively on God's will for their salvation. God was doing a new thing in these latter days, extending the gospel to nations who had never heard it, specifically the native peoples of the Americas. The first Jamestown settlers were serious about evangelizing the "Indians." Pocahontas was a famous early convert. Initially the Virginia Company saw the New World not only as a financial investment but also as a mission field.

Unfortunately it was not long before the spiritual vision of the Virginia colony faded. By the mid-seventeenth century, religious life in the Chesapeake tidewater had become tepid and conventional. Parishes up and down the rivers were controlled by the tobacco-growing planters whose zeal for alcohol, cards, and horse racing far exceeded their desire to emulate the Sermon on the Mount. There were several reasons for this decline.

First, because of the appalling hardship of life, there was instability in the religious leadership. Although Virginia attracted over a hundred English clergymen in the period 1607–1680, few lasted more than five years. Disease and poor nutrition killed off both clergy and laypeople rapidly. War with the natives also shortened life expectancy. The colonists' initial commitment to evangelize them quickly turned sour. Indian raids like the 1622 Good Friday massacre took many lives. So there was no continuity in the religious leadership of the colony—unlike New England, where the Congregationalist clergy kept the vision and purpose of their "errand into the wilderness" vivid and clear in the northern settlers' minds.

Second, the Church of England back home was too distracted in the seventeenth century to pay much attention to Virginia, or to remedy the lack of consistent clerical leadership there. From 1607 the bishop of London had assumed a vague responsibility for the colonies, there being no precedent (other than chaplaincies) for the care of English souls overseas. But the bishops of London were preoccupied first with the growing conflict between Crown and Parliament before 1642, then with the Civil War in 1642–1651, then with the religious chaos of the Cromwellian period, and latterly with the Catholic-versus-Protestant issues that led up to the Glorious Revolution of 1688–1689. No one was interested in giving Virginia its own bishop, even if there had been a statutory way to do that in the seventeenth century. The colony mostly had to fend for itself.

One way in which Virginia ordered its own affairs was for the planters to seize control in the parishes, a third reason for the spiritual slumber. In 1643 the Virginia legislature decreed that "vestries" composed of wealthy laypeople could appoint the clergy in each of the forty-odd parishes. (Local control seems obvious to us, but that wasn't the way patronage operated back in England.) The vestries soon became self-perpetuating. Exercising their legal power with considerable vigor, these aristocratic bodies generally hired their clergy on one-year contracts. This dampened whatever enthusiasm the ministers might have had for criticizing the piety or the morality of their employers. The clergy certainly did not object to the introduction of African slaves into Virginia in 1619.

So by the late seventeenth century, the early Evangelical flavor of the church in Virginia had dissolved into a bland formalism. In 1689 the bishop of London did appoint a deputy, a "commissary," to look into matters in Virginia. The Rev. James Blair was able and energetic, but his mission was too late. If the Church of England in the colonies were to find new life and fresh leadership, it would need to come from somewhere else than the Chesapeake tidewater parishes themselves.

Let's Pause and Reflect

2. What were the major reasons for the decline in spiritual vigor among the Church of England parishes in the Chesapeake tidewater over the course of the seventeenth century?

_____

_____

_____

_____

_____

_____

_____

_____

_____

High Church Missionaries (1701–1775)

An early winter snowstorm is frosting the muddy streets of Cambridge, Massachusetts in November 1702. The timbered houses are shuttered against the cold wind, and smoke pours from their brick chimneys. Inside a tavern near Harvard College, a dozen young men are huddled around the fireplace in the large front room. Sitting on benches and heavy wooden chairs, they are leaning forward with their eyes on an elderly gentleman standing to the right of the hearth. He is the Rev. George Keith, a Scot, a former Quaker, and now a missionary to the colonies from the Church of England. Speaking bluntly and gesturing forcibly, Keith tells the students that their Congregational polity is all wrong. For example, says Keith, you Congregationalists think that churches are formed when individual Christians agree to walk together in the Lord's ways. You say that each such congregation is independent of any higher church authority. On the contrary, Keith argues, the true church is an institution governed by bishops who can trace a direct line of succession back to the apostles. Only if you are a baptized member of the Church of England, in fact, can you be sure that you are within God's covenant of salvation. At this point three students spring to their feet, shouting at Keith and shaking their fists. Harvard College is not a very receptive environment for Keith's High Church ideas.

The Rev. George Keith was the first missionary to the colonies sent out by the new Society for the Propagation of the Gospel. Outside Virginia in 1702, the colonial Church of England was an embattled minority. Massachusetts and Connecticut were solidly Congregational with a few Presbyterians. There was only one Church of England congregation in Boston, called King's Chapel, not a very winsome name in a colony that had recently lost its independent charter to the new King James II. The "middle colonies" of New York, New Jersey, and Pennsylvania were an open religious marketplace, with the Presbyterians, Quakers, and Reformed (Dutch and German) churches well represented. There were only four Church of England congregations in those three colonies. Maryland looked more promising. The original Roman Catholic haven had become a royal colony in 1691, and a vigorous new governor there was working to establish the Church of England by law. Already there were seventeen active Anglican clergy in Maryland. But south of the Chesapeake, the Church of England was weak. South Carolina had only one Church of England clergyman outside Charleston, so the overall religious situation in the colonies was a challenge to the mother church back home. Was America to grow up virtually outside the influence—let alone the authority—of the English state church? George Keith's mission was to survey the battlefield and to plan the recapture of the American colonies.

In fact, it had not been the institutional Church of England that had sent Keith to America. The voluntary missionary society that sent him was the brainchild of one English clergyman, the Rev. Thomas Bray. Bray had been the bishop of London's commissary in Maryland. Unlike his counterpart James Blair, who lived in Virginia for fifty-seven years, Bray chose to exercise his ministry mostly from England, where he thought he could do more good. In 1698 he had founded an initial voluntary society to provide colonial clergy with libraries—the Society for Promoting Christian Knowledge (SPCK). He visited

America in 1700 and met the Maryland clergy in Annapolis, but he stayed only three months. Bray recognized the need for clerical manpower in the colonies, even in relatively well-served Maryland. So he returned to England and founded the Society for the Propagation of the Gospel in 1701 (which like the SPCK still does useful work today). Over the next seventy-five years, until the War of Independence ended its mission, the SPG would send over three hundred missionary clergy to the colonies. They would focus their activity outside Virginia and Maryland, and would face considerable opposition. On the whole they were better educated and more competent than their Church of England predecessors in the colonies. Thanks to the efforts of Keith and those who followed, the colonial Church of England would grow to more than four hundred congregations by 1775. Even in the stony soil of Congregational New England there would be twenty-two parishes in Massachusetts and thirty-seven in Connecticut on the eve of the American Revolution.

Thomas Bray and the SPG represented the "High Church" perspective that drew its inspiration from Archbishop Laud and the Caroline divines in the early seventeenth century. As that tradition survived in the period after the Stuart Restoration in 1660, it did not involve incense or holy water, crucifixes or candles. Since the Elizabethan Settlement of 1559, the ornaments and ceremonies of the English church had been plain and minimal. Even Archbishop Laud could not overcome the hostility of English people toward Rome and its symbols. By the eighteenth century, the term "High Church" had come to mean a high estimation of the English church's authority and identity. It meant that the Church of England was the one true church. Rome had erred, the Protestant denominations were schismatic, while the Church of England had preserved the true faith of the early church through that essential link, the institution of bishops in apostolic succession. The High Churchmen called on Rome to repent of its bad theology, and the Protestant "sects" to repent of their schisms, and return to the one true body of Christ, namely, the Church of England.

In one respect the High Churchmen made a bow toward the Age of Reason, namely, in their admiration for Newton and Locke. The SPG missionaries emphasized "general revelation" or "natural religion" as the foundation of faith. God has revealed his nature to us through the well-ordered construction of the universe. People should acknowledge the latter, and then go on to accept the claims of Christ and his unique spokesperson, the Church of England. You can see how this viewpoint might have excited some vigorous opposition in colonial America.

The controversial message of the SPG missionaries was exacerbated by their proselytism among the Congregationalists and Presbyterians. Keith and his fellows were inviting the others to "come up higher" and join an Anglican parish. SPG clergy did not fail entirely to evangelize neo-pagan colonists or the Native Americans (John Wesley had tried his best in Savannah, Georgia), but the focus of their mission was largely on the already-churched. They did enjoy some famous successes. In 1722 seven faculty and graduates of Yale College in Connecticut confessed that they were unsure about the validity of their ordination as Congregationalists. Four of them sailed off to England to seek Anglican orders. Three returned as SPG missionaries. This "Great Defection" did nothing to endear the High Church Anglicans to the Congregational ministers who still dominated public opinion in New England.

Even more inflammatory was the demand by SPG clergy for bishops in America. Most colonists saw English bishops as hateful symbols of everything they had crossed the Atlantic to escape. Bishops back in England were great wealthy lords, pillars of the royal government, and repressive agents of the aristocracy. Many rode about in gilded coaches surrounded by bodyguards all wearing the bishop's colors. The mere whisper of bishops for America raised the specter of British imperialism and royal despotism. This fear came to a crescendo in the decade before Lexington and Concord in 1775. So when the SPG clergy spoke or wrote in favor of bishops for the Church of England in America, they provoked the rage of the Sons of Liberty, who saw them as evil agents of the increasingly unpopular government in Britain. Only in the Chesapeake tidewater, where the SPG clergy were largely absent, did the colonial Church of England avoid this stigma.

In one sense, the SPG missionaries gave the colonial church a vision and purpose that it had previously lacked. Unfortunately this vision ("the one true Church") was anathema to most of the colonial population. In the War of Independence, this identification with the country's military enemy would practically destroy the Church of England in America. The survivors would need to rebuild a new denomination from the ground up.

Let's Pause and Reflect

3. What was the vision of the Church of England that the eighteenth-century SPG missionaries communicated in the American colonies?

_____

_____

_____

_____

_____

_____

4. What did the term "High Church" mean in this period?

_____

_____

_____

_____

_____

_____

The Age of Reason in the Colonial Church (1750–1775)

Thomas Jefferson's home, Monticello, near Charlottesville, Virginia, symbolized the Age of Reason in America. Begun in 1770, Jefferson's design expressed a confidence in the balance and harmony of the universe. The mansion is built of warm red brick with dazzling white wooden trim. As you face the house from the lawn in front, you see a high central porch supported by six Doric columns, the most geometrically perfect example of the classical Greek styles. Behind the portico, over the center of the building, rises a low dome on an octagonal base, with eight delicate round windows in each panel of the octagon. On either side of the central dome are two perfectly balanced wings, giving the whole mansion the elegant symmetry that Jefferson saw in the natural universe. The rational order of the world, as the Age of Reason

celebrated it, finds its reflection in the calm and confident balance of Thomas
Jefferson's Monticello.

English Deism echoed only faintly in the American colonies before the Revolution, but it did find representatives among the Southern plantation owners like Jefferson and the wealthier merchants in the seaport towns like Boston and Philadelphia. As we shall see, this watered-down Christianity would be a perennial temptation for Anglicans in the United States.

You may remember that in reaction to the carnage of the English Civil War, some British aristocrats emphasized the authority of human reason, and a lowest-common-denominator religion that they hoped all people of goodwill could affirm, and thus stop fighting. The authority of human scientific reason was the basic axiom of this viewpoint. We must not put our faith in anything that reason cannot verify. Reason teaches us that God is a distant creator who produced an orderly and harmonious universe, but who then stepped out for coffee and has not been heard from since. We can verify this God's existence by observing the perfect balance of nature's laws. Just as the complex and elegant order of a watch implies a watchmaker, so also the symmetry of the universe implies a watchmaker God. But this God is (to mix the metaphor) an absentee landlord. He does not interrupt the serenity of the cosmos by performing miracles, nor does he upset the course of nature by answering prayers.

So human beings are effectively alone in the universe. But thanks to our reason and to the scientific method, we can become masters of the cosmos. Human beings are also naturally good. When education frees us from ignorance and religious superstition, we are able to live balanced and harmonious lives. Jesus Christ was our great moral teacher, the consummate educator, who displayed the full human potential for perfection. (He did not rise from the dead, of course.) We are fully capable of following his example, achieving happiness in this life and immortality in the next. Aristocrats would all go to heaven, of course. Deists tended to think of hell as a useful idea, to keep the lower classes in line. Meanwhile, they thought life would progress onward and upward on earth, as human beings applied science and technology and built the perfect society.

Not too many colonial Anglicans were willing to profess this "reasonable" faith before the 1770s. However, we can see hints of the optimistic humanism that will challenge the Anglican way later in the nineteenth century. The Rev. Thomas Cradock preached a sermon in this vein to a gathering of clergy in Annapolis, Maryland in 1753. He argued that Isaac Newton and John Locke had purged Christianity of superstition and error, but had shown that science can at least bless a minimalist faith if it excludes miracles and the supernatural.

The Rev. William Smith of New York offered an even bolder version of "rational" Christianity that same year. A young Scottish immigrant, Smith published in 1753 a utopian vision of an imaginary college called Miriana, where education was strictly guided by scientific principles. Most young people at Miriana were trained in the mechanical arts, while an intelligent minority enjoyed a classical education in the liberal arts. Deliberately and significantly, Smith excluded Christianity from the Mirianan curriculum. Science, mathematics, philosophy, history, and rhetoric all featured prominently. But students encountered Christianity only in extracurricular sessions on Sunday evenings, and then only in a watered-down Deist version. Benjamin Franklin thought this educational program so attractive that he called Smith to be the provost of his new College of Philadelphia in 1755.

Mention of Franklin brings us to the radical Deism of the Founding Fathers. Franklin, Washington, and Jefferson were tenuously connected with the colonial Church of England. They all accommodated this affiliation with their own Enlightenment attitudes. In 1773 Franklin and his friend Francis Dashwood published an abridgement of the *Book of Common Prayer*, and dedicated it to Thomas Jefferson. They cut out all references to the supernatural and to Jesus' miracles, as well as any derogatory allusions to alleged human pride or "sin." Washington was a vestryman, though he evidently never received Holy Communion. He never spoke the names of our Lord, but referred only to the "Supreme Ruler of the Universe" and the "Great Disposer of Events" and other nonsectarian titles. Jefferson famously took a pair of scissors to the New Testament, and cut out everything but the moral teachings of Jesus.

Deism was an aristocratic phenomenon in the colonial Church of England, and not a very widespread one. It did have a limited appeal in that it offered aristocrats a refuge from the great explosion of enthusiastic fervor that swept all the colonies in the Great Awakening.

Let's Pause and Reflect

    5. What were the central ideas and values of the Enlightenment in mid-eighteenth-century America?

_____

_____

_____

_____

_____

_____

_____

_____

_____

The Great Awakening in America

On Monday morning, September 15, 1740, Trinity Church in Newport, Rhode Island is filled to overflowing. The box pews on the ground floor are packed with wealthy merchants and their families, while the second-floor galleries are crowded with poorer folk. Nearly a thousand people are listening in perfect silence as a young clergyman from England preaches from the tall "wine glass" pulpit toward the east end of the church. He is speaking about the new birth, the radical conversion that every Christian needs to experience.

He uses his voice as if it were a musical instrument, evoking emotions of longing from the congregation. They sense that they are on holy ground, that God is using this young preacher to give them a once-in-a-lifetime opportunity to receive pardon and forgiveness. The young man speaks for nearly an hour, as the large audience listens with rapt attention. Meanwhile in a box pew in front of the pulpit the Rev. James Honeyman, rector of Trinity Church, grinds his teeth and scowls. He thinks that he will have to work hard next

Sunday to remind his parishioners of the difference between true Christianity and this degrading "enthusiasm."

The Rev. George Whitefield became the hero of the Great Awakening that swept the thirteen colonies between 1735 and 1742. He was the best known figure in America, and almost every colonist could have heard him preach at least once. Yet most of his fellow Anglican clergymen reacted in horror as James Honeyman of Newport did, and then barred Whitefield from their pulpits.

Whitefield finished his Oxford degree in 1736 and was ordained deacon in the Church of England. At once he began preaching to large crowds with amazing results. People said that Whitefield could reduce strong men to tears simply by pronouncing the word *Mesopotamia*. While preparing to follow the Wesleys to Georgia, Whitefield began preaching outdoors to the coal miners in the Kingswood near Bristol, beginning that huge work of evangelism that Wesley would take over in 1739. Whitefield sailed to Georgia in 1738 to survey the situation there and discover what the work in Savannah might require. He stayed for three months, and the spiritual needs of the colonists (especially the many orphans) captured his heart. Over the next thirty-two years until his death in 1770 in Newburyport, Massachusetts, Whitefield would make six more visits to America, often preaching four times a day while he was there.

Whitefield's second visit to America was the most dramatic. In many of the colonies Christians were already praying expectantly for revival. In Northampton, Massachusetts, the preaching of Congregationalist pastor Jonathan Edwards had inspired a dramatic season of repentance and joy in that frontier town in 1735. From Northampton revival had spread to Congregational churches up and down the Connecticut River. New England had long yearned for renewal. Back in 1630 Governor John Winthrop had led the Massachusetts Bay settlers across the Atlantic. Speaking to the colonists aboard the flagship *Arbella*, Winthrop defined the new venture as a "city set upon a hill" that would model a holy Christian commonwealth for the whole world to emulate. Indeed, times of revival and spiritual power had swept the colony repeatedly in the century that followed. In Northampton, for example, Solomon Stoddard (Edwards's grandfather and predecessor as pastor) had seen five seasons of revival in his sixty-year ministry there. But people were still hungry. And not only in

New England. Evangelists like the Tennant brothers in New Jersey had recently sparked renewal there. So when Whitefield returned to America in October of 1739 and began preaching to thousands in Philadelphia, news spread quickly up and down the Atlantic Seaboard.

By September 1740 Whitefield had been preaching several times daily to larger and larger crowds in the middle colonies and in South Carolina. He then set sail for New England and landed at Newport, Rhode Island, on Sunday, September 14. The Rev. James Honeyman reluctantly loaned him the pulpit in Trinity Church the following day (which the horrified Church of England rector would instantly regret). After four days of almost continuous speaking in Newport, Whitefield rode north to Boston. There he conferred with his Church of England colleagues, and soon reached an impasse. As the latter were mostly of a High Church persuasion, they objected strongly to Whitefield's participation in the Lord's Supper with Congregationalists and Presbyterians, whose sacraments they considered invalid. Likewise Whitefield could not accept the High Church belief that infant baptism wholly saved a child, with no need for subsequent repentance and conversion. So from that point on Whitefield did not bother to seek admission to Church of England pulpits in New England. He did, however, speak to a crowd of seventeen thousand on Boston Common on October 12, before traveling westward to the Connecticut Valley.

Whitefield preached at Jonathan Edwards' Congregationalist church in Northampton on Sunday, October 19. Edwards and his flock wept copiously during the entire sermon (though after Whitefield left, Edwards did caution them about relying too heavily on emotional experiences). Whitefield greatly admired Edwards, his excellent and learned wife Sarah, and their several well-behaved children. Scholars have pointed to this visit as a turning point in Whitefield's theology, converting him to Edwards' Reformed Calvinism. In fact, Whitefield's appreciation of God's sovereign grace had been growing ever since his conversion in 1735. His association with New England Calvinists merely strengthened this tendency in his thought. Nevertheless, Whitefield was gradually growing away from his mentor John Wesley's Arminian confidence in the sinner's capacity to repent, toward a more exclusive emphasis on God's sovereignty. Both men did their best to remain on civil terms with each other. But the theological rift led to an organizational parting of the ways. Whitefield's

Evangelical Calvinism would stay mostly within the Church of England, while Wesley's Holiness movement became the Methodist Church in the 1780s and 1790s, as we have seen.

Meanwhile George Whitefield would visit the American colonies five more times. The afternoon before he died in September 1770 he preached in a large field in southern New Hampshire, standing on a large barrel and encouraging the flock to keep seeking the new birth. An asthmatic attack took his life early the following morning.

During his early ministry in America, Whitefield's preaching had a huge impact on the other Protestant denominations, inspiring renewal and schism in both congregations and denominations. Many new converts formed their own renewal churches, mostly Baptist in theology and democratic in polity. The Great Awakening was the first pan-colonial event, and stirred deep currents of moral fervor that helped lead to the War of Independence. But the Awakening largely bypassed the colonial Church of England, as we have seen. Not until after 1750 did younger leaders in the latter tradition begin to appreciate Whitefield's example. Young rectors like the Rev. Devereux Jarrett in Virginia began to preach for personal repentance and conversion, and to organize Bible studies and prayer groups in their parishes and beyond. Partly for this reason, and because of continuing immigration from the mother country, the colonial Church of England enjoyed a season of growth from 1750 to 1775. The number of parishes doubled to more than four hundred, still behind the Congregationalists, the Presbyterians, and the Baptists, but nevertheless a good showing.

On the fringes of the colonial church, the Methodist societies were multiplying as well. In 1772 the Rev. Francis Asbury assumed direction of Wesley's lay evangelists, who had begun to work in America six years earlier. Hundreds of converts joined the networks of Methodist class meetings, especially in the Chesapeake tidewater region.

But what would be the relationship between the Methodist societies and the Church of England in the colonies? And indeed, what would become of colonial church as a whole? Should America go to war with England? The superficial prosperity of the colonial church in 1775 proved to be short-lived. In April 1775 the "shot heard round the world" at Concord bridge in Massachusetts would throw the colonial Church of England into a crisis that would nearly end its life.

Let's Pause and Reflect

> 6. Why were the Church of England clergy in America so hostile toward George Whitefield and the Great Awakening?

_____

_____

_____

_____

_____

_____

_____

_____

_____

The War of Independence (1775-1783)

On April 18, 1775, British troops in Boston marched out of the city at night, aiming to seize the cannon and other military stores that the colonists had gathered in Lexington and Concord. Shots rang out, "heard round the world," as Ralph Waldo Emerson later claimed. Within weeks, other colonies had joined the Massachusetts rebels against British rule. But not all the colonists supported the rebellion. We often forget that the American Revolution was a civil war, with perhaps a third of the population resisting the cause of independence. Nevertheless, the British forces were unable to cope with the guerilla warfare that the rebels waged outside the coastal towns. Gradually, the ragtag armies of the Continental Congress wore down the will of the government in England to repress the rebellion. The colonies ultimately won their independence in the Treaty of Paris in 1783.

The colonial Church of England found itself in a very uncomfortable position when the war broke out. As the local representative of the British state church, it was rightly identified in the colonists' minds with the government against which many of them were in rebellion. All its clergy had taken an oath of obedience to the king on the occasion of their ordination. Were they not therefore political traitors? Likewise as we have seen, the colonial Church of England was an episcopal institution (even with bishops an ocean away), and it reminded many colonists of the hierarchical society they had fled to America to escape. The SPG clergy in 1775 continued to draw their salaries from England. This was all very awkward.

For all these reasons—and despite the fact that many clergy in the Chesapeake tidewater supported the rebellion—the colonial Church of England suffered the most among all the denominations during the war. By 1783 it had practically ceased to exist. Divided in its loyalties, the colonial Church of England lost its identity.

In the whitewashed pulpit of the parish church in Woodstock, Virginia stands the Rev. Peter Muhlenberg. Now twenty-nine years old in 1775, he has studied theology in Philadelphia under his father, the Rev. Henry Muhlenberg, founder of the Lutheran Church in America. Peter moved to the Shenandoah Valley to work among German settlers in that area. But he also has been ordained in the Church of England so that he can legally marry, bury, and collect tithes. Last year he was elected to the Virginia legislature, and earlier this year he was present at St. John's parish in Richmond, where Patrick Henry delivered his famous speech that ended, "Give me liberty or give me death!" Muhlenberg was deeply touched by Henry's rhetoric, and has decided to accept a commission in the Continental Army.

Now back in Woodstock to deliver his farewell sermon, Muhlenberg has chosen to preach on the third chapter of Ecclesiastes He says, "There is a time to preach and a time to pray. But there is also a time to fight." Having said that, Muhlenberg takes off his clerical robes to display the uniform of a full colonel in the Virginia line. He proceeds to the west door of the church, where he recruits men from his congregation as a drummer outdoors beats a martial roll.

About the same time, the Rev. Jonathan Boucher of Queen Anne's parish in Maryland is also standing in his pulpit. He is facing a very hostile congre-

gation. Boucher is not preaching on Ecclesiastes, but on Titus 3:1, "Remind them to be submissive to rulers and authorities..." True liberty, says the rector, does not mean political self-government, but rather freedom from sin, especially the sin of rebellion.

There is a mutter of angry dissent in the congregation, and scowls on the faces of men and women who obviously disagree vehemently with the rector's politics. But no one stirs in the box pews or threatens to interrupt the sermon. For on either side of the pulpit, resting on cushions, lie two loaded and cocked horse pistols. The Rev. Jonathan Boucher is determined to maintain his oath of loyalty to King George III.

Muhlenberg rose to be a major general in the Continental Army. Boucher's irate parishioners finally mobbed him in church and desisted only when Boucher held a pistol to the head of his senior warden. Boucher and his wife escaped unscathed, boarded a ship for England, and never came back.

These two vigorous leaders of the church symbolized the political division that tore apart the colonial Church of England in the months after Lexington and Concord. There were some 250 clergy in the colonies, spread over the 409 congregations, although unevenly distributed. Virginia alone had 105 while Delaware had 5 and Georgia 4. The war would reduce the total number by more than half.

The Virginia, clergy solidly favored colonial independence (roughly 85 to 20). In Virginia the Church of England had been established by the legislature since the seventeenth century and supported by tax revenues. When the Virginia legislature voted for independence, their clergy could cite their obligation to that duly constituted authority, offsetting their previous oaths of allegiance to the British Crown. As we have seen, aristocratic Virginia vestries tended to keep their clergy on one-year contracts. It was a bold rector who would dare to criticize the political views of the parish leaders, even in the unlikely event that he should desire to do so. Muhlenberg's views were typical of his colleagues in Virginia.

Elsewhere the Church of England clergy tended to support the Crown. None of the twenty Connecticut clergymen supported independence, only one of nineteen in New York, and even in tidewater Maryland only thirteen of the forty resident there. Outside Virginia and South Carolina, the colonial church was a countercultural phenomenon, making its way either in a hostile environment like Congregationalist New England or in a pluralistic open marketplace like Pennsylvania. In these areas the SPG clergy were apt to take their ordination vows to George III very seriously. Some, like the Rev. Samuel Seabury of Connecticut, enlisted as chaplains in American Loyalist regiments. Some took refuge in New York City, where the British army protected them until the end of the war. Others stayed in their parishes and suffered persecution at the hands of patriotic hooligans. (One Connecticut rector was tied to a chair and forced to look at a portrait of Oliver Cromwell for thirty whole minutes.) When the pressure grew too strong, most finally emigrated to Canada or back to England. By 1783 the colonial Church of England had lost at least half of its clergy.

The political views of the Church of England laity are harder to estimate. If colonial Loyalists represented some 35 percent of the population, which seems a reasonable guess, then the percentage of "Tories" in the church was probably a bit larger. Small in Virginia, the numbers were probably greater in High Church Connecticut. What is certain is that from 1775 to 1783 the numbers in the colonial church shrank catastrophically. What with emigration and the religious apathy that accompanies any civil war, by the Peace of Paris in 1783 the ranks of communicants seem to have dwindled to about twelve thousand.

The church also found itself in dire financial need. Those former SPG clergy who remained in America could no longer look to England for their salaries, because the SPG charter made no provision for clergy who could not swear an oath of allegiance to the British Crown. In some areas like Connecticut, where the SPG clergy had won the loyalty of their flock, parishes were able to shift to voluntary contributions fairly rapidly. In other states it took some time for congregations to adopt the idea of stewardship. In Virginia, where the colonial church had been supported by tax revenue, the "disestablishment" that followed the war left the church in considerable poverty. Parishes had little experience of self-support, in contrast to those denominations like the Baptists whose churches had been used to paying their own way from the very start.

So in the 1780s, when the covered wagons were crossing the Alleghenies and creaking through the Cumberland Gap in greater numbers, the former colonial Church of England was uniquely ill prepared to follow them westward.

It lacked leaders, it lacked structure, it lacked money, and it lacked any mission-ary strategy. What would the former Church of England be and do in a nation that had just thrown off British rule?

The one part of the erstwhile colonial church that prospered in the 1780s was of course the Methodist movement. Back in England, John Wesley had opposed the rebellion, and during the first three years after 1775, nine of the ten preachers he had sent over (all but Francis Asbury) had left the colonies. But local Methodist societies carried on. The preachers had done good work in preparing laypeople to take the initiative for themselves, running the weekly class meetings and inviting new members to join them. In 1784 there were over fifteen thousand Methodists in America, already outnumbering the remnant who identified themselves as Church of England. Most of the Methodists lived south of the Mason-Dixon Line. Their lay leaders could thrive on very little money and no traditional episcopal leadership. They were ready to follow the wagon trains westward into Ohio and Kentucky, and were beginning to think and act as an independent denomination.

But would the parent church survive the birth of the new nation? At the end of the War of Independence its vital signs were not promising.

Let's Pause and Reflect

7. How and why did the War of Independence shatter and almost de-stroy the colonial Church of England?

_____

_____

_____

_____

_____

_____

_____

_____

_____

Rebirth and Reorganization

The colonial Church of England suffered most among all the denominations during the war. By 1783 it had practically ceased to exist. Astonishingly in the following six years, the colonial church came back to life. It established an independent identity and chose a new name, The Protestant Episcopal Church in the United States of America. It managed to reconcile severe internal disagreements over the structure that it should adopt. It established a constitution, a set of church laws or canons, and a *Book of Common Prayer* adapted to the new American environment. It succeeded in procuring the consecration of four new bishops in England to ensure that the apostolic succession would continue in the newly independent nation. And in the person of Bishop William White of Pennsylvania, it produced a statesman who could preside over this miraculous rebirth.

By 1789, therefore, the Episcopal Church had successfully severed its ties with Britain and had arisen from the grave in which the War of Independence had seemingly buried it. True, the new church was a pitifully weak body at the beginning, with perhaps twelve thousand communicants in a nation of nearly four million. But it was alive. Barely.

On an evening in early October 1789, two men are sitting quietly in a snug corner at the back of a tavern in Philadelphia. One of them is a large florid man with a fierce expression. He is the Rt. Rev. Samuel Seabury, the new Episcopal bishop of Connecticut. His companion is slender and aristocratic, the Rt. Rev. William White of Pennsylvania. The two men could scarcely be more different in temperament and opinion, but they are conversing amiably over dinner.

Seabury was born in Connecticut and had been a staunch Loyalist from his early youth. He had served as an SPG missionary in New Jersey and New York before the war, and subsequently as chaplain to a Loyalist regiment after 1778. During the war his brusque personality grew even more abrasive. He was a classic High Churchman, not in reference to any penchant for "smells and bells" but to his stubborn conviction that bishops in apostolic succession were essential to the Church, and that the Church of England alone embodied true Christianity. It wasn't easy to be on the losing side in the war, and the experience of defeat strengthened his convictions.

White was a native of Philadelphia, son-in-law of the mayor, and brother-in-law to the financial wizard Robert Morris. During the war White had served as chaplain to the Continental Congress. In contrast to Seabury's High Church views, White's outlook was deeply shaped by the democratic ideals of the new American nation. He came to believe strongly in lay representation in the church's government. In shaping any successor to the colonial Church of England, White wanted to pattern the denomination after the federal government that the nascent Constitution would provide. Firmly orthodox in his theology, although no "enthusiast," and hard to assign to any church party, White was providentially a genial and open-minded man. He always believed in cooperation with non-episcopal denominations, and warmly affirmed their validity.

How can Seabury and White be dining in such a friendly manner, when their views of the church are so radically different?

After the Methodists became a separate denomination in 1784, there were two parties in the tiny remnant of the colonial Church of England in America, represented by Seabury and White.

As we have seen, Seabury's High Churchmanship maintained that authority in the body of Christ came directly from our Lord through the line of bishops in apostolic succession. Therefore authority was "top down" rather than "bottom up," as opposed to the Congregationalist and Baptist view that authority derived from the consent of the converted laity. A group of ten episcopal clergy gathered in Connecticut in 1783 to nominate one of their number to seek bishop's orders in England. They wished to ensure that their High Church viewpoint be represented in any successor body to the colonial Church of England in America. The prickly Seabury was not their first choice. But the front-runner demurred, and so Seabury got the nod and sailed for England in June of 1783.

Seabury's problem on arrival was that the Church of England had "never done it this way." There was no established procedure for making bishops to serve dioceses outside the British Isles. So after some disappointing interviews in London, Seabury looked for an alternative. In Scotland there remained a tiny remnant of a group that had left the Church of England in 1689, after King James II was deposed and William and Mary arrived from Holland in the Glorious Revolution. The Archbishop of Canterbury and six diocesan bishops had refused to swear allegiance to the new monarchs, on the grounds that James II was still alive. People called them the "Non-Jurors" after the Latin verb *jurare,* "to swear." They went into exile in Scotland, and continued to consecrate bishops right through the eighteenth century, in due apostolic succession. Seabury found three of them in Aberdeen who were willing to make him a bishop. He gladly promised in return that he would press for High Church principles in any new American denomination. So on November 14, 1784, in Aberdeen, the three Non-Juror bishops consecrated Samuel Seabury for Connecticut.

Meanwhile another small group of clergy in Pennsylvania and Maryland were conceiving a very different ideal for a new episcopal denomination. A group of Maryland clergy proposed a new name, the Protestant Episcopal Church. The word "Protestant" distinguished them intentionally from the Roman Catholics in Maryland, while "Episcopal" contrasted them with groups like the Presbyterians and Baptists who had no bishops. Around the same time, the Rev. William White of Philadelphia published a pamphlet titled *The Case of the Episcopal Churches in the United States Considered* (1782). White proposed that conventions of clergy and laity should elect candidates for bishop as well as representatives to national conventions. White clearly had in mind a very bottom-up structure in contrast to Seabury's top-down vision.

White was no great evangelist on the model of George Whitefield, but his theology was entirely creedal and orthodox. Later on in 1801 as presiding bishop of the new Episcopal Church, he would persuade the General Convention to adopt the Thirty-Nine Articles of Religion as its doctrinal standard (with minor amendments to suit the new political situation in the United States). While William White was not an "enthusiastic" Evangelical in terms of the Great Awakening, he was certainly true to the terms of the Elizabethan Settlement, the Articles of Religion, and the 1662 *Book of Common Prayer.* And he was "Low Church" in the sense that he held a low view of the English church's claim to be the only true representative of Christ's body.

With White's ecclesiastical vision in mind, state conventions began to meet in the mid-1780s. Two of them took advantage of recent parliamentary legislation in London that permitted the Church of England to consecrate bishops for foreign parts. Pennsylvania, not surprisingly, elected William White to cross the ocean. New York chose the Rev. Samuel Provoost, the only clergyman in the diocese who had supported the War of Independence. Provoost resolutely hated his erstwhile colleague Samuel Seabury as a Loyalist and a traitor, not a hopeful sign of future cooperation within the American episcopate. On February 4, 1787, the Archbishop of Canterbury and two other English bishops consecrated White and Provoost in London. At this point America had three bishops, the minimum number for further consecrations on American soil. But would these three new bishops ever agree on anything?

In the end it was White's statesmanship that allowed the two rival Episcopal churches to unite. In the summer and early autumn of 1789 a General Convention assembled in Philadelphia. It was a tiny meeting in contrast to the mammoth two-week affairs that would come to afflict the church in the twentieth century. At its largest gatherings, the Convention of 1789 numbered only twenty-two clergy and sixteen laymen. Yet this small group managed to agree on a constitution, a set of laws or canons, and a *Book of Common Prayer*. Astonishingly the Convention made a way for the two mutually hostile parties to live together in the same church.

During the first sessions in July and August, no representatives from New England appeared. Fortunately Bishop Provoost of New York was ill for part of this time, and White took advantage of his timely absence by making some concessions that persuaded the New England High Churchmen to attend a further session in September. Under White's leadership over the summer, Convention affirmed the validity of Seabury's consecration—not a foregone conclusion, as some of the middle-states clergy wondered if the Scottish Non-Jurors were really part of the Church of England at all. Then White persuaded Convention to establish a separate House of Bishops, addressing Seabury's commitment to episcopal authority. And finally, Convention assured the New Englanders that they need not bring lay delegates to Philadelphia if that offended their sense of propriety. These initial concessions induced Seabury and three New England clergy to attend the next session in late September. Provoost was so offended that he boycotted the meetings entirely.

In the autumn sessions, Convention made further concessions to Seabury's High Church convictions. They strengthened the House of Bishops, allowing it to initiate legislation and to veto the House of Clergy and Lay Deputies by an 80 percent majority (twenty years later reduced to a bare 51 percent). White and Seabury then left the lower House and constituted themselves as the House of Bishops. Since Seabury had been consecrated first, White graciously asked him to preside when they met together for dinner.

The new Episcopal Church that emerged in 1789 combined Seabury's belief in the divine authority of bishops with White's democratic and representative polity. *The Book of Common Prayer* also showed marks of compromise between the two parties. It obviously omitted any prayers for the British monarch. On the other hand, it contained several features that Seabury had promised the Aberdeen Non-Jurors that he would seek to insert. In the service of Holy Communion, the 1789 book included an "invocation," or *epiclesis,* that asked the Holy Spirit to sanctify the elements of bread and wine. No English liturgy since 1549 had contained such a prayer, which Protestants viewed as dangerously suggestive of transubstantiation. Bishop White agreed to put it back in.

So by the middle of October 1789 the two bishops and all the delegates had agreed on a structure and a liturgy that would permit the two tiny parties to come together as one. They represented a denomination of only twelve thousand or so, as we have seen. Could this small group find a new identity and a mission in America? Would the Episcopal Church ever be more than a small antiquarian sect? In 1789 it was much too soon to tell.

Let's Pause and Reflect

8. What were the key elements of the new Protestant Episcopal Church in 1789? How were they achieved?

_____

_____

_____

_____

_____

_____

_____

_____

_____

_____

_____

Review

A. In 1775 there were two principal theologies of the Church among members of the Church of England in the American colonies—the High Church and the Evangelical views. There were also two minor perspectives, held by fewer people—the Enlightenment and the Holiness beliefs about the Church. Describe each of these briefly. Which of the four do you consider to have been the most credible and persuasive? Why?

_____

_____

_____

_____

_____

_____

_____

_____

_____

_____

_____

_____

_____

For Thought and Application

B. Imagine that you are sitting in a tavern in Cambridge, Massachusetts, in 1701. You are listening to the Rev. George Keith expound his High Church ideas. You are a Congregationalist pastor, feeling exhausted from your efforts to pastor your unruly flock—each one of which seems to have his or her own ideas about everything. What might you find attractive among Keith's ideas, and what would still offend you? Why?

_____

_____

_____

_____

_____

_____

_____

_____

_____

_____

_____

C. When John Winthrop and his companions came to Massachusetts in 1630, they were seeking *freedom for* building a godly society, a "city set upon a hill." When the Boston Tea Party rebels threw the British tea into Boston Harbor in 1773, they were seeking *freedom from* the oppressive government of King George III. Are these two kinds of freedom more similar or more different? Why?

_____

_____

_____

_____

_____

_____

_____

_____

_____

_____

For Further Reading

Robert W. Prichard, *A History of the Episcopal Church, Third Revised Edition.*

- Chapters 1-4

Chapter 7

Anglican Evangelicals in England and America

(1787–1873)

The Episcopal Church in the United States managed to survive the American War of Independence and to establish its own identity in 1789, as we saw in the last chapter. For the next century or so, however, events in England would continue to influence the daughter church in America. The two strongest groups in the early nineteenth-century English church were the Evangelical movement and the Anglo-Catholic revival. The same would be true for the Episcopal Church in America. Likewise both in Britain and America those two parties would begin to battle each other fiercely in the 1840s. This unedifying spectacle would weaken both parties and open the door for a modernist movement to grow unchecked, beginning in the 1860s. We will consider that modernist religion in Chapter 10.

For the moment, we need to grasp what was happening in England in the eighteenth and early nineteenth centuries in order to understand the history of the American Episcopal Church. The latter was formally independent, but in many ways it continued to depend theologically on the church from which it sprang. Because both the Evangelical and the Anglo-Catholic movements were so important in the development for the emergence of what we can call "Anglicanism" in the nineteenth century, a chapter will be devoted to each one. The Evangelical movement emerged first, so we'll begin with its story.

The Evangelical Movement in Britain

Near the coast of West Africa in 1789, a line of men are plodding along a track through the jungle, heading for a beach on the shore. They have been marching for three days, and have received nothing to eat along the way. Most of them are faint and staggering. Not only are they starving, but they are also cruelly fastened to one another in pairs. The man in front has a forked wooden beam pressing against the back of his neck, and tied with rope around his throat. The beam extends five feet behind him, pressing against the throat of the man in back. A rope secures the open end of this fork behind the man's neck. A chain connects his manacled hands to the foremost man in the pair behind him.

Tired, hungry, humiliated, and in pain, these slaves are marching to the coast to be loaded into British ships bound for the Americas. Their captors are fellow Africans whom British traders have bribed to catch and sell their neighbors. The slave drivers have muskets, and carry whips with which they lash their captives constantly. As long as British ships rove up and down the coast by the dozens looking for cargoes, there will be slaves on the beach.

Several thousand miles to the north on this same day in 1789, St. Stephen's Chapel in Westminster is crowded with members of the British House of Commons. Word has circulated that the most eloquent young member of the House, William Wilberforce, plans to pronounce an oration today attacking the African slave trade in British vessels. The trade is a gargantuan institution with investors from all ranks of British society. From great lords down to butchers and bakers, practically everyone has some investment in a "Guinea cargo." Profits are huge despite the predictable death rate of 25 percent for cargoes in the middle passage between West Africa and the Caribbean. How can Wilberforce have the audacity to challenge a trade on which (as nearly everyone agrees) the prosperity of Britain directly depends?

The young orator proceeds to hold his audience spellbound for three and a half hours. But still the slave trade owns the House of Commons. Pro-slavery members easily find procedural reasons for delaying any action. Wilberforce's motion never comes to a vote.

Will the African slave trade go on forever?

William Wilberforce and his allies would eventually transform the moral consciousness of the British nation. They would not only move Parliament in 1807 to abolish the slave trade in British vessels, but in 1833 they would eradicate the entire institution of slavery in the British Empire. Wilberforce's brand of Anglican evangelical piety would revive the old Puritan dream of England as a holy nation. Wilberforce's movement would also exert a strong influence across the Atlantic. It would help to create the climate of opinion that would make the abolition of slavery the focus of American politics, and ultimately move Abraham Lincoln to issue the Emancipation Proclamation on January 1, 1863.

The Evangelical Transformation of English Society

Wilberforce was born in 1759 into an enormously wealthy merchant family in Hull, on the northeastern coast of England. Wilberforce was a tiny, nearsighted boy, and he suffered from a host of ailments. Nevertheless he was so witty and friendly that people immediately forgot his unimpressive appearance. After loafing through university at Cambridge, Wilberforce won election to Parliament from the borough of Hull on his twenty-first birthday. His best friend in the House of Commons was William Pitt the younger, who would soon become prime minister at the age of twenty-four. It looked as if Pitt and Wilberforce would dominate British politics for the next fifty years. Wilberforce belonged to all the right London clubs, and he was the life of the most glittering parties and balls. But after some five years he inexplicably fell into a depression. By his early twenties he had climbed effortlessly to the top of British society. Was this all there was?

To take his mind off his misery Wilberforce took the grand tour of the Continent in 1785. As a traveling companion he invited his Cambridge contemporary Isaac Milner, also a native of Hull (and unbeknownst to Wilberforce a recent Evangelical convert). Milner had a brilliant mind and a huge body—on one occasion while crossing the Alps in winter, he singlehandedly heaved their coach away from a sheer cliff and back onto the icy road. Milner's company inspired Wilberforce to take another look at the Evangelical Christianity that he had encountered as a boy, but from which he had drifted at university. Back in London he resolved to visit John Newton and ask for guidance.

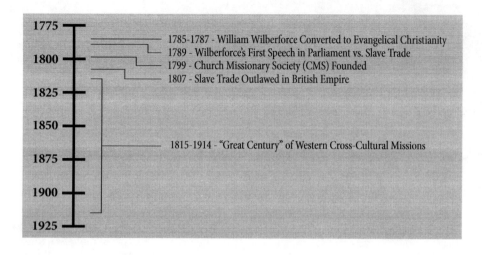

By the time Wilberforce saw Newton (secretly, lest the young politician be suspected of enthusiasm), he had more or less decided to become a serious Christian. But since political life in England was such a moral cesspool, he assumed that he should follow Newton into holy orders. Not so fast, said Newton. Suppose God has called you to the House of Commons? Wilberforce was stunned. He knew all too clearly how venal, corrupt, and immoral Parliament was in the 1780s (one reason why the American colonies had rebelled). How could God possibly call Wilberforce to be a politician? All through 1786 and 1787 he wrestled with God about his vocation. By October of 1787, he had come to a clear vision. He wrote in his diary that month, "God Almighty has set before me two great objects, the suppression of the slave trade and the reformation of manners." (By the latter he meant cleansing the debased moral squalor of British society). A tall order!

Slavery and corrupt British morality offered enough challenges for a thousand lifetimes. Wilberforce could not have attempted them if God had not surrounded him with the ablest group of reformers in British history. All of them were Wilberforce's friends and keen Evangelicals. In the 1790s many of them moved with him to the village of Clapham, about an hour's horseback ride south of the houses of Parliament in Westminster. In Clapham they were in and out of each others' homes. For many years a core of them spent three hours a day in prayer. That "engine room" was the library of Henry Thornton's house in Clapham. Thornton was a fabulously wealthy banker, who gave away almost three-quarters of his income every year. Another regular was Charles Grant, former chairman of the vast East India Company. A third was the famous lawyer James Stephen. Together this band of Evangelical Anglican reformers directed the campaign against slavery that Wilberforce had begun in May of 1789, with his first speech on the horrors of the slave trade in British vessels.

The House of Commons was controlled (bought and paid for) by the slave ship owners and their investors, and by the wealthy sugar planters in the Caribbean. Wilberforce had to introduce his abolition bill twelve times in the years between 1789 and 1807. Eleven times the slavery interests brushed it aside with contempt. Wilberforce and his allies took the campaign to the country. Even though the British electorate was still tiny, the Clapham allies believed that they could evoke the latent moral conscience of the nation and put pressure on Parliament to act. The "Clapham sect" (as their enemies called them) invented modern politics in the process—especially by their foundation of voluntary societies organized around a specific issue. Wilberforce and company formed an Abolition Society, with hundreds of local branches around the country. The latter organized mass rallies, torchlight parades, and petitions with hundreds of thousands of signatures. They mounted a successful boycott of West Indian sugar. The famous potter Josiah Wedgwood created a cameo for the campaign, showing a black man kneeling in chains, with the inscription "Am I Not A Man and A Brother?" Wilberforce gave huge dinner parties at his town house in Westminster, and when the guests finished the soup course they would find Wedgwood's picture staring at them from the bottom of their bowls.

Finally the campaign swayed the moral conscience of Britain against the slave trade, whose horrors the Clapham allies had made brutally clear to the nation. The House of Commons passed the twelfth bill in 1807 by a margin of 283 to 16, prohibiting the slave trade in British vessels. But as an institution, slavery still persisted in the nascent British Empire. It took Wilberforce and his allies twenty-six more years to abolish slavery altogether. As Wilberforce lay on his deathbed in July 1833, he heard that Parliament had voted twenty million pounds sterling from tax revenue to buy out the West Indian planters and abolish the last vestiges of slavery in the British Empire.

The antislavery campaign—huge as it was—did not prevent Anglican Evangelicals from undertaking Wilberforce's second great cause, the transformation of British morality. The Clapham sect took up dozens of other issues, from campaigns against alcohol abuse to parliamentary legislation forbidding coal mine owners from using women as beasts of burden in cramped tunnels five hundred feet beneath the surface. Wilberforce and his friends were also equally active in measures to spread the gospel. Hannah More (their ally in the West Country) had been a famous playwright and poet before her conversion. She founded the "Penny Tracts" that the poor could afford, which told the gospel through stories of everyday life, and sold millions of copies. The Clapham allies formed the Church Missionary Society in 1799, and helped create the British and Foreign Bible Society several years later. They campaigned in Parliament to open India to missionaries. (The East India Company recognized all too well the socially explosive nature of the gospel, and hated it.) The Evangelical revival in Britain was a crucial base for what historian Kenneth Scott Latourette called "the great century of world evangelization" between 1815 and 1914.

Wilberforce and the Anglican Evangelicals helped transform Great Britain from a nation that was notoriously the most violent and corrupt in late eighteenth-century Europe into a country that was famous by the mid-nineteenth century as the most peaceful and honest in the West. Problems continued to abound, as any reader of Dickens will immediately recognize. The mills continued to eat whole families alive. The squalor of industrial ghettoes was abysmal. Tenements packing in three hundred souls typically had one privy in the courtyard—next to the well. But Wilberforce and his allies had firmly established the principle that the British government was morally responsible for the welfare of all its subjects (a notion that would have elicited drunken guffaws from the aristocracy in 1775). Gradually other groups took over leadership in British reform from the mid-nineteenth century onward—socialists, utilitarians, labor activists, and other secular idealists. But the Anglican Evangelicals had opened the door.

Let's Pause and Reflect

1. Illustrate the role of the new "voluntary societies" in the transformation of English society from the late 1700s onward.

_____

_____

_____

_____

_____

_____

_____

_____

_____

_____

Evangelicals in the American Episcopal Church

The British Evangelicals helped stimulate a similar wave of social trans-formation in America between 1789 and 1861. The Second Great Awakening erupted in the 1790s in New England, after the religious depression of the American Revolution. Voluntary reform societies proliferated there, and spread throughout the North. As in Britain, the societies aimed at factory reform, Sunday schools for poor working children, new hospitals and schools, and finally what became the cause of causes—the abolition of slavery. The Episcopal Church in America would have to decide how to relate to this wave of revivalism and reform in the North, an issue that became particularly fraught as the Church gained numbers and strength in the South.

The Episcopal Church may have risen from the dead in 1789, but it sleepwalked through the next generation. Bishop William White of Pennsylvania did manage to persuade the General Convention to adopt the Thirty-Nine Articles (suitably edited for American use) as its doctrinal standard in 1801. White also published a syllabus for ordinands, giving the Church's new leaders a common theological foundation in the early nineteenth century. Other than that, the Episcopal Church mostly slumbered in eastern comforts while the new nation spread westward across the Appalachians.

On a frosty Sunday morning in February 1811, three men are riding in a carriage down Duke of Gloucester Street in Williamsburg, Virginia. The owner of the carriage is the Rt. Rev. James Madison, cousin to the president of the United States. Not only the first Episcopal bishop of Virginia, he is also president of the College of William and Mary. With Bishop Madison in the carriage are the Rev. John Bracken, rector of Bruton Parish Church in Williamsburg, and young William Meade. The latter has just now before breakfast passed his examination for the diaconate. He and his two examiners are now riding to the church for the service of ordination.

As the carriage rolls down Duke of Gloucester Street, it passes a group of cheery undergraduates carrying guns, with bird dogs at their heels. It's a crisp morning and good for hunting. The students have no intention of going to church on this or any other Sunday. The College of William and Mary is secular. The debating society entertains such topics as "Whether there be a God?" Half of the members vote no. Meade's mother has insisted that he study at Presbyterian Princeton, rather than at Anglican William and Mary. Meade is frank to admit that every young white man in Virginia is either a skeptic or an atheist. As Meade looks out the carriage window this morning, he smiles ironically as the students wander by, hallooing toward the fields with their guns and their dogs.

When the carriage pulls up outside Bruton Parish Church, the prospects for Christianity do not look much more promising. The churchyard is unkempt and littered with trash. The windows in the church are mostly broken, and the white trim on the exterior is cracked and peeling. Inside, the church is cold; a stiff wind blows across the nave. The box pews have not been painted in decades. A tiny congregation huddles together under the pulpit, two ladies and about a dozen gentlemen, most of them Meade's relatives.

After Morning Prayer and the service of ordination, Meade himself climbs into the high pulpit in his plain homespun clothes—no vestments. The bishop has not bothered to prepare an ordination sermon, so Meade is on his own. As he stares down at the acres of empty box pews, the newly minted Rev. Mr. Meade does not estimate the Episcopal Church's chances of survival very highly.

Three months later, in May 1811, the tide began to turn, with the consecration of two men who would lead their Episcopal parties into significant growth: the Evangelical bishop Alexander Viets Griswold and the High Church bishop

John Henry Hobart. We will contemplate Griswold and the Evangelicals in this chapter, and get to know Hobart and the High Churchman in chapter 8.

To understand the Evangelical movement in the early nineteenth-century Episcopal Church, we need to look at the wider environment of revivalism in America. By 1811 the Second Great Awakening had been energizing Congregational and Presbyterian churches in New England for two decades. Led by the sons, grandsons, and other theological heirs of Jonathan Edwards, the awakening also touched colleges like Yale and Williams, where the famous Haystack Prayer Meeting in 1806 saw the first American undergraduates commit their lives to evangelism overseas. Soon, mission boards were forming—denominational and interdenominational—to support this surge of idealism.

Also by 1811, the New England revival was beginning to produce a variety of voluntary societies aimed at social transformation, just as was happening across the Atlantic in Britain. The early Industrial Revolution and the American and French political upheavals suggested that social change was in fact possible. As America began to swarm into the vast expanse of the continent westward, many people (especially in the North) believed that God was offering them a fresh start, and opportunity to build the kingdom of heaven on earth. Finally at last, the human race had the chance to get it right! John Winthrop's vision might come true of a holy commonwealth, "a city upon a hill" that would inspire the Old World to throw off its chains and escape the tyranny of corrupt human governments. In New England especially, this titanic transformational energy turned toward the building of hospitals and schools, to reforming prisons, to attacking alcoholism and spousal abuse, and to mitigating the exploitation of child labor in the new textile factories. In the 1830s

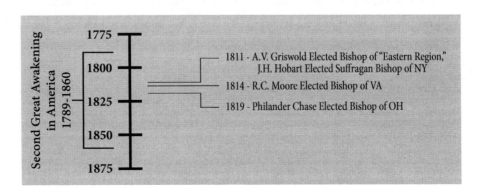

(as hitherto in England) the "cause of causes" became the abolition of slavery. What attitude would the new Episcopal Church take to this energetic passion for reform in the North?

While the second Great Awakening was transforming New England, a very different kind of revival was exploding in Kentucky and Tennessee as the covered wagons creaked westward through the Cumberland Gap. The settlers were hardscrabble people, battered by weather and often on the edge of starvation. Like young Abraham Lincoln's family, they moved about restlessly, looking for farmland that would guarantee their survival. Ruggedly independent yet often isolated, these hardscrabble farmers and their families needed fellowship and company. When rumor spread of a great Christian revival meeting to be held at Cane Ridge, Kentucky in August of 1801, the response was electric. Over ten thousand people showed up at Cane Ridge. (Lexington, the largest town in the state, had barely two thousand citizens at the time.) Wagons were circled, preachers leapt and shouted from their tailgates around the clock, and the lively event went on for a whole week before the food ran out. The Cane Ridge revival set a pattern for frontier revival that would last for decades. Baptists and Methodists took it up eagerly, Presbyterians and Congregationalists a bit more hesitantly. It is not true (as some mean-spirited critics have alleged) that the Episcopalians waited until the invention of the Pullman car before venturing beyond the Appalachians. But in 1801 they were still asleep.

Meanwhile the frontier revivals were washing back to the northeast. In the 1820s and 1830s urban revivalists like Charles Grandison Finney were adapting the techniques of the frontier camp meeting to a white-collar, middle-class constituency. Finney developed a "New Measures" evangelism that appealed first to small cities along the Erie Canal in New York. He sent out advance men, he used parades and massed choirs from local churches, he challenged local sinners (often by name) to come forward and repent, and he designated an "anxious bench," where people under conviction but not yet "saved" could sit and absorb the concentrated prayers of the assembly. Finney claimed to have discovered a science of evangelism. (How the prestige of the Industrial Revolution had invaded Christianity with its confidence in "technique"!) Finney later took his New Measures to coastal cities like New York, and gradually (reluctantly) the older revivalists in New England came to embrace many of Finney's techniques. Later Finney became professor of theology, and then president of the new Oberlin College in Ohio. The college soon became a center not only for Finney's activist theology but also for social causes like abolition. Evangelical trust in human capacity to "decide for Christ" led directly to a confidence in humankind's ability to eradicate evil and build a purely Christian society in America.

Needless to say, this Northern Protestant "Methobapterian" activism did not play well in the South. As Northern abolitionists stepped up the violence of their antislavery language after 1830, the South increasingly circled its wagons to defend "the peculiar institution." Revivalism continued in the South, but without the socially transformationist idealism that had swept the North. On the whole, Southern preachers affirmed the duty of Christians to bring the good news to the slaves, but they insisted on a hierarchical universe where white men ruled and slaves huddled below in their servile ranks. While the North was embracing a progressive worldview in which change was the norm—and for the good—the South maintained a static traditionalism that viewed social change as the enemy.

Let's Pause and Reflect

2. Describe briefly the three main revivalist movements in early nineteenth-century America—the Second Great Awakening in New England, the frontier revivals that began at Cane Ridge, Kentucky, and the New Measures evangelism of Charles Grandison Finney and his allies.

_____

_____

_____

_____

_____

_____

_____

_____

Evangelical renewal began to lift the Episcopal Church out of its post-partum depression in the second decade of the nineteenth century. Leaders emerged in Virginia and in New England who rediscovered the old Reformation message of God's love for humankind in Christ Jesus, and they began to preach in a warm and persuasive fashion that invited conversion. Because of the growing rift between the South and North after 1830, southern Evangelicals in the Episcopal Church tended to linger on the themes of the individual's "Great Change" and of personal devotion thereafter. In the North, Episcopal Evangelicals generally followed the British pattern and insisted that individual conversion must lead to social transformation. Right down to the Civil War, however, Evangelicals on both sides of the Mason-Dixon Line maintained warm relations and saw each other as comrades in the work of evangelism.

The Episcopal Church in Virginia had seemed a hopeless cause on that icy February day in 1811 when young William Meade preached at his own ordination to the diaconate. Two years later, riding home from a small and desultory diocesan convention, Meade found himself repeating disconsolately, "Lost, lost, lost." But in 1814 Meade helped persuade the diocesan convention of seven clergy and eighteen laypeople to elect the New York clergyman Richard Channing Moore (1762–1841) to replace the deceased Bishop Madison. Moore had practiced medicine in New York, had studied for ordination under Bishop Provoost, and was ordained deacon and priest in 1787. Twenty-five years of fruitful ministry in New York City followed. Moore's excellent education and his natural courtesy appealed to aristocratic Virginians, as did his warm message of grace. To be sure, Moore was quick to affirm that the Great Change implied moral consequences. He had the boldness to demand that Virginian Episcopalians renounce horse racing, gambling, theater going, and public dancing. Not likely. Despite his countercultural moral vision, Moore's constant travel and eloquent preaching brought the Episcopal Church in Virginia back to life. When he died, the diocese had a hundred clergy and almost twice that number of active parishes.

Three months after Meade's gloomy ordination in Bruton Parish Church, the first Northern Evangelical bishop was consecrated in New York City. Alexander Viets Griswold (1766–1843) was a native of Connecticut and had been serving a parish in Bristol, Rhode Island, where his preaching had focused mainly on law rather than gospel. On the occasion of his consecration (at the bedside of old Bishop Provoost of New York, whose pair of hands were necessary for a valid rite) Griswold experienced a Wesleyan warming of the heart. Thereafter his preaching changed radically and for the rest of his life emphasized the love of God in Jesus Christ. He shared the conviction of the British Evangelicals that everyone needed to have a specific conversion experience in response to the gospel. Out of this revolutionary Great Change would flow the fruits of conversion—personal holiness, a commitment to evangelism, and a dedication to Christian social action. The one true Church included all persons (regardless of their denomination) who could testify to a Great Change. Griswold gladly cooperated with other Protestants in building the kingdom of God in New England.

Griswold's leadership helped awaken the Episcopal Church in the Northeast from its Laodicean slumbers. The new diocese (the "Eastern Region," all of New England save Connecticut) had only 15 clergymen in 1811. In the thirty-two years of his episcopate, Griswold ordained 111 priests, confirmed more than 10,000 Episcopalians, and traveled more than 20,000 miles. He was a quiet, humble man who helped formerly Puritan New Englanders get over their visceral hatred of bishops. One Congregationalist said of Griswold that he was "the best representative of an Apostle that I have ever seen, particularly because he doesn't know it."

While Griswold was building the Episcopal Church in New England on the foundation of the gospel, a second Evangelical bishop was following the mobile population westward. Philander Chase (1775–1852) was born on a rocky New Hampshire farm, and throughout his life would always return to farming in support of his missionary labors. His father was a Congregationalist deacon, but while a student at Dartmouth College, Chase read the new Episcopal *Book of Common Prayer,* and was entranced. Determined to seek Anglican orders, he found an English priest in Albany, New York, who agreed to tutor him. Six feet four inches tall, he appeared at the clergyman's door and demanded instruction. Fortunately the Englishman had the wisdom to admit him. Chase was a seismic force. Provoost of New York ordained him in 1798.

After serving happily in a Hartford, Connecticut, parish, Chase felt called to the wilderness of Ohio in 1817. He bought a farm near Columbus, founded St. John's Church and a Christian school, and in 1819 was elected first bishop (nonstipendiary, bivocational) of the new diocese of Ohio. Recognizing that his new flock was small and poor, Chase decided to go and raise money among British Evangelicals in 1823. He had phenomenal success. A gigantic backwoodsman in the elegant drawing rooms of Wilberforce's aristocratic friends in England, Chase spoke so persuasively that he came back with more than $30,000 in hand, an enormous sum for the early nineteenth century. Chase used some of the money to found Kenyon College, of which he became president. His volcanic energy, his autocratic personality, and the conflict between his roles as president and as bishop led to a faculty revolt in 1831, whereupon Chase resigned both offices. He spent the next five years farming in Michigan, where he also built and operated a successful lumber mill. But he was too able for the church to ignore him for long. In 1835, three clergymen and a group of laymen founded a new diocese in Peoria, Illinois, and elected Chase their bishop. Once again Chase went off to England, where Lord Kenyon and other Evangelical aristocrats agreed to bankroll a new diocese once more. Chase spent the rest of his life as bishop of Illinois, and as senior (or "presiding") bishop of the Episcopal Church from 1843 until his death in 1852.

While Chase was building two new dioceses in the wilderness of the "Old Northwest" (Ohio, Indiana, Michigan, and Illinois), a third great Evangelical leader worked for social transformation in the eastern cities of Philadelphia and New York. Always a parish priest, Stephen Higginson Tyng typified the Protestant "Benevolent Empire" in the northeast that linked revivalism with social transformation. His evangelical preaching was powerful, and congregations grew large under his leadership. St. Paul's, Philadelphia, was known (not entirely charitably) as "Tyng's Theater." There, and subsequently at St. George's, New York City, Tyng labored energetically for the American Bible Society, the Sunday School movement, and various temperance organizations. (The annual American consumption of whiskey per capita in 1830 was reckoned at about ten gallons.) Tyng's fifty-seven years in parish ministry epitomized the Evangelical Episcopal party in the North, and its eagerness to take part in the over-all Northern Protestant tendency to link gospel preaching with an optimistic confidence in divine transformation, and to advance the kingdom by rolling up their sleeves and keeping busy.

The most important second-generation Evangelical bishop was Charles Pettit McIlvaine (1799–1873), who succeeded Chase in Ohio in 1832. While chaplain to the United States Military Academy from 1825 to 1827, McIlvaine had occasioned a revival among the cadets through his evangelistic preaching. One prominent convert was the young Leonidas Polk, future bishop of Louisiana and a general in the Confederate army. McIlvaine was elected bishop of Ohio the day after Chase's resignation. He served in that capacity for more than forty years, his long tenure contributing to his leadership in the Episcopal Evangelical movement.

In McIlvaine's ministry we see the distinctive Episcopal attitude toward the Protestant mainstream in the North before the Civil War. McIlvaine fully shared the revivalists' commitment to gospel preaching and to social transformation, but he loathed and feared the emotional excesses that revivalism often incited, both in the Southern camp meetings and the Northern New Measures urban crusades. McIlvaine even favored metrical psalms in Episcopal worship instead of hymns, lest the latter excite the "animal passions" of the worshipers. The Prayer Book was the gold standard of decent and orderly worship, and McIlvaine commended its decorum and dignity to his fellow Protestant revivalists. While he recognized the other Protestant denominations as valid churches, McIlvaine stressed the apostolic authority of Episcopal bishops as a bulwark against emotional anarchy on the frontier. Under McIlvaine's leadership, the Northern Episcopal Evangelicals were part of the revivalist mainstream, but not altogether of it.

McIlvaine's gifts and his abolitionist credentials led President Lincoln to appoint him to a crucial diplomatic mission in the fall of 1861. British textile mills had depended on slave-grown cotton in the American South, and it was touch and go whether Parliament would support the Confederate cause. Lincoln asked McIlvaine to go and test the winds in Britain and to advise him how to proceed. McIlvaine discovered that Wilberforce's legacy of abolitionism still strongly predisposed the British electorate against slavery. British mills could do without Southern cotton thanks to new sources in India. If the Northern cause in the war proved not to be simply the preservation of the Union but also about the abolition of slavery, McIlvaine discovered, the British would stay out of the war. The bishop advised the president to that effect. After the battle of Antietam in 1862 gave Lincoln a barely credible Union victory, the president issued the Emancipation Proclamation, which took effect on the following January 1. McIlvaine's was not the only influence that produced the proclamation, nor was he the only author of British neutrality, but the Archbishop of Canterbury later asserted that "few men living have done so much to draw England and the United States together."

Meanwhile, for the two decades leading up to the Civil War, another issue had come to preoccupy Episcopal Evangelicals and to take their eyes off evangelism and social transformation. This was the Anglo-Catholic revival that began in Britain in the summer of 1833 and began to influence the American Episcopal Church by 1840. Tragically the two orthodox streams of Anglican life were soon at loggerheads—on both sides of the Atlantic. In America it almost seemed at times that Evangelical Episcopalians were more intent on the struggle within their church over Anglo-Catholic ritual and theology than they were about the great issue of slavery that was coming to divide the nation. We will look at the Anglo-Catholic revival and its consequences in the next chapter.

Let's Pause and Reflect

3. Describe the relationship of Episcopal Evangelicals to the wider currents of revival in America before the Civil War.

_____

_____

_____

_____

_____

_____

_____

Review

A. What were the conditions that encouraged Evangelical Christians in America—especially in the North—to hope that their generation could build the City of God in their new land?

_____

_____

_____

_____

_____

_____

_____

_____

B. What means did revivalists use to pursue their goals of personal and social transformation?

_____

_____

_____

_____

_____

_____

_____

_____

_____

_____

For Thought and Application

C. Imagine that you have just attended a revival meeting led by Charles Finney in Utica, New York in 1828. Write a letter to your cousin in Rochester, New York, describing what you have just seen and heard, and alerting your cousin to what's likely to happen soon when Finney comes to that city.

_____

_____

_____

_____

_____

_____

_____

_____

_____

_____

_____

_____

_____

_____

D. Some Evangelical Christians in America today argue that they should adopt the Wilberforce strategy and press for both religious and social renewal in this country. Other Evangelicals dismiss this proposal as naive and prefer to withdraw into gathered enclaves, so as to protect Christians from a hostile society that seeks to destroy their faith.

Of the two strategies, which would you favor? Why? Or would you argue for a third alternative? Why?

_____

_____

_____

_____

_____

_____

_____

_____

_____

_____

_____

_____

_____

_____

For Further Reading

J.R.H. Moorman, *A History of the Church in England, Third Edition.*
- Chapter 18

Robert W. Prichard, *A History of the Episcopal Church, Third Revised Edition.*
- Chapter 5

Chapter 8

Anglo-Catholics in the Church of England

(1833–1867)

The typical Anglican or Episcopal parish church in the 1780s was an austere and spartan building. It was designed as a lecture hall, and all its features were intended to focus the congregation's attention on the spoken word. The most prominent object in the rectangular building was the pulpit, often a three-decker affair. It would have a reading desk at the bottom, where the clerk read the prayers. Then a lectern halfway up, for the lessons. Finally, the pulpit proper topped the structure, perhaps fifteen feet above the floor. Often the pulpit was placed toward the east end of the church, on the right, facing the squire's box pew. Sometimes it was located on the north (or left-hand) wall, for better audibility. In any case, the pulpit was the most prominent object in the church.

By contrast, the holy table at the east end was plain and inconspicuous. Behind it on the east wall there might be tablets inscribed with the Lord's Prayer and the Ten Commandments. The congregation was allowed to look at written words—but absolutely no pictures or symbols or stained glass (except what might accidentally have survived in England from the Reformation's destructive outbursts). Any recent windows would have clear glass panes. There were no crosses, no candles, and no colors. Certainly no flowers on the holy table. The clergy dressed simply, in a white surplice over street clothes, sometimes exchanging the surplice for a black academic gown when they ascended to the

Right: The "triple decker pulpit" at Trinity Episcopal Church, Newport, RI. This church was built in 1726, and is a good example of a typical Anglican or Episcopal Church in the late 1700s.

Below: St. John Chrysostom Episcopal Church, Delafield, WI. This church was built in 1852 in the Gothic Revival style.

pulpit. Everything in the building and in the service combined to underline the supremacy of the Word.

The typical parish church built (or restored) in England or built in America in the 1850s offered a radically different visual experience.

Architecturally, the building focused the congregation's eyes on the holy table, now known as the altar, at the east end of the building. These Gothic Revival churches were longer and narrower than the lecture halls of the 1780s. Their interiors were divided into two separate domains. The nave was the larger space, where the congregation sat in parallel pews, all facing forward (no more family "boxes" all facing inward). At the head of the nave stood a brass-eagle lectern on one side, and a pulpit on the other, for the ministry of the Word— still important, but the entire decorative scheme emphasized the visual and the symbolic, not the verbal. Stained glass windows in Gothic arches told the Christian story in pictures. Light and color combined to delight the eye and spark the imagination. The spoken word still had its place, but in these Gothic Revival churches, the altar replaced the pulpit as the visual focus.

Up three steps from the nave, a rood screen led into the chancel, the domain of the clergy. The screen often featured wooden carvings, topped by a crucifix (or a "rood") in the center of an archway. This opening focused the eyes of the congregation forward, through the choir, with pews on either side. Then another three steps led up to the sanctuary, where a Communion rail enclosed the holy of holies. The altar was adorned with light and color. There were beautifully embroidered hangings, there were candles, and there were flowers. In the liturgy of the Mass, the priest stood with his back to the congregation, facing the altar and dressed in a richly embroidered and brightly colored chasuble. Behind the altar rose a screen called a "reredos," often adorned with wooden carvings of the saints and a rich variety of Christian symbols. At the climax of the service the congregation processed up past the lectern and the pulpit, through the opening in the rood screen. They knelt at the Communion rail and received the holy elements from the hands of the priest. Then they returned to their places, down the steps, in the nave.

The revival of medieval architecture and ceremonial sparked enormous controversy in the Church of England and the American Episcopal Church beginning in the 1840s. For three hundred years, the Reformation had determined the identity of the Anglican tradition. Now in the 1840s, it seemed as though both churches might well turn their backs on the Reformation, and return to the Catholic Christianity that Thomas Cranmer and his generation had rejected. Naturally the Evangelicals were outraged. Their ensuing conflict with the Anglo-Catholics distracted and diminished their passion for social transformation, and entangled both parties in unseemly public brawling—over issues that British and American societies were coming to view as fussy and irrelevant.

The Oxford Movement

Strictly speaking, the Anglo-Catholics fired the first shot. On July 14, 1833, the Rev. John Keble, the young Professor of Poetry at the University of Oxford, preached a sermon at St. Mary the Virgin in which he accused Parliament (and by implication Wilberforce and the Evangelicals) of "national apostasy." Ironically, Keble's attack came at precisely the moment of the Evangelicals' greatest triumph. As Wilberforce lay on his deathbed that month, the House of Commons would pass the legislation that would ban slavery in every part of the British Empire. Nevertheless, Keble believed that Parliament had sinned so gravely in other respects that God was calling the English church to throw off its three-hundred-year yoke of obedience to king-in-Parliament. What did this mean?

You may recall that in the 1530s, Parliament had declared that the English monarch—not the pope—was now the Supreme Head of the English church on earth. In fact, Henry VIII carried out this revolution through parliamentary legislation, so that, in fact, the English church was subject to king-in-Parliament. The Thirty-Nine Articles affirmed the supremacy of Scripture in matters of faith and morals, and the monarch was expected to uphold and to enforce this preeminence. But in all other respects, king-in-Parliament (or queen, as might be) supervised the life of the English church. Throughout the eighteenth century and on into the nineteenth, the English monarchs grew less and less interested in actually carrying out this mandate. As Parliament was now admitting Methodists and Presbyterians—and soon Roman Catholics—its authority over the Church of England was growing more and more anomalous. Still the Reformation settlement prevailed.

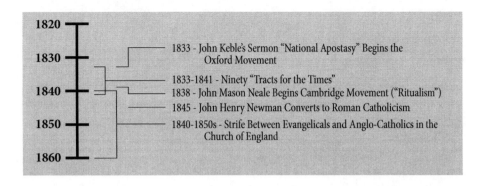

1820

1830 — 1833 - John Keble's Sermon "National Apostasy" Begins the
         Oxford Movement

1833-1841 - Ninety "Tracts for the Times"

1840 — 1838 - John Mason Neale Begins Cambridge Movement ("Ritualism")

1845 - John Henry Newman Converts to Roman Catholicism

1850 — 1840-1850s - Strife Between Evangelicals and Anglo-Catholics in the
         Church of England

1860

The Old High Church tradition since the early seventeenth century had generally supported this settlement. Beginning with Archbishop William Laud in the 1630s, this movement had tried to revive certain medieval features that they thought the Reformation had unnecessarily rejected, like a more central place for the sacraments in worship, and a higher view of bishops as necessary to the Church's identity. (The term "High Church" at this time referred especially to this high belief in episcopacy, not to ritualism.) At the same time they accepted the governance of the Church by king-in-Parliament. So did later High Churchmen like Thomas Bray and the Society for the Propagation of the Gospel, who sent so many clergy to the American colonies between 1700 and 1775. So did the "Non-Juring" bishops who consecrated Samuel Seabury in Aberdeen in 1784. (They just disagreed with the English about who the legitimate king was.) Not only did the eighteenth-century High Church party conform to the Reformation establishment of king-in-Parliament, but they were also aware that anti-Roman feelings still ran high in England. So they also accepted—at times uncomfortably—the Reformers' distaste for visual images, and the simplicity of church decoration and of ceremonial that had typified Anglican worship since the Reformation.

The Oxford movement that Keble began would gather up and support all the old positive values of High Church Anglicanism, like the centrality of the sacraments and the importance of episcopacy. But the Oxford movement would oppose the English church's captivity to king-in-Parliament. The subsequent Cambridge movement (as we'll see) would repudiate the plain and word-focused environment of the English church's worship since the Reformation.

The immediate occasion for Keble's "National Apostasy" sermon was a bill in Parliament the previous year, to abolish and recombine several ancient dioceses in the Church of Ireland (a symbol of English hegemony over this mostly Roman Catholic nation). The legislators had reasoned that a few solvent dioceses would make better sense than a lot of penniless ones, and would reduce the burden of tithes on the starving Irish peasantry to pay for a "foreign" Church they hated. The Evangelicals in the House of Commons had agreed with this line of thinking, but Keble the High Churchman thought it was blasphemous for king-in-Parliament to lay violent hands on the bride of Christ by daring to abolish bishoprics that stood in line of apostolic succession back to Jesus. This was the "apostasy" of which Keble spoke. The remedy he proposed was that the Church of England should cease to draw its authority from God through king-in-Parliament. Instead of being the English nation at prayer—which was no longer the case anyway—the Church should recover its true identity as the body of Christ, and draw its true authority from God via the apostolic succession of its bishops. Keble renounced the centuries-old High Church insistence on the Church's national establishment and proposed that it acknowledge the reality of its divine nature and its countercultural identity. While the Anglo-Catholic movement in England never succeeded in completely dissolving the Church's ties with the state, over the next century the Church would move toward considerable autonomy.

Let's Pause and Reflect

1. Why did John Keble not celebrate the achievement of Wilberforce and the Evangelicals in July of 1833, but rather accuse them of national apostasy?

_____

_____

_____

_____

_____

Keble's vision raised wider issues than simply the Church's relationship with the state. In four areas in particular, Keble and his allies in Oxford wanted to strengthen the Church (liberated constitutionally from the state) against a society that was becoming more secular, as science and industry grew more and more influential. During the 1830s, Keble and his friends published a series of ninety "Tracts for the Times," which expounded this vision. An early supporter was the Rev. Edward Bouverie Pusey, the well-respected Professor of Hebrew in the University of Oxford. But the leader who emerged to spearhead the movement—far more energetically than Keble the poet could have done—was the Rev. John Henry Newman, vicar of St. Mary's Church in Oxford. An eloquent preacher and an inspiring leader of young men, Newman gave the emerging movement both intellectual power and clarity of expression. Together the tracts set out a powerful vision for the Church's reform in four particular areas, in such a way that the Church could withstand the erosion of its life by a secularizing industrial society.

First of all, the emerging Oxford movement wanted to reestablish *apostolic tradition* as the basis of the Church's authority, and the heart of its life. Only thus could the body of Christ withstand the corrosive acids of secularism and scientism (we'll say more about the latter in the next chapter) that were turning English society upside down. Keble and company had no wish to dispute the authority of Scripture, but rather to see it in its true context. Before the New Testament began to be acknowledged in the late second century, there existed a body of oral teaching that the apostles had passed down. When Christians like Irenaeus of Lyons in the 180s began to ask what the true new covenant writings were, the answer was those that had been written or dictated by an apostle, or that summarized an apostle's direct teaching. So the New Testament emerged *within* the apostolic tradition, which was the source of its authenticity. When the canon of Scripture (the list of its valid books) took final shape in the late fourth century, of course, Scripture became the touchstone for any tradition that subsequently claimed apostolic authority. Even after the New Testament writings began to be recognized, however, the apostolic tradition continued to play a key role in the Church's life in two additional ways. First, it supplied the lenses through which Christians read Scripture, namely, the early creeds. For example, the early Apostles' Creed grew up alongside Scripture, and expressed the heart of the Christian story—enabling Christians to tell the difference between major and minor themes in the much more lengthy Gospels and Epistles. "Tradition" produced the creed in nearly identical versions in Rome, Antioch, and Alexandria. Christians could memorize it, and stake their lives on it. The creed was authentic because it was faithful to Scripture. But in the apostolic tradition, the creed stood alongside Scripture, and had its roots not only in the New Testament, but also in the oral tradition that continued to flourish alongside it. This lively tradition influenced the early church in a second way, namely, by providing some key guidelines for organizing the Church's life and worship. For example, nowhere in Scripture do we find the principle that Christians are to observe the Lord's Day on Sunday. But almost everywhere, that's what tradition taught Christians to do.

Keble and his friends had no desire to push Scripture off center, but to see it as part of the wider apostolic tradition—which contained important elements besides Scripture, such as the Apostles' Creed. The Oxford reformers thought that the traditions of the early church had continued to agree with Scripture, and to reflect valid apostolic truth, down to the year 600 or so. At that point, the Church of Rome had begun to propose new traditions that were flat contrary to the New Testament, such as the primacy of the pope over all other bishops. So the Reformation was entirely correct in pruning back these false traditions. But in setting up the Bible as the sole touchstone of truth, the Reformers had weakened its authority by leaving its interpretation up to king-in-Parliament. God never intended earthly rulers to exercise this ministry. Rather, from the apostles' time on down, God meant bishops to have this authority, bishops presiding over communities of faithful Christians who could affirm (or if necessary, fail to affirm) their teaching. So Keble and his friends wanted the Church's bishops to acknowledge and reclaim their rightful authority, as successors to the apostles by means of the apostolic succession, the chain of consecrations back to the first century.

Second, the Oxford reformers believed that true bishops should preside over *Christian communities* that were distinct from the increasingly secular society around them. Keble and his friends believed that the Evangelicals had been far too individualistic, much too preoccupied with individual conversions. The Evangelicals had assumed that a person could come to faith through a "Great Change," listening to George Whitefield preaching to a crowd in a field. This view was naive and simplistic, the Oxford reformers thought, and it failed to grasp how human beings actually come to faith. True and lasting conversion comes about by participating in a community of faith—by worshiping, learning, and growing gradually over time. True conversion requires more than simply saying "yes" to the gospel on a specific occasion. It involves more than rational assent. It's a holistic change in one's life, in which heart and head and hands all participate and cooperate in renewal together. It requires a community—and a community's mutual support if a secular society is busily trying to tear down what the Holy Spirit is building up. But if the process of true conversion is gradual and cumulative, at what point is a Christian actually saved?

Here is the third issue the Oxford reformers wished to address. They taught that *justification and sanctification* went hand in hand simultaneously. The sixteenth-century Reformers had attacked the late medieval church's teaching that human beings must initiate their own salvation, and accumulate merit toward salvation by doing the good works that the Church specified. No, said the Reformers, human beings cannot possibly do anything good at all, before they hear the gospel and respond in faith. (Thus the Thirty-Nine Articles: "Works done before the grace of Christ, and the Inspiration of the Spirit are not pleasing to God, forasmuch as they spring not of faith in Jesus Christ," Article 13). Thus the Evangelicals believed that the Great Change would immediately produce good works, grounded in faith, and differing absolutely from anything the person had done previously. Justification before true sanctification. Infant baptism simply promised that when a person welcomed the Great Change as an adult, God would faithfully declare that person just. But the Oxford reformers—Edward Pusey in particular—did not distinguish so radically between justification and sanctification. A baby born into a Christian family and baptized into the Christian community was already declared "justified" and was already undergoing sanctification—unconsciously, gradually, invisibly but completely and truly. Therefore the minister at Holy Baptism could accurately say, "We yield thee hearty thanks, most merciful Father, that it hath pleased thee to regenerate this infant with thy Holy Spirit." An Evangelical minister would need to interpret this (to himself) as a charitable prediction of the baby's later conversion as an adult. An Anglo-Catholic would mean it literally. Did this mean that the sacrament of Holy Baptism worked "automatically," as outraged Evangelicals claimed the Anglo-Catholics were teaching?

This leads us to the fourth area in which the early Anglo-Catholics wished to challenge the current teaching and practice of the Church of England, namely, the *sacraments and holy orders*. The sixteenth-century Reformers had viewed the sacraments of Baptism and Holy Communion as "visible words," guaranteeing the promises of God in Holy Scripture, and strengthening the hearts of believers to embrace those words. The sacraments were not optional. Jesus had commanded us to baptize and to celebrate the Eucharist. But for the Reformers the sacraments were extensions of the Word, grounded in the authority of the Word, and working to establish the Word in our hearts. So Baptism was a promise of later justification in the Great Change, and Holy Communion was a meal intended to strengthen our faith in Christ, and our ability to obey his commandments.

Let's Pause and Reflect

2. What were the four major areas in which Keble and the Oxford reformers wished to modify the doctrine and practice of the Church of England?

_____

_____

_____

_____

Keble and the Oxford movement wanted to allow the sacraments a much more independent efficacy than the Evangelicals did. By no means did they sever the sacraments from the Word, but they believed that the sacraments worked not only as the Evangelicals believed, but also subliminally, invisibly, secretly, nonverbally, and inaudibly. Something really happened to a baby in Baptism, even though the baby had no idea what the minister was saying. John Henry Newman put it this way:

> *Christ shines through the Sacraments as through transparent bodies, without impediment. He is the Light and Life of the Church, acting through it, dispensing His fullness, knitting and compacting together ev-*

*ery part of it; and these its Mysteries are not mere outward signs, but (as
it were) effluences of grace developing themselves in external forms. . . .
He has touched them, and breathed upon them, when he ordained them;
and thenceforth they have a virtue residing in them.*

Evangelicals would hear these words with outrage, fearing that Newman and
company were proposing a return to the superstitions of the late Middle Ages,
when people fed consecrated Communion wafers to their sick cows, or threw
them down dry wells to make water flow. The Oxford reformers were not teaching a magical view of the sacraments, but rather trying to expand the Reformation's preoccupation with our conscious understanding of *words*. God communicates with us not only through words and propositions, but also through
things that work in us even as we are unaware. Thus the Oxford movement emphasized God's "real presence" in the Eucharistic bread and wine. They didn't
teach "transubstantiation" in the Roman Catholic sense (that Christ's body and
blood replace the inner essence of the elements, while the outward appearances remain the same), but they did teach that a change definitely takes place.
Christ's presence in the elements was real, and the consecrated elements feed
our souls, even if we aren't conscious at that moment of God's promises that the
bread and wine represent.

The sacraments, according to the Oxford movement, were a great deal
more important than the Evangelicals had supposed. Therefore it was crucial
for the Oxford movement to establish whether a given sacrament was valid.
Could you receive Holy Communion from a Methodist, and thus partake of
Christ's "real presence"? No, said Keble and company very firmly. A valid sacrament required a valid celebrant. And according to God's plan, a valid celebrant
had to be a priest ordained by a bishop consecrated in the apostolic succession.
No exceptions. This meant that Communion services among the Methodists
and Baptists were not true celebrations of the Lord's Supper (whatever else they
might be). It also meant that Anglican clergy (consecrated and ordained in
apostolic succession) were different in kind and in calling from Protestant ministers. Anglican bishops were true bishops. They were essential to the Church
(of the Church's *esse)* and not simply "good for the Church" (of the Church's
bene esse), as Protestants would say. And the priests whom they ordained were
the only true priests. Episcopal ordination conferred a special "indelible char-

acter" on them, which set them apart uniquely from the rest of God's people. Their calling was not simply to preach and teach the Word. Crucially, they were to provide the sacraments, without which salvation was extremely unlikely at best. They were "priests" and not "ministers of the gospel," as the Reformation had supposed. As such they stood at the Lord's Table *in persona Christi,* representing Christ and his sacrifice on Calvary. Receiving the elements from their hands, God's people could be assured that they were partaking of Christ's true body and blood, which were necessary to their salvation.

Unfortunately for the Oxford movement, by the late 1830s John Henry Newman began to lose his confidence that the Church of England could give its people this assurance. In 1841 he published Tract 90, in which he argued (mostly trying to persuade himself) that the Thirty-Nine Articles actually permitted certain beliefs that Newman found in the early church, such as purgatory and the sacrifice of the Mass, and which he had come to think were necessary for salvation. Newman was entirely unprepared for the firestorm of protest that Tract 90 ignited. English anti-Roman sentiment was deep and persistent. English people still remembered Bloody Mary, and the threat of the Spanish Armada in 1588. They still saw "Roman aggression" as a clear and present danger in 1841. Newman sounded not only like a Roman Catholic, but like a political traitor as well. The bishop of Oxford forbade Newman to publish any further tracts. Personally devastated, he resigned his post at St. Mary's, Oxford, and moved out to his residence in the countryside. In 1845 he joined the Church of Rome. All the Evangelicals' most dire predictions seemed to have come true.

But Keble and Pusey stood firm back in Oxford, persuaded that Rome was in error on many points, and that the Church of England offered the best venue to promote their program. It had bishops in apostolic succession, but without the theological errors that had tainted the Church of Rome. It's important to note that the Oxford reformers had no interest in architectural or ceremonial changes, in medieval church architecture or in clerical vestments. They accepted the plain glass windows and the prominent pulpits of the English churches since the Reformation. Pusey said he feared that any outward changes would confuse people, and shift their attention away from the crucial matters of apostolic faith that he and his Oxford allies were commending.

But toward the end of the 1830s, a movement was beginning in the sister university of Cambridge which would emphasize precisely these outward appearances. The Cambridge movement would presuppose the theology of the Oxford reformers, but give it a very "Catholic" look. Together the two strands would produce the modern Anglo-Catholic tradition in the Anglican story.

Let's Pause and Reflect

3. How did the Oxford reformers' beliefs about the sacraments and the priesthood differ from the Evangelicals' perspectives?

_____

_____

_____

_____

_____

_____

_____

The Cambridge Movement

By the late 1830s, the leadership of the Catholic revival had shifted to Cambridge and to the young undergraduate John Mason Neale. The Cambridge movement would affirm all the theological proposals that Keble and company had made, but they would give this theology a very visible, audible, and even olfactory reality (as the Evangelicals scoffed, "smells and bells"). Specifically, they intended to revive the Gothic architecture, the stained glass windows, the candles and incense, and the ornate clerical vestments of the thirteenth century. They did this for a very urgent reason.

By the 1830s the Industrial Revolution was changing the face of England profoundly—more than any force since the introduction of agriculture around 4500 BC. By 1830 new urban factories were swallowing the former peasant population of England. As landlords drove them off their farms, to enclose their land for "scientific agriculture," the peasants fled to the huge new cities for work. Families of these wage slaves lived in crowded tenement houses, as many as twelve to a room, with one bathroom per building and no clean water. Twelve or fourteen hours a day they labored in cotton mills and other dangerous factories. These belched black clouds of smoke that covered the cities with toxic grit. The new urban landscape was hideously ugly.

The wealthier classes—from shopkeepers up to captains of industry—suffered from the same blighted urban environment as well. Many of them dreamed nostalgically of an imaginary "Merrie England" of medieval villages, maypole dancers, and daring knights and their beautiful ladies. The Waverley novels of Sir Walter Scott catered to this fantasy of an unspoiled world of cottages and castles and Gothic cathedrals. The revival of medieval worship—light, color, and beauty—might offer an alternative universe, a temporary relief from the soot-and-smoke ugliness of the new industrial cities. In light of all this, Neale could make a persuasive case that his fellow English people deserved an experience of thirteenth-century Christianity at least once a week.

Neale took a holiday from his studies in 1838, riding on horseback around the East Anglian countryside. He was a tall, angular youth, nearsighted, tousled, and careless of his dress. He was terminally shy and usually in ill health. This unlikely youth was to transform the plain worship of the Church of England, and to revive an appreciation of visual beauty in the Anglican tradition.

Everywhere he rode in Cambridgeshire, Neale saw parish churches untended and decrepit. Medieval parish churches had once been colorful and lovely. Their Gothic architecture drew the eye of the worshiper through the chancel toward the elaborate altars at the east end of the buildings. In the Reformation, with its emphasis on the Word, altars had been dismantled and the chancels boarded up and used for storage. For three hundred years, English church interiors had been plain and whitewashed, the prominent pulpit underscoring the primacy of preaching and hearing. Often the plain Communion table at the front of the nave was small and obscure, sometimes even used as a coatrack. Neale grieved at the decay of beauty in Anglican worship. How could the industrial working class imagine heaven if their erstwhile rural churches were decrepit and the relatively few urban churches equally ugly?

Neale absorbed the ideas of the Oxford movement and took them a step further. How to embody the primacy of worship in the formation of Christians? Neale believed that the revival of Gothic architecture and medieval cer-emony would draw the masses back into the churches, and shed the light of heavenly beauty into their grimy and squalid lives. He and his friends founded a journal called *The Ecclesiologist,* which aimed to restore ancient principles of church architecture and the Christian piety that had inspired it. Over the next thirty years, the program of *The Ecclesiologist* would transform the worship of the English church and its daughters throughout the expanding British Empire.

The Ecclesiologist proposed a revolution in Anglican worship, rejecting church buildings as lecture halls and reimagining them as pageantries of heav-en. Neale wrote,

> *A Church is not as it should be, till every window is filled with stained glass, till every inch of floor is covered with encaustic tiles, till there is a Roodscreen glowing with the brightest tints and with gold, nay, if we would arrive at perfection, the roof and walls must be painted and frescoed.*

Light, color, and symbolism beautified the worship of the new Anglo-Cath-olic movement. Inspired by *The Ecclesiologist,* Anglo-Catholic parishes began to repair their stained glass windows. They opened up their chancels so that worshipers could see through them to the restored altars, now replacing the pulpits as the visual focus of the churches. Crosses, candles, and liturgical colors reappeared in all their glory. Colored stoles and chasubles came out of the clothes presses where they had lain in the sacristies. Bishops once again donned copes and miters. All this outward symbolism reminded Anglicans that their God is high and lifted up, majestic and worthy of all worship. Neale reminded Anglicans that the Church is not only missional (as the Evangelicals had insisted) but also liturgical and sacramental.

One aspect of Neale's program drew particular Evangelical ire, namely, its deliberate emphasis on the distinction between priest and people. For three centuries the chancel in many parish churches had been boarded off, with a wooden table used for Communion at the front of the nave. Neale and *The Ecclesiologist* argued that the chancels should be reopened, and the sanctuaries at the east end refurbished. The point was to distinguish between the priest's domain—the east end, the chancel and the sanctuary—and the nave where the laypeople watched and waited. Neale wanted to destroy the box pews of the recent past, which highlighted the social distinction between rich and poor, between the haves, who could afford them, and the have-nots, who had to stand in the aisles. Now the crucial distinction was between the clergy, who dispensed the sacraments, and the laity, who received them. The revival of medieval vestments like the chasuble further emphasized the otherness of the priestly caste.

Let's Pause and Reflect

4. What were Neale's chief proposals for the reform of church architecture and decoration, and for ceremonies and vestments? How did Neale justify these proposals?

_____

_____

_____

_____

_____

_____

_____

_____

_____

By the late 1840s a number of parish churches were adopting Neale's program, and redecorating their interiors accordingly. Naturally, residual English anti-Roman partisans responded as if traitors were trying to drag the Church of England over the Alps to Rome. Various battles ensued. The later 1840s and 1850s saw an unedifying spectacle as Evangelicals and Anglo-Catholics went to war over the identity of the Church of England. The Evangelicals defended the heritage of the Reformation, the supremacy of Scripture, the priesthood of all believers, and the doctrine of justification by grace through faith. The Anglo-Catholics asserted the heritage of the early and medieval church, the centrality of the sacraments, the authority of the clergy, the real presence in the Eucharist, and baptismal regeneration. These were all features of medieval

Christianity that the Reformation had rejected, not to mention distaste for the full majesty of thirteenth-century Gothic architecture and ceremonies. Both parties could say the creeds with full conviction; they were not quarrelling over the existence of God or the resurrection of Jesus Christ. But both sides believed that their beliefs about the Church and the sacraments were central, and necessary to salvation. Neither side would back down.

The latter-day "wars of religion" took place in two venues. One was the English legal system. Almost as soon as "ritualist" clergy began introducing minor innovations (like the use of credence tables behind the altar), Evangelical champions arose to attack them in the Church of England's courts. The Anglo-Catholic defendants appealed verdicts that required that they cease and desist, and the cases wound their ways upward through the ecclesiastical legal system. Because of the royal supremacy over the Church of England, the final appeal lay with the Judicial Committee of the Privy Council. This group consisted of laymen who were skilled in common law but knew nothing of theology—plus one lone bishop. In the 1850s the Judicial Committee found nothing in church law that actually prohibited the use of credence tables, any more than doors or pews or stoves. But other judgments went against the ritualists. No crosses were allowed on the altar, for example. Some Anglo-Catholic clergy actually went to jail for contempt of court when they persisted in using incense or holy water. The deplorable spectacle ground on through the 1860s. The tide of battle finally turned in favor of the Anglo-Catholics. *The Ecclesiologist* ceased publication in 1868, having achieved all of its goals.

Clergy who so desired could introduce virtually any pre-Reformation practice and get away with it. The English public considered the ritualists odd and quirky, but they respected their courage and their persistence—and the willingness of their "slum priests" to stay in their parishes and die during the cholera outbreaks of the 1850s. They no longer appeared to be dangerous seditionists, traitorously dragging England back toward Rome.

Meanwhile, the other field of combat lay in the parish churches themselves. In the 1850s a number of prominent Anglo-Catholic parishes became the target of vandalism and actual mob violence. In London, St. George's-in-the-East saw the most notorious Evangelical hooliganism. For several months in 1859 and 1860, the Sunday-afternoon services at St. George's became a circus.

Crowds interrupted worship by hooting and hissing, by banging fireworks, by throwing pew cushions at the altar, by using pew 16 as a privy, and by setting a pair of hounds howling through the aisles. By the summer of 1860, it took seventy-three policemen to keep order in St. George's on a Sunday. When the vicar left on holiday, Evangelicals hired a brass band to escort him to the train station. Eventually the parish calmed down, and the mobs found other Sunday entertainment. But the damage had been done. Evangelicals had appeared to be bullies and boors (however few of their clergy had actually supported the riots). Among the English middle and upper classes, the Evangelical cause steadily lost credibility. Its defenders appeared to prefer slinging mud to engaging in reasonable conversation.

All of this helps us understand why a "modernist" movement found increasing support among Church of England clergy in the 1860s. But before we consider that development, we need to return to America and see how the conflict between Evangelicals and Anglo-Catholics played out in the Episcopal Church in the later nineteenth century.

Let's Pause and Reflect

5. Why did the Anglo-Catholic ritualist movement gradually achieve toleration among the wider English populace?

_____

_____

_____

_____

_____

_____

_____

_____

_____

Review

A. How did Anglo-Catholicism differ from the Old High Church movement, as the former developed from the 1830s through the 1860s?

_____

_____

_____

_____

_____

_____

_____

_____

_____

_____

B. How did the Anglo-Catholic movement differ from the nineteenth-century Evangelicals, in their beliefs about what the Church should be and do?

_____

_____

_____

_____

_____

_____

_____

_____

_____

_____

_____

For Thought and Application

C. Anglo-Catholics and Evangelicals held very different views about conversion, about justification and sanctification, and about good works. With which of these do you agree, and why?

_____

_____

_____

_____

_____

_____

_____

_____

_____

_____

D. Suppose that you were an Anglo-Catholic priest standing at the edge of a crowd at an outdoor Methodist evangelistic service outside London in 1845. People are falling on their knees, lifting their hands, and praising God who has just saved them. As an Anglo-Catholic, what are you thinking about the validity of these apparent conversions?

_____

_____

_____

_____

_____

_____

_____

_____

_____

_____

For Further Reading

J.R.H. Moorman, *A History of the Church in England, Third Edition.*

- Chapter 19

Robert W. Prichard, *A History of the Episcopal Church, Third Revised Edition.*

- Chapter 6

Chapter 9

The Episcopal Church in the United States

(1789–1873)

We come back across the Atlantic in this chapter to see how the struggles between Evangelicals and Anglo-Catholics played out in the American Episcopal Church. The American situation differed in that the War of Independence had nearly killed the colonial Church of England. The American church needed to be reconstructed from the ground up, and a whole new identity conceived. Miraculously that resurrection took place in 1789.

Once the American Episcopal Church was on its feet in 1789, it sleep-walked through the next generation. Nothing much happened between 1789 and 1811, though in this fallow time Bishop William White of Pennsylvania did manage to persuade General Convention to adopt a revised form of the Thirty-Nine Articles of Religion, and a syllabus of readings for ordinands to study. White thus gave the Episcopal Church a basic theological foundation for the next few decades. Otherwise the Episcopal Church lay dormant, while the new American nation grew and spread westward across the Appalachians. Let's see how all that happened.

High Churchmen and Evangelicals (1811–1840)

After a long ecclesiastical nap, the consecration of two new bishops in 1811 symbolized a reawakening in the Church. One of them was the Evangelical Alexander Viets Griswold of New England. The other was a High Churchman,

John Henry Hobart of New York. Hobart had a very different vision for the Church than Griswold. The Evangelicals thought that the Episcopal Church was part of the broader Protestant revival in America, though more sedate and thoughtful than the camp meeting excesses or the urban crusade torchlight parades and anxious benches. By contrast, Hobart thought the Episcopal Church was the true Church in America, the ark of salvation, riding serenely above the turbulent waves of Protestant effervescence. Griswold's and Hobart's rival visions of the Episcopal Church would clash in the early 1800s, but the leaders of the two parties would remain on friendly terms with one another. They would share a broad theological tradition in common, symbolized by the Thirty-Nine Articles and the syllabus of books that Bishop White provided for all the Church's ordinands.

After 1840, however, the influence of the Oxford and Cambridge movements would transform Hobart's Old High Church party, and destroy the consensus of the earlier decades. Ritualist Anglo-Catholics would outflank Bishop Hobart on one side, while outraged Evangelicals would outflank Bishop Griswold on the other. The ensuing "wars of religion" would disturb the peace of the Episcopal Church from the early 1840s into the 1870s, offering an unedifying spectacle to American society. By the late 1870s a third party, a modernist "Broad Church" movement would rise to leadership in the Episcopal Church. Broad Churchmen would offer a solution to the party strife of the previous decades, and a new theological outlook that would dominate the Episcopal Church well into the next century. But that's a later story. Our task in the present chapter is to contemplate the struggle between Anglo-Catholics and Evangelicals from 1811 to 1873, and see why their earlier peaceful coexistence could not survive the spread of ritualism after 1840.

Hobart had been assistant minister at Trinity Church, Wall Street, in New York when he was elected suffragan bishop in 1811. Because of diocesan bishop Benjamin Moore's poor health, Hobart led the diocese from the beginning, until Moore died in 1816 and Hobart replaced him. Hobart traveled incessantly around his enormous diocese—more than forty thousand square miles—from the eastern tip of Long Island westward to Niagara Falls, from Staten Island north to Lake Champlain. Hobart walked, rode horseback, took stagecoaches, and sailed on steamers up the Hudson and longboats on the Erie Canal.

He confirmed, he ordained, and he planted churches. On one trip around the diocese, he traveled four thousand miles. He inherited 27 clergy and left 133. He inherited 40 parishes and he left 165. Hobart was a powerful advocate for his vision of the Episcopal Church, and he wore himself out with his labors. Hobart died in 1830 at the age of fifty-five.

Hobart's ideas about the nature of salvation were very different from Bishop Griswold's. Hobart held to the Old High Church belief that Christian conversion was gradual, a matter of small steps over a lifetime, and not the revolutionary "Great Change" that the Evangelicals asserted. For Hobart, the sacrament of Baptism first incorporated a child into the Church. Thereafter, regular participation in worship and Holy Communion was the path to maturity in the Christian life. Hobart maintained a high view of the sacraments, and of the Anglican clergy as uniquely authorized to administer them. He believed that only the Church of England and its American daughter possessed an ordained ministry that was authentic, and traced its lineage reliably back to the apostles. The Protestant churches had willfully broken with the apostolic succession. The Roman Church had tainted its heritage by lapsing into superstition and error. Therefore the Episcopal Church was the true Church in America. You might perhaps find salvation in another denomination, but it was risky. Only the Episcopal Church and its sacraments guaranteed you a place within God's covenant. Bishop Hobart thus firmly declined to participate in Protestant revivalism, or to join interdenominational groups like the American Bible Society. In fact, he rejected the idea that the true Church was called to transform the world at all. Rather, it was to float securely above the flood, offering its members a refuge from the turbid waters of American revivalism.

As mentioned above, Bishops Griswold and Hobart always maintained cordial relations with one another, despite their different beliefs about the identity and mission of the Episcopal Church. In fact, they shared a great deal in common, both in their theology and in their styles of worship. Both of them were close to the center of Anglican thought, and both emphasized the four principles that would later form the Lambeth Quadrilateral in the 1880s. They both pointed to Scripture as the norm and standard of faith. Both of them affirmed the Apostles' and Nicene Creeds. Both of them emphasized the necessity of Baptism and Holy Communion. Significantly, neither Griswold nor

Hobart believed that Baptism actually guaranteed salvation. Griswold thought that Episcopalians needed to claim the promise of mercy that Baptism extended, when they experienced the Great Change later in life. Hobart believed likewise that we must accept God's offer of salvation made in Baptism, though he thought that this process consisted of many small steps over a lifetime. The two bishops were not that far apart on the efficacy of Baptism.

On the matter of apostolic succession Griswold and Hobart did disagree, of course, but not to the point of breaking fellowship. Griswold believed that bishops in apostolic succession were good for the Church (for its well-being or its *bene esse)* but were not absolutely necessary. The Baptists and the Presbyterians were true churches even though they lacked bishops. Hobart (as we saw) thought that bishops were essential (of the Church's *esse).* So apostolic succession was a sore point between Evangelicals and High Churchmen in the early nineteenth-century Episcopal Church, but neither side pushed too hard, and they lived together in reasonable charity.

Likewise in worship the two parties were closer together in the early nineteenth century than they would be after 1840. Episcopal churches varied in size and tidiness—many enjoyed better upkeep than Bruton Parish Church in 1811—but a casual visitor would not have noticed any great differences between parishes of the two parties in architecture, or in the worship that they both shared according to the *Book of Common Prayer.* Both parties still maintained the plain and word-focused interiors of the eighteenth-century churches. Walls were whitewashed, window glass was clear, and at most there were brass chandeliers for lighting. Absolutely no candles on the Holy Table (never "altar")! The pulpit was still the most visible piece of furniture, often of the three-decker variety and fifteen feet tall. The Holy Table stood humbly and inconspicuously against the east wall, often with tablets above it inscribed with the Ten Commandments and the Lord's Prayer. No crosses were visible, nor any pictures. There were certainly no colored altar cloths, nor any decorative flowers. The celebrant wore a simple white surplice. Most Sundays, the service consisted of Morning Prayer and sermon. (For all the High Church emphasis on the Eucharist, old habits died hard.) The theology in the sermon might vary between Evangelical and High Church preachers, but if you weren't paying very close attention, you might not notice which party the rector favored. So in terms of worship as well as basic theology, the differences between Evangelicals and High Churchmen in the early nineteenth century were not so great as to threaten the Church's unity, or to prevent its modest growth in numbers. All this would change after 1840.

Let's Pause and Reflect

1. Summarize the differences about the Church and the sacraments between Bishop Hobart and Bishop Griswold.

_____

_____

_____

_____

_____

_____

_____

_____

The Anglo-Catholic Movement

Southeast of Massachusetts lies the island of Nantucket. Waves crash on its wide sandy beaches, and coarse grass blows in the stiff wind over its dunes. Nantucket in 1844 is Herman Melville country. Whaling ships sail out from the harbor on Nantucket's northern side, and venture to the Arctic and around Cape Horn into the Pacific in search of their quarry. Nantucket is Yankee and Congregationalist to the core. The whaling captains and their crews are weather-beaten, withdrawn, and monosyllabic. Their ancestors emigrated to New England to escape from the kings and bishops in the old country. Now they are fiercely independent and very Protestant. Their Congregationalist pastors still preach hour-long Calvinist sermons.

But in the year 1844, a new clergyman lands on the island to serve Trinity Church, Nantucket—an Episcopal outpost in this bastion of Yankee culture. The Reverend Frederick Pollard has new ideas about the identity of the Episcopal Church, and about the architecture and decoration of Trinity Church in particular.

This morning he is supervising the local painter as the latter applies the finishing touches to "Father" Pollard's redecoration scheme. Pollard has ordered the destruction of the venerable three-decker pulpit from which his predecessors have pronounced impeccably Protestant sermons. Using the wood from the pulpit, Pollard has ordered the local carpenters to build a tall painted panel that he calls a "reredos" to replace the Ten Commandments and the Lord's Prayer on the east wall. Upon this reredos the artist (curling his lips in scorn) is now finishing a painting of the Virgin Mary. In front of the reredos, the old Communion table has now become an altar, attached to the wall. Upon it Pollard has placed two candlesticks, into which he firmly intends to place lighted candles during the service of Holy Communion next Sunday.

The senior warden stands in the west door, shaking his head mournfully. But Father Pollard ignores him, and confidently orders the painter to add a little more gold to the Virgin's halo.

Until 1840 (as we have seen), Episcopal Evangelicals and High Churchmen both shared a wide basis of common theology, and they often looked much the same when they gathered for worship. After 1840, the introduction of Anglo-Catholic ideas and practices from England produced a new generation of High Churchmen, who looked and sounded much more like Rome. The Evangelicals in turn reacted violently (in some cases hysterically) to what they perceived as a threat to the very identity of the Episcopal Church, namely, its Reformation heritage. In the ensuing combat, some radical Evangelicals rejected Bishop Griswold's gentle spirit of tolerance and began to define themselves in terms of their opposition to the Anglo-Catholics. It was a mess.

Let's look at the Anglo-Catholic movement in the Episcopal Church, and see how it moved progressively Rome-ward after 1840. Not all High Churchmen approved of this development, but the new Anglo-Catholics possessed considerable energy, and a conviction that they were recovering a precious heritage that the Church of England had lost in the Reformation. Gradually the Old High Churchmen died off or were swept up into the Anglo-Catholic ranks.

The General Seminary in New York City was the port through which Anglo-Catholicism entered the Episcopal Church. It was in that school that the first controversy over the new movement erupted. General Seminary, founded by Bishop Hobart, was now some twenty years old and occupied a whole block in the suburbs (between West 20th and 21st Streets in Chelsea). In 1840 its most able student was one Arthur Carey. During his ordination examination, Carey refused to repudiate the Council of Trent (1545–1563), the council that had been the definitive Roman Catholic response to the Reformation. Bishop Onderdonk of New York ordained Carey anyway.

Evangelicals throughout the Episcopal Church flew into a rage. In 1844 the House of Bishops appointed a panel of episcopal visitors to study General Seminary and report on its health. The visitors included several leading Evangelicals, and they gave the school a good report. Nevertheless, suspicions rankled, particularly as the influence of the seminary spread through the ministry of its graduates, and of its faculty who became bishops.

William Whittingham was the most prominent of those early Anglo-Catholic bishops. Professor of church history at General Seminary, he became bishop of Maryland in 1840 and proceeded to infuriate the Evangelical clergy in his diocese. Theologically Whittingham stood a good deal closer to Rome than Bishop Hobart had. For example, Whittingham taught that Baptism actually effected a child's regeneration, that through the sacrament, the child received salvation. Whittingham did not specify the need for subsequent repentance and faith, as Hobart had done. Concerning Holy Communion, Whittingham taught that the consecrated elements do represent (in a way that the bishop declined to articulate) the real presence of Christ's body and blood. Whittingham also insisted on referring to the Eucharist as a "sacrifice," though not an actual repetition of Christ's death on Calvary. So although Bishop Whittingham frequently denounced the Church of Rome for its alleged superstition and error, his clergy might have been pardoned for wondering if their bishop hadn't in fact crossed the Alps and "swum the Tiber."

Meanwhile another event in 1840 signaled further growth toward Rome in the Anglo-Catholic movement. Bishop Jackson Kemper visited General Seminary searching for recruits. Since 1835 Kemper had been the first missionary bishop in the Episcopal Church—responsible for a vast tract of land known as

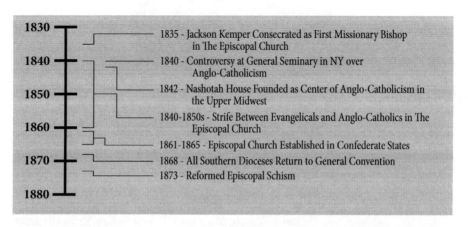

1830
1840
1850
1860
1870
1880

1835 - Jackson Kemper Consecrated as First Missionary Bishop in The Episcopal Church

1840 - Controversy at General Seminary in NY over Anglo-Catholicism

1842 - Nashotah House Founded as Center of Anglo-Catholicism in the Upper Midwest

1840-1850s - Strife Between Evangelicals and Anglo-Catholics in The Episcopal Church

1861-1865 - Episcopal Church Established in Confederate States

1868 - All Southern Dioceses Return to General Convention

1873 - Reformed Episcopal Schism

"the Northwest" (effectively Wisconsin and its neighboring states of Illinois and Indiana). Kemper had very little support from other dioceses, and there was as yet no national church structure to speak of, so he was responsible for finding volunteers to go with him. Kemper had been a High Churchman, so naturally he appealed to the General Seminary for help. Three young men in the class of 1841 responded to his challenge, including the late Bishop Hobart's son. Making their way westward into the howling wilderness, they planted a missionary base at Nashotah Lakes in Wisconsin. There they founded a community loosely modeled on the Benedictine order. Then they traveled widely on foot and on horseback, visiting the isolated cabins of the lonely settlers, and preaching the gospel. The work was hard, and it took its toll on the volunteers, but by 1847 the mission base had become a new seminary, later called Nashotah House, when it graduated its first class of six.

The Nashotah mission produced clergy who were much more Anglo-Catholic than the first generation. For example, the Rev. James DeKoven moved from General Seminary to Nashotah House, where he became a tutor, and later became warden of Racine College (a new Anglo-Catholic school). There he greatly expanded the boundaries of what was permissible in Episcopal worship. He incorporated the whole panoply of medieval ceremonial: elaborate vestments, candles, incense, bells, seasonal colors, acolytes, vested choirs, medieval plainsong, and so on. His disciples built their churches in the Gothic Revival style that was becoming the fashion all over England and America. They denied that Episcopalians belonged to that family of churches that descended from the Reformation. Nor would they admit that Anglicanism was a *via me-*

dia between Protestantism and Rome. Rather, they claimed that the Episcopal Church was fully capital *C* Catholic. To the extent (and a very large extent it was) that the new generation of Anglo-Catholics got away with all this, Episcopal Evangelicals watched their church being redefined and redesigned right under their eyes.

Bishops Griswold and Hobart had lived amicably together through the 1820s because Hobart's theology was still arguably Protestant, within the boundaries of the Thirty-Nine Articles, and because his style of worship was recognizably Protestant. Now in the 1850s the new breed of Anglo-Catholics was evidently determined to lead the Episcopal Church out of Protestantism altogether. The Evangelicals were not disposed to contemplate all this without a vigorous response.

Let's Pause and Reflect

2. In what ways did Anglo-Catholic ideas alter the Old High Church movement in the American Episcopal Church after 1840?

_____

_____

_____

_____

_____

_____

_____

_____

The Wars of Religion in the Episcopal Church

In Boston, Massachusetts, in the year 1845, Bishop Manton Eastburn is making his first episcopal visitation to the new Anglo-Catholic parish in the city, the Church of the Advent. As the bishop enters the church from the vestry at the beginning of the service, he glares around him at the furnishings in the chancel. The Holy Table is covered with a red cloth. On it are four golden candlesticks and a large wooden cross. As the bishop watches the clergy of the parish bow before the altar, as they call it, his eyes bulge and a large vein in his neck begins to throb. It is not clear that he will survive long enough to confirm the candidates lined up before him in the front pew.

Several days later Bishop Eastburn is writing a letter to his diocesan clergy, to be published in the church's newspaper. He grinds his teeth and clenches his fists as he remembers what he witnessed last Sunday. He writes that he has noted "with inexpressible grief and pain, various offensive innovations upon the ancient usage of our Church." He asserts that the decoration of the Communion table (the candles and the cross) represented "superstitious puerilities" displaying an "offensive resemblance to the usages of that idolatrous papal communion against which our Prayer Book so strongly protests."

Bishop Eastburn silently resolves never again to visit the Church of the Advent until that parish removes those Romish enormities and returns to the historic Protestantism that constitutes the true identity of the Episcopal Church.

Bishop Eastburn (Griswold's successor in Massachusetts) had been one of the first American Episcopalians to suspect the Oxford and Cambridge movements of leading Anglicanism toward Rome. Eastburn's response emerged straight out of the English Wars of Religion, its anti-Roman paranoia worthy of the Puritan Roundheads in the 1840s. The Anglo-Catholic movement, wrote Eastburn, "was of Rome, the work of Satan; if allowed to continue, it will destroy the Evangelical faith and tradition which has descended from the Reformation; and while suasion has its place, condemnation and even force must be brought to bear to silence these advocates of the Dark Ages and followers of the Scarlet Woman."—Shades of Oliver Cromwell. Eastburn remained in this take-no-prisoners mode throughout the 1840s, and although he was the most voluble curmudgeon among the Evangelical leaders, he articulated what many of his allies were thinking in their hearts.

The Evangelicals initially hoped that General Convention would put a stop to this creeping Anglo-Catholicism and rule out the use of candles and crosses and all the rest. But they discovered in 1844 that the rot (as they saw it) had already eaten away the Protestant integrity of the Church. That year they introduced a resolution at Convention that condemned Anglo-Catholicism as containing "serious errors in doctrine and practice." But when the vote came, only nine dioceses supported the resolution while twelve opposed it, with six dioceses divided. The Evangelicals had to be content with an inoffensive resolution in which General Convention deplored whatever was deplorable, but declined to consider or critique any specific "errors of individuals."

The failure of General Convention to address their grievances stoked Evangelical anger to higher temperatures, and that animosity corroded relationships within the Church in many ways. Episcopal elections became a battleground, for example, between Evangelical and Anglo-Catholic parties in many dioceses. A radical Evangelical wing began to emerge in the 1840s, much more touchy in the defense of Protestantism than old Bishop Griswold had been. Clergy like the Tyng dynasty of New York and Philadelphia (Stephen Tyng Sr., and his sons Stephen Jr., and Dudley) marshaled their congregations behind bishops like Eastburn, insisting on the Episcopal Church's identity as part of the revivalist Protestant mainstream in America. The Rev. Dudley Tyng of Philadelphia was a prominent leader of the 1858 revival that swept the North and the Midwest, with daily noontime prayer meetings by the dozen and nightly tent-meeting revivals in many cities. But within the Episcopal Church itself, the Evangelicals began to feel more and more marginalized and disinherited.

The party struggles of the 1840s and 1850s help explain a curious phenomenon, namely, that when the American nation split in two during the Civil War, the Episcopal Church divided only reluctantly and temporarily. Protestant denominations like the Baptists, Methodists, and Presbyterians had split North versus South over the issue of slavery long before the war broke out in 1861. The Episcopal Church, however, stayed together until after the Southern secession, when the dioceses in the Confederacy formed their own denomination for the duration of the war. Nevertheless, when General Convention met in New York City in 1862, tables for the Southern dioceses stood empty, and their names were solemnly intoned at roll call. In the summer of 1865 representatives from three erstwhile Confederate dioceses (North Carolina, Tennessee, and Texas) appeared in Philadelphia and were warmly welcomed by their Northern brothers. In 1868 all the Southern dioceses were back in the fold. Why?

One reason was that many Anglo-Catholic bishops continued to affirm Hobart's Old High Church dictum that the Episcopal Church should float serenely above the stormy waves of democratic America, and not take sides in political controversy. Furthermore, as Hobart had taught, if the fathers of the early church had not addressed a certain topic—like slavery—neither should the bishops of the Episcopal Church do so now. So most Anglo-Catholic bishops in the North tried to stay neutral on the great issue that was driving Americans apart. That policy (as their critics immediately observed) effectively meant a vote in favor of the status quo, and the toleration of slavery. And of course many Northern Anglo-Catholic bishops were good friends with their counterparts in the South, and personally disinclined to break relationships over an issue that they thought the Episcopal Church should ignore anyway.

Among the Evangelicals as well, party affiliation and personal friendship played an important part in keeping the Episcopal Church together in the 1850s. Feeling progressively marginalized by the apparently inexorable spread of Anglo-Catholicism, Northern Evangelicals needed the help of their Southern counterparts in the councils of the Church—and were reluctant to alienate the latter over the issue of slavery in the nation. Likewise deep bonds of affection kept Evangelical leaders together. Bishop Charles Petit McIlvaine of Ohio was the foremost Evangelical leader in the 1850s, and a strong opponent of slavery. President Lincoln would send McIlvaine on an informal diplomatic mission to England after the war broke out. The bishop's letters would help persuade Lincoln that if he made slavery—and not preservation of the Union—the chief issue in the war, England would stay out of the conflict. So no one could accuse McIlvaine of being soft on slavery. Yet he remained personally devoted to Bishop Leonidas Polk of Louisiana, who owned more than three hundred slaves. McIlvaine had served as chaplain at West Point back in 1825, and had led young cadet Polk to the Lord. Up to the outbreak of hostilities in 1861, McIlvaine stayed in touch with the Evangelical bishop of Louisiana. Polk unfortunately put off his episcopal robes, rose to be a lieutenant general in the Confederate army, and died in action.

When the war was over, the Evangelicals led the way in welcoming the Southern dioceses back to General Convention. In the House of Deputies in 1865, a prominent Evangelical clergyman, George Cummins of Illinois, introduced a motion that gave thanks to God for the return of delegations from North Carolina, Tennessee, and Texas. But if the Evangelicals supposed that

Southern help would roll back the tide of Anglo-Catholicism, they were bitterly disappointed in the years that followed.

For one thing, Evangelicals were beginning to distrust their own *Book of Common Prayer* at several critical points. Ever since Archbishop Cranmer in the mid-1500s, the service of Holy Baptism had used the word "regenerate" in reference to the newly baptized, who were almost invariably infants. Evangelicals had since then understood the word "regenerate" in a conditional sense, charitably assuming that a future adult conversion would follow. Now in the 1860s, however, Anglo-Catholics were arguing that "regenerate" meant exactly what it said: that infants were completely born again through the sacrament of Baptism. Read the Prayer Book, they insisted. Does the service say anything about a future "Great Change"? Not a word. So how can you deny that a baptized baby is completely regenerate? Evangelicals found it hard to refute this train of logic. All they knew was that, in the past, their theology of Baptism had been mainstream Episcopal doctrine, and it was no longer so. Did this mean that they should stop using the *Book of Common Prayer,* or politely cough as they approached the word "regenerate," and leave it out?

One Evangelical clergyman who followed this line of thought was the Rev. Charles Cheney of Christ Church in Chicago. Like others of his persuasion, he omitted the words "regenerate" and "regeneration" from the service of Baptism. Whereas many bishops might have winked at this practice, Bishop Whitehouse of Chicago elected to make it an issue. He ordered Cheney to say the whole service, including the offensive word. When Cheney refused, the bishop suspended him in 1871, and later deposed him from the ordained ministry.

The Cheney case signaled to a number of Evangelicals that there was no longer a place for them in the Episcopal Church. Not only were more and more parishes adopting Anglo-Catholic decoration and ceremonial with the tacit permission of successive General Conventions, but also Anglo-Catholic theology now seemed to be obligatory (at least in Bishop Whitehouse's Chicago diocese) with no toleration for Evangelical consciences. Whether or not this perception matched reality, it seemed to some Evangelicals that they were being run out of their own denomination.

This sense of alienation helps us understand the first significant exodus from the Episcopal Church, the Reformed Episcopal schism of 1873. The young Evangelical leader George Cummins was now assistant bishop of Kentucky. The Cheney incident worried him deeply. He had also been criticized (though not punished) for participating in a service of the Lord's Supper at a Presbyterian church in New York City. Cummins concluded that the Episcopal Church no longer had a place for him. In December of 1873 he formed a new denomination, the Reformed Episcopal Church, along with eight clergy and nineteen laymen.

Practically no one else followed. Some Evangelicals like Stephen Tyng, Jr. deplored the spread of Anglo-Catholicism, but did not think schism was the answer. Meanwhile old leaders like Bishop McIlvaine were dying, and they left no successors to carry on the Evangelical tradition. Decades of warfare against Anglo-Catholicism had given the Evangelical party a negative orientation that was unattractive to many younger Episcopalians in the 1870s. The old Evangelicals seemed to have been fighting the ancient battles of the Reformation, while many Americans no longer believed that baptismal regeneration was worth dying for. Whereas in the 1830s, the Evangelicals had been actively promoting the social transformation of America, now in the 1870s the "wars of religion" seemed to have drained away all their spiritual energy. Not to mention that those battles had presented an unedifying spectacle to the nation.

After the 1870s, while Anglo-Catholics continued to extend their liturgical and ceremonial program within the Episcopal Church, the Evangelical party gradually dwindled and died. In its place arose a movement that would speak clearly to the new Smokestack Era in America. This was the so-called Broad Church party, with a new and up-to-date brand of modernist theology. In the next chapter we will explore the roots of this new movement, and its domination of the Episcopal Church for the next sixty years.

Let's Pause and Reflect

3. How and why did the previous truce between the High Church and the Evangelical movements break down after 1840?

_____

_____

_____

_____

_____

_____

_____

_____

_____

_____

_____

_____

Review

A. Trace the changes in viewpoint between Bishop Alexander Viets Griswold and his successor Manton Eastburn, and likewise between Bishop John Henry Hobart and Bishop Jackson Kemper.

_____

_____

_____

_____

_____

_____

_____

_____

_____

_____

_____

_____

_____

For Thought and Application

B. In 1820, High Church parishes in America didn't look very different from Evangelical ones in terms of church architecture, decoration, or ceremonial. In 1870, Anglo-Catholic parishes looked very different. What do you suppose attracted people (both clergy and laity) to these latter congregations? Do you think that people today are drawn to Anglo-Catholic parishes for similar reasons? Why or why not?

_____

_____

_____

_____

_____

_____

_____

_____

_____

_____

_____

C. Would you be inclined to emulate Bishop George Cummins of Kentucky, and leave a denomination that required that you use the word "regenerate" in reference to baptized babies? Why or why not?

_____

_____

_____

_____

_____

_____

_____

_____

_____

_____

_____

_____

For Further Reading

Robert W. Prichard, *A History of the Episcopal Church, Third Revised Edition.*

- Review Chapters 4-6

Chapter 10

Modernism in England and America

(1860–1940)

In 1912 an Oxford don named B. H. Streeter published an essay in a theological volume titled *Foundations*. In his essay he likened faith in Jesus' resurrection to a "flat earth" view of the universe.

> *The theory that the actual physical body laid in the tomb was raised up seems to involve . . . that it was subsequently taken up, "flesh and bones," into heaven—a very difficult concept if we no longer regard the earth as flat and the centre of the solar system, and heaven as a definite region locally fixed above the solid bowl of the skies.*

Similar doubts about the central doctrines of the Christian faith were soon being expressed—openly and without penalty—by clergy in the Episcopal Church.

The rector of St. Bartholomew's Church in New York City in 1924 is the Rev. Leighton Parks. The previous year he has published a book titled What is Modernism? *in which he commended the authority of science and called on Christians to adjust their faith and bring it into conformity with the results of modern scientific research. Recently he has taken sides in a controversy in the national Episcopal Church over the doctrine of the virgin birth. Parks argues for tolerance toward those (like himself) who find the doctrine impossible to believe in the light of modern science.*

To symbolize the conflict that he perceives in the Episcopal Church between superstition and science, the Rev. Mr. Parks has decided to perform a striking gesture this Sunday. Before he goes into the pulpit to deliver the sermon, he removes his surplice and stole and puts on an academic gown. The surplice and stole represented the Christian faith, composed (the Rev. Mr. Parks thinks) of biblical and traditional doctrines, now rendered unbelievable by the results of modern science. The academic gown stands for objective scientific truth, supplied by the universities and offering us facts of which we can be absolutely certain.

The Rev. Mr. Parks's symbolic gesture in 1924 represented an attitude that had been percolating through the Episcopal Church since the 1870s. He was unusual in his willingness to fly his flag so boldly, but he embodied a direction in which much of the Episcopal Church's leadership was tending.

What gave these deviations from the Christian faith credibility in the Church of England and the American Episcopal Church in the early twentieth century? And what protected their advocates from discipline by the bishops whose job it was to defend the faith?

The current of thought that came to call itself "modernism" was the source of these critiques of the Christian story. The task of this present chapter is to look at the origins and growth of this movement in Europe before the 1860s, and then its influence on Anglican thought both in Britain and in America—all of which encouraged critics like Streeter and Parks to question the central tenets of the Christian faith.

The impact of modernism on Anglicans in England and America was in fact delayed until the 1860s because of the satisfying truce between science and Christianity in the century after Isaac Newton's *Principia Mathematica* in 1687. As we saw earlier, the great philosopher John Locke (1632–1704) taught that Newtonian science could prove at least some of the Christian story—that the beautiful complexity of order in the universe argued for a Creator God, and that the credible New Testament records of Jesus' miracles showed him to have been the Messiah. Despite his immediate critics (Deists who said Locke was being unscientific to believe in miracles, for instance), Locke's arguments satisfied the majority of Anglican Churchmen throughout the eighteenth century and into the nineteenth. Archdeacon William Paley's *Evidences of Christianity* (1794) supported Locke by proposing the popular "watchmaker" argument from design—that if you found a pocket watch in a field, its precise and elegant internal workings would argue for a designer. So likewise the order in the universe argued the existence of God. Even young Charles Darwin (before his voyage around the world) found Paley's arguments convincing. The more radical Deist ideas found little purchase in the Church of England or the American Episcopal Church in the early nineteenth century. However, when acids of doubt finally began to erode the faith of Anglican theologians in the 1860s, some of these thinkers would reject the compromise with science that Locke and Paley had symbolized. Neither the Evangelicals nor the Anglo-Catholics could provide a reassuring alternative, and their "wars of religion" seemed petty and outdated. Movements in theology on the Continent began to appear increasingly attractive to leaders in the Church of England and the American Episcopal Church. It is to that European tradition that we now turn.

The Erosion of Faith and the Rise of Modernism on the Continent (1618–1860)

In November 1618, a young French soldier called René Descartes stepped into the sleeping alcove of the home where he was billeted for the winter near Ulm in southern Germany. Descartes was fighting on the Roman Catholic side in what would become the Thirty Years' War (1618–1648), but in fact he had no confessional stake in that conflict. He had joined the army to see the world. And in fact he was deeply concerned about the apparently irreconcilable wars between Roman Catholics and Protestants. Both sides claimed to speak for God, but who was the truly authorized spokesman? Holy pope? Holy reformer? Holy Spirit, in the mind of the pious peasant reading his Bible alone by candlelight? No one could tell.

So that day in November of 1618, Descartes stepped into the alcove and resolved not to come out until he had doubted everything he could doubt, and come down to some bedrock that he hoped everyone could accept . . . and stop fighting. He was looking for a new starting point, a new "first principle" (just as Locke would do, later on in England—finding a different new place to begin). Every system of thought depends on some axiom that can't be proved. For

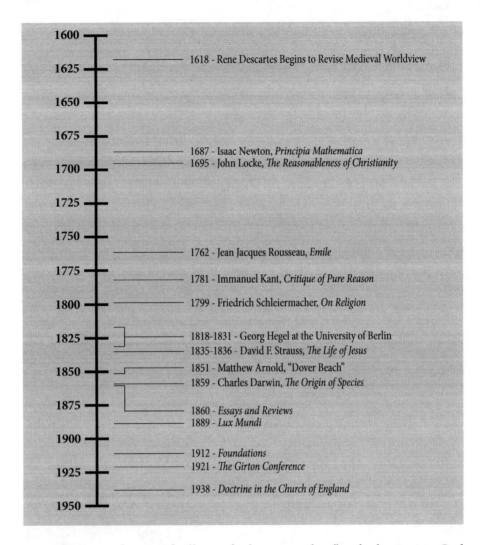

1600

1625 — 1618 - Rene Descartes Begins to Revise Medieval Worldview

1650

1675

1687 - Isaac Newton, *Principia Mathematica*
1695 - John Locke, *The Reasonableness of Christianity*
1700

1725

1750

1762 - Jean Jacques Rousseau, *Emile*
1775

1781 - Immanuel Kant, *Critique of Pure Reason*
1800 — 1799 - Friedrich Schleiermacher, *On Religion*

1825 — 1818-1831 - Georg Hegel at the University of Berlin
1835-1836 - David F. Strauss, *The Life of Jesus*
1850 — 1851 - Matthew Arnold, "Dover Beach"
1859 - Charles Darwin, *The Origin of Species*
1875 —
1860 - *Essays and Reviews*
1889 - *Lux Mundi*
1900

1912 - *Foundations*
1921 - *The Girton Conference*
1925 —
1938 - *Doctrine in the Church of England*
1950

example, you can't scientifically verify the axiom that "in the beginning God created the heavens and the earth." Locke would think (later in the century) that he could in fact prove it, arguing from the design and order in the cosmos. But Descartes knew that Locke would be wrong. How could you stand outside the universe and scientifically test for God? Descartes was searching for a new axiom, one other than "In the beginning, God . . . ." He was trying to *help* Christianity by putting the faith on a solid foundation which everyone could affirm and which would end the Wars of Religion.

Descartes did come up with a new axiom. Not all on that day, but he got started. He worked through the whole process of doubting whatever he could possibly doubt. At the end, he concluded that the one thing he couldn't doubt (after this laborious analytical examination) was the truth of ideas that were left, which now seemed "clear and distinct" to him. That was his new axiom, his new bedrock, and his new "first principle." He believed that anyone who followed the same arduous process would come down to the same "clear and distinct" ideas, and would find them to be as indubitable as he had.

One of Descartes' "clear and distinct" ideas was the famous *Cogito ergo sum* (I think, therefore I am). But for our purposes, Descartes' most important indubitable idea was the concept of God. He found in his mind the idea of a God that was so "clear and distinct" that he could not doubt it. There is a God who is all good, all wise, and all powerful, and who created the universe. This idea was totally internal to Descartes' mind. It did not depend on the authority of the Bible, or the pope, or the local king. Descartes believed that any honest and diligent thinking person would immediately recognize its truth. This was, he thought, a great gift to Christianity, putting the existence of God beyond doubt. But in fact, Descartes had put "In the beginning Me . . ." in place of "In the beginning God . . . ." He had made the indubitability of his own "clear and distinct" ideas the bedrock of a new worldview. This "turn to the self" was the ultimate root of modernist theology. But what if someone else came along with a different "clear and distinct" idea about God? What then? Who would judge?

This is precisely what happened in European philosophy in the century and a half after Descartes. People didn't find Descartes' idea of God in their own minds. Meanwhile the prestige of modern science was increasing so powerfully that intellectuals on the Continent came to believe that the scientific method was the royal road to truth. For example, the German thinker Gotthold Lessing (1729–1781) argued that since God's existence couldn't be verified scientifically, it must be considered a matter of personal opinion. It's fine if you like that sort of thing, but it's not on a level with Newton's laws of gravity.

Before 1618, "In the beginning God . . ." had been the *axiom* on which Western thought was built. Now in 1799, Genesis 1:1 was demoted to a *hypothesis*. If you could explain reality without that hypothesis, why drag it in? As C. S. Lewis later observed, God was now in the prisoners' dock in a courtroom—put on the defensive, accused of nonexistence, challenged to justify himself.

Meanwhile European thinkers had concluded that Descartes' turn to the self might offer a way forward. If God's existence couldn't be verified by the scientific method studying the universe around us, the alternative was to look inside ourselves. Perhaps in the depths of our own consciousness, we might be able to detect signs that would ground our belief in God. But if the scientific method were the royal road to truth, and one's inner feelings were a matter of opinion, why would anyone think that inner consciousness provided a basis for faith in God?

The answer lies in a movement that came to be known as Romanticism, which gained traction on the Continent in the late eighteenth century. The high priest of this movement was a Frenchman called Jean-Jacques Rousseau (1712–1778), a brilliant novelist and political theorist whose ideas still resound in a thousand high school graduation speeches in America every year. Rousseau made a number of influential assertions. First, he claimed that human beings are born "good," and that society subsequently corrupts us. Second, the road to the recovery of our original goodness lies in recapturing the childlike instincts that society has repressed; he popularized the myth of the "noble savage." Third, we reconnect with this innocent inner child-savage by getting in touch with the spirit of nature. Once Rousseau was sitting idly in a boat on a lake in southeastern France. All of a sudden he felt an overwhelming sense of unity with the world, and he cried out, "O Nature! O my Mother!" This oceanic experience temporarily mollified the hurts and psychic wounds that Rousseau felt society had inflicted on him. (With good reason—Rousseau was a horror of a man, who forced his common-law wife to put all their five children in the Paris foundling home, where babies died of neglect by the thousands.)

Rousseau's ideas caught on with many intellectuals in Western Europe. The eclipse of the Christian God had left a vacuum. Rousseau offered a substitute deity—Mother Nature. He provided a path for contacting her, namely, by immersing oneself in nature's goodness and letting one's subconscious feelings bubble to the surface. This method did not supply hard verification the way the scientific method did *vis-à-vis* the external physical world, but Rousseau and his followers believed that inner feelings offered an alternative road to truth, especially as they found expression in art, music, poetry, and the novel. They believed that the scientific revolution had overemphasized analytical and rational knowing, what we might metaphorically call "left brain" cognition. Elite European society needed the compensation that intuitive and affective "right brain" experience offered. These ideas were at the heart of the Romantic movement. They had a crucial impact on the rise of modernist theology on the Continent, and in the Anglican world after 1860.

Let's Pause and Reflect

1. How did Romanticism support the turn to the self in Continental theology that Descartes had initiated?

_____

_____

_____

_____

_____

_____

_____

_____

Three thinkers in particular developed the turn to the self and the rise of modernism. The first was the German philosopher Immanuel Kant (1724–1804); the second was Friedrich Daniel Ernst Schleiermacher (1768–1834); and the third was Georg W. F. Hegel (1770–1831).

Kant wrestled with the problem that John Locke had raised. The Englishman had taught that we can know the outside world directly, that our sense impressions are accurate evidence of what's out there. Kant disagreed. He thought that raw sense impressions came to our minds all in a jumble. If the world seems orderly to us, it's because our minds have a grid through which we filter this sense data so that we can know it. Otherwise it would be just a roaring blur of white noise (my phrase, not Kant's). One of the grids in our mind sorts external actions into "good versus bad." When we reflect on the good, we feel compelled to do it. In terms of survival, this makes no sense—doing the good may compel us to jump into a raging stream to save a drowning baby, and lose our lives. Kant thus inferred that there must be a God, who created us and put this moral imperative in our minds. It's an easy argument to criticize—how could Kant assume that an Aztec or a Hindu would feel the same moral imperative that a Protestant German philosopher did? But the profundity and complexity of Kant's thought reinforced the idea among European intellectuals that the turn to the self offered a way forward in trying to reground some kind of belief in a God.

Schleiermacher, the second great founder of modernist theology, was a German Reformed pastor and later professor at the University of Berlin. Schleiermacher took very seriously the opinion of his educated friends in Berlin, who asked how he could be a Christian when "science had disproved Christianity." (Obviously science could do no such thing.) Schleiermacher decided that his friends were right, and that science had won—that Christianity as a religion of historical revelation was dead. All its claims about a God intervening in the cosmos were empty. But Schleiermacher didn't want to give up. So he resolved to reinvent Christianity as a religion of internal self-exploration. He argued that the cosmos inspired in human beings a feeling of awe and gratitude and "absolute dependence" on Something. This existential consciousness, he said, is the basis of Christianity.

> What we feel and are conscious of in religious emotions is not the nature of things, but their operation on us . . . . The Universe is ceaselessly active and at every moment is revealing itself to us . . . . Now religion is to take up into our lives and to submit to be swayed by them, each of these influences and their consequent emotions.

In other words, Christianity equals existential consciousness. Schleiermacher did not shrink from the consequences of this theological revolution. All human religions, according to Schleiermacher, are based on what he called "God consciousness." All religious scriptures, traditions, ethical systems, liturgies, and so on are purely human artifacts. Jesus was a Galilean prophet who (for the first time in human evolution) achieved 100 percent God consciousness. He did not rise from the dead. But if we continue to remember him and to follow his teachings, we have the best chance of reaching 100 percent God consciousness ourselves.

Hegel, a professor of philosophy at the University of Berlin, was the thinker who put the finishing touches on modernist theology. While his friend Schleiermacher had assumed the idea of evolution (long before Darwin), Hegel developed a philosophical system to support that notion in detail. He taught that deep within the cosmos there is Something, which he variously described as "Spirit" or "Idea." Spirit was the driving force of development in the universe. The course of history was a series of back-and-forth conflicts, called a dialectic, each of which produced a new situation with new conflicts, and so on. This dialectical progress gradually moved the spiral of history upward, producing the human race and shaping its ongoing development. Hegel thought of this progressive Spirit as the expression of the mind of God, but a God who was in the process of becoming along with the universe. And human beings could contribute to that upward spiral by becoming aware of the Spirit within, and cooperating with its upward growth—in order to be on the "right side of history."

All three of these influential thinkers turned Christianity upside down, changing it from an embrace of God's sovereign interventions in the universe, to the cultivation of subjective and human-centered modes of consciousness. In this way all three hoped to protect Christianity from the attacks of its scientific enemies, and to create a safe space for its remnants to flourish. They could not predict, of course, that their thought would ultimately undermine Christian faith. For the time being, many intellectuals in Europe held to the new modernist theology with great conviction.

Let's Pause and Reflect

2. What were the central ideas in Kant, Schleiermacher, and Hegel that reinforced the turn to the self in Continental theology?

_____

_____

_____

_____

_____

_____

_____

_____

Kant, Schleiermacher, and Hegel each founded traditions of thought that would weave together in the late nineteenth century to make up the complex tapestry of modernist thought. Kant would influence the strand that emphasized moral behavior as the essence of religion, helping form Christian socialism and the "social gospel" movement in America. Schleiermacher would support those (especially for our purposes, late twentieth-century Anglican modernists) who treated Christianity as a form of subjective self-exploration. And Hegel shaped the developmental worldview that Darwin would epitomize in 1859, but also Karl Marx, whose dialectical materialism would borrow Hegel's back-and-forth upward spiral of "progress."

One final modernist tradition would later have much influence on Anglicans, namely, what came to be known as "higher criticism" of the Bible. ("Lower criticism" had to do with establishing a reliable text, while higher criticism investigated the text's meaning and purpose.) Early nineteenth-century biblical scholarship in Germany naturally reflected all the philosophical currents we've looked at above, and it embodied their presuppositions. The universe is a closed system. There is no creator God. There may be "Spirit" within the cosmos, like the Hegelian "Idea," but this Spirit is more principle than Person. Jesus was a Galilean prophet (not divine) who was filled with "Spirit." "Salvation" means experiencing "Spirit" as Jesus did. "Faith" means letting the experience of "Spirit" influence our lives. And the Bible is a purely human artifact, to be interpreted just like any other historical book.

The most forthright (and therefore controversial) of the early nineteenth-century German higher critics was a scholar named David F. Strauss (1808–1874). His *Life of Jesus,* published in two volumes in 1835–1836, won him wide notoriety. Strauss made no bones about working with the presuppositions we've seen above. There is no divine intervention in the universe, no miracles like the virgin birth or the resurrection. Jesus was a purely human Hebrew prophet. The New Testament presents faint echoes of his career and his death. But in the subsequent decades, his credulous followers "mythologized" Jesus into the Messiah, the Son of God and the risen Lord. The task of higher criticism was to unmask these myths, and to try and get back to what Jesus actually said and did. Strauss's contemporaries in the German scholarly world generally tried to conceal their presuppositions, so as not to offend pious laypeople (and so as to keep their jobs—Strauss lost his). But Strauss had the courage of his convictions, and proclaimed modernist theology with boldness and clarity. Strauss's ideas would win wide acceptance in the late twentieth century in the Anglican world, as we will see.

Let's Pause and Reflect

3. What were the main features of German higher criticism as it developed in the mid-nineteenth century?

_____

_____

_____

_____

_____

_____

_____

_____

Modernist Theology in the Church of England (1860–1938)

In 1860, seven theologians in the Church of England published a book called *Essays and Reviews* in which the camel of modernist theology poked its nose inside the Anglican tent. The authors of the chapters were trying, first, to acknowledge what had happened in German theology over the past century. Second, having noticed these developments, they were trying to see how far they might be allowed to influence Anglican thinking. The *Essays and Reviews* were moderate, as we will see. But it was a sign of a changed environment that they could be published at all.

How had the environment of the English Church altered to allow modernism a voice (however muted) in 1860? First of all, three revolutions had shaken the old premodern worldview, which assumed that reality was basically stable. These revolutions suggested that change might actually be the basic characteristic of the universe. The old metaphor of the body politic in Europe had implied that (beneath the superficial wars and rumors of wars) society would generally balance itself over time. Change meant disease and ill health in the body, and needed to be resisted and (so far as possible) eliminated. But three great seismic forces in European society were gradually altering this basic assumption of a stable reality in the early nineteenth century.

The first of these great changes was the political revolutions in America and France. The American War of Independence had shown that one could overthrow the institution of monarchy and replace it with a durable government that rested on the active consent of the people. The French Revolution expressed the same ideas of "liberty, fraternity, and equality," though it collapsed into chaos, then into Napoleon's dictatorship, and finally the restoration of a monarchy. Still the bloody upheaval had signaled that an ancient regime could be overthrown, with world-historical changes that no one could have foreseen.

The second of these great upheavals was part of the scientific revolution, which had been at work in Europe since the time of Copernicus in the 1540s. Isaac Newton had summed up all the advances in astronomy and physics in his great *Principia Mathematica* (1687). But the universe that Newton described was basically static, and Archdeacon Paley's watchmaker metaphor aptly described it. Once created, the universe kept ticking along according to the laws that governed its operation. Now in the early nineteenth century, this static view of nature was giving way to a dynamic picture. Geology was emerging as a coherent field of study. Amateur geologists with their sharp hammers were picking away at the chalk cliffs of Dover (and elsewhere). They were revealing a series of strata in which fossils suggested a developing process, from the oldest and lowest levels to the highest and newest. In 1830-1833, Charles Lyell published his three-volume *Principles of Geology*, in which he argued that a very long (million-year) uniform process of stratification had produced the record as we see it today. Hitherto, people had accepted the date of 4004 BC for the creation of the universe as Archbishop James Ussher of Armagh had proposed in 1650. And they had accepted a six-day process of creation, as a literal reading of Genesis suggested. Lyell overturned that familiar and comfortable view of nature. Was Genesis wrong? Opinions varied. (Some still argue a six-day creation.) But the cumulative scientific revolution was shaking the hitherto static view of the universe, and implicitly calling into question a literal reading of the Bible.

The Industrial Revolution was the third seismic force that was shaking English consciousness and undermining the older static view of reality. Beginning in the early eighteenth century with the harnessing of steam power, the Industrial Revolution in England had its "big bang" in 1783 when James Watt and Matthew Bolton produced a steam engine that could power the machinery in a textile mill. Cheap, factory-produced cotton goods revolutionized human life. (Imagine being able to afford a change of clothes, and to wash them occasionally!) But the mills required human beings to work them. In the late 1700s, factories proliferated in England, while at the same time landlords evicted their tenants so as to farm more "scientifically" on larger fields. Great crowds of former peasants swarmed into the new industrial cities. An England of peasants and villages—six thousand years old—gave way to a world of "dark Satanic Mills." Living in tenements, dark and cold and without running water or sanitation, the new industrial underclass often worked twelve hours a day, as did their small children. Steam power was quickly adapted for use on the new railroads. George Stephenson's "Locomotion No. 1" powered the trains on the twenty-five-mile Stockton and Darlington line in northern England that opened in 1825. This event revolutionized transportation, both of goods and of people. (Imagine traveling at thirty miles an hour!) The steam engines kept getting better, more powerful, and more efficient. Perhaps change *was* the basic nature of reality.

Let's Pause and Reflect

4. Briefly describe how each of the three great revolutions (political, scientific, and industrial) shook the old notion of reality as stable, and the previous faith in the Bible in Britain and America.

_____

_____

_____

_____

_____

_____

It is important to note here that for all these reasons, the idea of an "evolving" universe predated Darwin's *Origin of Species* (1859) by nearly a century. Darwin simply offered scientific evidence for a worldview that the European intelligentsia had already widely embraced. Although there were many who rejoiced in the hope of progress, and a spiraling ascent toward a perfect society on earth, there were many who longed for the stability of the old world picture, and who knew that the upward swirl of "progress" claimed many victims along the way. By the mid-nineteenth century in England, poets and others were expressing a new mood of doubt in the old "truths" of a stable cosmos, and fearing that without Christianity the universe was a very bad joke. Matthew Arnold, for example, wrote his famous poem "Dover Beach" in 1851, lamenting the demise of Christianity and the vacuum of meaning it had left behind. Looking over the moonlit English Channel, Arnold mused that

> *The Sea of Faith*
> *Was once, too, at the full, and round earth's shore*
> *Lay like the folds of a bright girdle furled.*
> *But now I only hear its melancholy, long, withdrawing roar,*
> *Retreating, to the breath*
> *Of the night-wind, down the vast edges drear*
> *And naked shingles of the world.*
>
> *Ah, love, let us be true*
> *To one another! For the world, which seems*
> *To lie before us like a land of dreams,*
> *So various, so beautiful, so new,*
> *Hath really neither joy, nor love, nor light,*
> *Nor certitude, nor peace, nor help for pain,*
> *And we are here as on a darkling plain*
> *Swept with confused alarms of struggle and flight,*
> *Where ignorant armies clash by night.*

Many British intellectuals overcame this anxiety by clinging to hope in human progress. There was a widespread sense that thoughtful people could not turn back to the old premodern certainties. Courageous people needed to acknowledge the shaking and heaving in their nineteenth-century scientific and industrial world. Likewise, they needed to take into account the ways in which German scholarship was trying to adapt Christianity to that world in the turmoil of change. So beginning in 1860, and continuing right down through the 1930s, leading intellectuals in the Church of England sought to incorporate more and more of German modernist theology into the doctrine of the Church of England.

As mentioned above, the first of these tentative attempts was that modest volume titled *Essays and Reviews,* published in 1860 and containing seven essays by Anglican clergy (and one lone layman). The most prominent of the authors was Benjamin Jowett, Regius Professor of Greek at Oxford. In a letter to a friend, Jowett made his intentions plain. Speaking for his colleagues, he said that their purpose was "to say what we think within the limits of the Church of England." Of course the effect of the essays was to begin extending those limits more and more, so that by the 1920s it would be possible to deny all the tenets of Christianity and still claim to be a member of the Church, and an ordained member too. *Essays and Reviews* would sound quite moderate to later radicals, but it did propose many of the central assertions of modernist theology, and legitimize them for consideration by Anglican scholars. For example, the authors proposed the usual radical distinction between science and fact and public truth on the one hand, and religion and opinion and private experience on the other. Although science alone offered certainty, nevertheless subjective experience was important as the well from which all religions draw their feelings. The Bible, said Jowett, shows the evolutionary development of this consciousness among the Israelites, culminating in Jesus. And of course the Bible must be read, criticized, and dissected like any other human document from the ancient Near East.

Of course, Anglican Evangelicals reacted to *Essays and Reviews* with horror and scorn. But their star was setting, and they failed to produce a single leader who could criticize German modernist theology clearly and comprehensively. The first two generations of Anglo-Catholics likewise viewed the waves of German theology with alarm. But a new generation of Anglo-Catholics emerged in the 1880s, convinced that they could no longer ignore modernist scholarship as if it didn't exist. Led by Charles Gore (1853–1932), the principal of Pusey House in Oxford, a group of younger Anglo-Catholics published *Lux Mundi* ('light of the world') in 1889, another landmark in Anglican thought. They claimed to write as servants of the Church and its creeds, but that the great transformations of the era required of Christian theology "some general restatement of its claim and meaning." In particular, they hoped that by emphasizing Christ's incarnation, they might find some common ground with modernist concerns. Gore's essay "The Holy Spirit and Inspiration" addressed the evident disparities between the Old Testament and modern science, and the problem presented by Jesus' acceptance of Old Testament teaching (e.g., that Moses wrote the Pentateuch). Gore suggested that in his incarnation, our Lord had voluntarily given up his divine omniscience and submitted to the intellectual limitations of the first century. Gore found New Testament support for this idea of Jesus' renunciation in Philippians 2:7, where Paul says that our Lord "emptied himself, taking the form of a servant." Many Anglo-Catholics believed that Gore had gone too far, that he had given up too much. (What about the cosmic activities of the preexistent Word during Jesus' human lifetime?) But Gore had successfully shown that any study of Jesus must take full account of his first-century environment, a conviction of which both Anglo-Catholic and Evangelical scholars a hundred years later would approve.

After *Lux Mundi* Gore moved in a conservative direction and became the Church's leading defender of creedal orthodoxy. Likewise, a group of Cambridge New Testament scholars—F. J. A. Hort, J. B. Lightfoot, and B. F. Westcott—were demonstrating that the tools of German higher-critical interpretation could lead to quite orthodox conclusions.

But the limits of permissible thought in the Church were expanding as the new Modern Churchmen's Union demonstrated in the early twentieth century. This expression of modernism was almost entirely negative. It sought to dismiss all the elements of Christianity that modern science had allegedly disproved. It offered no alternative system, such as Schleiermacher had done with his religion of God consciousness. The leader of this movement was Hastings Rashdall (1858–1924), dean of divinity at New College, Oxford. His allies produced another book of critical essays *(Foundations* in 1912, including B. H. Streeter's "The Historic Christ," which was quoted at the beginning of this chapter). The full expression of Rashdall's thought came at a conference of the Modern Churchmen's Union at Girton College, Cambridge, in 1921. Rashdall

believed that Anglican theology should dispense entirely with all the supernatural assumptions of the Bible, retaining only our Lord's ethical teaching,
which could stand on its own authority. Christ never asserted his own divinity,
claimed Rashdall, and neither should we. Rashdall blandly assumed that all
thoughtful scholars would agree with his rejection of the whole supernatural
dimension of the Bible in its entirety. By no means did all Anglican leaders do
so! But the Church of England's response was not to reassert the Bible and the
creeds. It was to appoint a committee.

In the wake of the Girton conference, many Evangelicals and Anglo-Catholics petitioned Archbishop of Canterbury Randall Davidson to respond. Wary
of making any move at first, Davidson agreed in 1922 to appoint a commission
on doctrine. This body took sixteen years to survey the present state of theology
in the Church of England. In 1938 it finally published a report titled *Doctrine
in the Church of England* (significantly not *Doctrine of*). It made no attempt to
draw the line at modernist denials of the Christian faith, but simply reported
the range of opinions currently being expressed in the Church of England.

By 1938, the storm clouds of war were gathering once more, and the optimism of the modernist faith in human progress was looking very thin. The
bankruptcy of modernism in the late 1930s may be gauged by the theological
career of the doctrine committee's chair, Archbishop of York William Temple
(and of Canterbury 1942–1944). The son of Archbishop of Canterbury Frederick Temple (in office 1896–1902), William Temple was a genius and a brilliant
leader. For most of his career as a theologian, as a teacher and then as a bishop,
Temple tried to interpret Christianity through the lens of Hegel's philosophy,
arguing that Christ was the culmination of the long upward spiral of historical
development directed by God. In this way, Temple tried to justify Christian
faith to a modern skeptical world. But by 1939, Temple had changed his tune
entirely. He rejected his former attempts to explain Christianity in terms of
Hegelian philosophy. He wrote,

> *There is a new task for theologians today . . . . Our task with this world is
> not to explain it but to convert it. Its need can be met, not by the discov-
> ery of its own immanent principle in signal manifestation through Jesus
> Christ, but only by the shattering impact upon its self-sufficiency and*

arrogance of the Son of God, crucified, risen and ascended, pouring forth
that explosive and disruptive energy which is the Holy Ghost.

Temple's conversion marked the end of an era. While modernist optimism had somehow survived the slaughter in the trenches of World War I, the combined impact of the Great Depression and the rise of Fascism served to obliterate it for a season. Modernism would storm back in the 1960s, but for a generation it gave way in the Church of England to orthodox expressions of Christianity, such as the great wartime BBC talks for which C. S. Lewis became famous. But that's another story.

Let's Pause and Reflect

5. Summarize the widening parameters of permissible teaching in the Church of England between *Essays and Reviews* in 1860 and *Doctrine in the Church of England in 1938.*

_____

_____

_____

_____

_____

_____

_____

_____

_____

_____

The Broad Church Era in the American Episcopal Church (1873–1934)

Standing in the high ornate pulpit in Trinity Episcopal Church, Copley Square, in Boston, the Rev. Phillips Brooks is preaching on Matthew 4:8–9, the temptation of Jesus.

"Again, the devil took him to a very high mountain and showed him all the kingdoms of the world and their glory, and he said to him, 'All these I will give you, if you will fall down and worship me.'"

Brooks' interpretation of this passage takes a very unusual turn. Instead of presenting the "kingdoms of this world" as the domain of Satan, Brooks understands these kingdoms to be the future "great society" that lies ahead for humanity—thanks to the upward spiral of historical progress. Developing this theme, Brooks says, "Mankind is greater than it has known itself to be. I see in a mist and haze—but still I do see—the pinnacles of a more glorious city, the outline of a larger world. So the world vaguely feels about itself. It has gone up—the Spirit of God surely sending it, and yet often the devil surely meeting it there—it has gone up into the mountain, and is seeing all its future kingdoms, and the glory of them."

No one rises to protest.

Philips Brooks was not a radical modernist. He was widely hailed as the greatest preacher of his era in the Episcopal Church. But after the debacle of the conflicts between Evangelicals and Anglo-Catholics, and the failure of either party to address either the Industrial Revolution or the tidal wave of modernist ideas crossing the Atlantic from Germany, Brooks called for openness and charity and freedom of debate. To this end, he helped found a Church Congress in 1874 that would meet every three years, in the year preceding General Convention. Papers would be welcome from all parties in the Church, and Evangelicals and Anglo-Catholics did indeed speak to the congress on matters of interest to them, especially in the first decades. But Brooks and his allies set the agenda, which more and more turned to the oppression caused by modern industrialism and the agony of the immigrant workers in cities like Pittsburgh (which one writer described as "hell with the lid off"). The Church Congress in 1874 featured a paper titled "The Mutual Obligations of Capital and Labor," which pointed the direction for future meetings of this body. If America was to grow into the "Heavenly City" that Brooks foresaw, Christians would have to roll up their sleeves and deal with the hideous suffering that polluted the industrial cities of the late nineteenth century.

The Episcopal Church was exhibiting an openness (sooner than most American denominations) to the social gospel and to the application of Christian principles to the agonies of immigrant labor—in dangerous factories and squalid tenement houses. The social gospel became a powerful voice in American Christianity in the 1890s, led by prophets like the Congregationalist Washington Gladden (1836–1918) and the Baptist Walter Rauschenbusch (1861–1918). Standing in the tradition of Immanuel Kant, who had written a century earlier, they identified morality as the heart of Christianity. Likewise, they generally followed Hegel in assuming an upward spiral of human progress. German theologians like Albrecht Ritschl (1822–1889) and Adolf Harnack (1851–1930) had developed these themes, emphasizing Jesus' preaching of God's justice and peace as the heart of his mission. Now Gladden and Rauschenbusch applied this teaching to American society. They believed that the kingdom of God was spreading in this world, and they called on American Christians to dig in and help it happen. There was an evolutionary optimism in this message that made it plausible to many in the 1890s. Because the social gospelers emphasized the humanitarian promise of Jesus' teaching ("the brotherhood of man and the Fatherhood of God") they had no occasion to deny the virgin birth or the resurrection. Their teaching seemed largely consistent with Episcopal standards of faith like the Thirty-Nine Articles (though it did not stress their supernaturalist assumptions). The Church Congress meetings in the period 1874–1914 proceeded in this spirit.

At the same time, however, some leaders in the Episcopal Church were beginning to make noises that sounded a great deal like Schleiermacher. In particular, they began to adopt the German theologian's argument that all religion had its roots in human subjective experience of a "Something" in the universe that gave them a feeling of absolute dependence and security. These ideas found expression in the thought of William Porcher Dubose (1836–1918), professor of theology at the University of the South. Dubose combined a Hegelian belief in human evolution with Schleiermacher's insistence on Christianity as a religion of internal subjective human experience. He believed that Christ was the highest expression of God in human flesh, but that all women and men are occasions for "incarnation." "The incarnation of God in man is still going on in the world." Likewise, the truth of Christianity depended not on any miraculous signs like the resurrection, but rather on the internal assent of the human consciousness. "How do we know Christ to be the truth and the life? Of whether he be the truth and the life, the criterion is within us." Dubose was widely recognized to be the most creative theologian the American Episcopal Church had ever produced, and his ideas occasioned no negative response from the House of Bishops.

After World War I, leaders in the Episcopal Church began to make similar noises about additional matters of the Christian faith. The focus of their critique was that the Bible, the creeds, and the *Book of Common Prayer* all insisted on propositions that were alien to the modern mind. At a Church Congress session in 1919, for example, liturgical scholar John Wallace Suter maligned the doctrine of original sin. Fortunately, Suter optimistically continued, there was now a widespread consensus in the Episcopal Church in favor of dropping such old-fashioned notions, which modern scientific knowledge had rendered obsolete.

Suter was probably correct in identifying such a consensus among the Episcopal Church's intellectual elite. But events in the 1920s revealed a widening gap between the seminary-trained clergy and the conservative laity in the pews. In 1923, Bishop William Lawrence of Massachusetts published an autobiography in which he argued that belief in the virgin birth was not essential to the Christian faith. A firestorm of protest erupted among Episcopal laypeople when Bishop Lawrence's faux pas became widely known. The House of Bishops had to issue a pastoral letter in 1924 to try and calm the uproar. They said that trusting in the virgin birth was more important than confessing it as a historical event (which again echoes Schleiermacher), but they ruled that no Episcopal clergyman should actually rock the boat by publicly denying any articles of the creed. (Surprisingly, it was this pastoral letter that disappointed the Rev. Mr. Parks, and provoked his symbolic gesture in St. Bartholomew's, New York.) Bishop Lawrence apologized to the Church Congress in 1924, not for the content of his statement on the virgin birth, but for his lack of good judgment in publishing it.

A similar defeat for the modernists occurred when the proponents of a revised Prayer Book presented to General Convention for its first reading in 1925 dropped the Thirty-Nine Articles from its pages. Over the next three years, conservative leaders organized a series of petitions (one with over thirty-four thousand signatures) asking that the Articles be restored. At the book's second reading in 1928, General Convention relented and put the Articles back in. Fearing this backlash of conservative sentiment, three Episcopal seminaries responded by moving under the wings of large universities, where they hoped that academic freedom would preserve their right to critique the central doctrines of the Christian faith.

Over the next few years, the impact of the stock market crash and the early Depression years revealed the inadequacy of the Church Congress' love affair with modernist optimism. Unfortunately the chairman of the congress chose this moment to assert his views all the more plainly. The Rev. Harold Prichard of New York referred to the Apostles' Creed as a "museum piece." He called for the Episcopal Church to replace it with a more up-to-date statement, playing down such distasteful themes as Jesus' suffering and death on the cross. All of this was too much. The Church Congress ceased to meet after 1934. In fact, a movement back toward biblical theology reversed the tide of modernism in American Christianity in general for about a generation. We will consider this brief return to orthodoxy in Chapter 12.

Let's Pause and Reflect

6. How did the ideas of Kant, Schleiermacher, and Hegel find expression in the teaching of Episcopal leaders in the period 1873–1934?

_____

_____

_____

_____

_____

_____

_____

_____

_____

_____

Review

A. What were the main features of modernist theology as it had developed in Germany by the 1830s?

_____

_____

_____

_____

_____

_____

_____

_____

_____

_____

B. What made this modernist theology attractive to many Anglican leaders in England and America in the period beginning in the 1860s?

_____

_____

_____

_____

_____

_____

_____

_____

_____

For Thought and Application

C. Do you accept the notion that modern science has ruled out any sort of "historical revelation," or the idea that a Creator God intervened in history—above all in Jesus of Nazareth? Why or why not?

_____

_____

_____

_____

_____

_____

_____

_____

_____

_____

D. Can you think of specific instances of modernist teaching, not only in your experience of the Christian churches today, but also in the ideas taught in the media, higher education, and government policy?

_____

_____

_____

_____

_____

_____

_____

_____

_____

_____

_____

_____

For Further Reading

J.R.H. Moorman, *A History of the Church in England, Third Edition.*

- Chapters 20-21

Robert W. Prichard, *A History of the Episcopal Church, Third Revised Edition.*

- Chapter 7

Chapter 11
The Anglican Communion
(1789–2018)

A young Chinese woman named Tang Li Di is riding in a smoky compartment of a local train, chugging its way out from Nanking into the countryside in 1936. Next to her is a young American woman named Mary Parke, an Episcopal missionary in training. She is serving an apprenticeship to Li Di, learning how to preach the gospel in Mandarin. After about an hour on the train, the two women alight at a local station, a simple gravel patch adjoining the rails. Here a farmer in a conical hat meets them with a wooden wheelbarrow. The barrow has a large wheel in the center, with benches on either side for passengers. The women climb aboard, and the farmer picks up the handles. Slowly he trundles them along a dirt track toward a village of thatched-roof huts. In the little marketplace he halts, and the women get off and sit on the ground. A small crowd gathers, wondering at this novelty.

Li Di begins to tell stories. First she starts with Chinese folktales. Then she introduces some Western stories. The woes of Cinderella especially interest the policeman, who is standing on the edge of the crowd, picking his teeth with a piece of straw. Finally Li Di begins to tell a story about Jesus, how he fed five thousand people with a few rice cakes and two small fish. The small crowd presses closer around Li Di and her "foreign devil" friend. The villagers have never heard (or seen) anything quite so astonishing.

Fifty years later and thousands of miles to the east . . .

We are standing in a corrugated metal shed, on a farm in Chile, amid the rolling fields near the town of Chol Chol. The people of this area are mostly Mapuche. They have lived here for thousands of years, long before the conquerors came and took all the best land. Alcoholism is the great reality in Mapuche country. The natives never formally surrendered to the Europeans, but alcohol finally brought them down.

The metal shed where we're standing is part of a farm owned and worked by Segundo ("Junior"). He is an evangelist and lay reader of the Anglican Church in Chile. His people first heard the gospel from Englishmen in the South American Missionary Society in the 1860s. Now Segundo is carrying on the work, gathering a little flock of Mapuche people every Sunday. The church in his metal shed—which he built himself—is part of a network of rural congregations, each five or six miles apart. Transportation is still by foot or by oxcart, so churches need to be close together. And Segundo needs to be close to his people, who frequently lose their sobriety and need to be picked up from the fields at night and taken home.

This is Segundo's work, reminding his people every Sunday about Jesus' love for sinners, and picking them up when they fall. It's often frustrating and disappointing. But it's his work. Segundo turns to his American guest and motions with his head toward the north. "Como trabajas alli?" he asks. "How do you work up there?"

And finally, thousands of miles to the north . . .

The village of Pangnirtung is on the shore of a deep fjord on Baffin Island in Canada, just beneath the Arctic Circle. About twelve hundred Inuit (and a handful of the qadlunat, or white people) live in prefabricated houses in the village. In the midst of the little town stands St. Luke's Anglican Church, a wide one-story shed with a tiny bell tower. It's Sunday morning in January, and the bell is ringing for church, its clanging sharpened acutely by the temperature of -40° Fahrenheit. The chill doesn't bother the Christians who stream into the building—some children are wearing nothing warmer than a jean jacket.

Inside the church, the choir is warming up. A lively elderly lady called Mika is leading them in a gospel song in Inuktitut, a cappella except for the drums, sealskin discs stretched on circular wooden frames about a yard wide. When the church is full, Abraham the native priest begins with, "Blessed be God, Father, Son, and Holy Spirit" in Inuktitut. The entire service is in the people's mother tongue, and they join vigorously in the responses.

There is a small seminary here in Pangnirtung, training Inuit clergy (women and men) amid their own culture. Part of their instruction is in English, so that they can participate fully in the Anglican Church of Canada. But worship at the school is always in Inuktitut, and they can read the entire Bible in their native language—and preach from it. "Every language, tongue, people and nation . . ."

This is the great new reality in the Anglican story—that we now belong to a worldwide church with 85 million members in thirty-nine independent "provinces." The three vignettes above are a tiny sample of this diverse body of Christians. How did the Church of England grow, over the last two centuries, into this global fellowship? That's the theme of this present chapter.

The Great Century of Global Missions (1815–1914)

The expansion of the Church of England overseas began first in North America, specifically in the Episcopal Church, which formally took shape in 1789. But the major expansion of Anglicanism happened in the "Great Century" of world evangelization, as the famous historian Kenneth Scott Latourette called the period from 1815 to 1914. This was the age of evangelical revival and mission, of the Industrial revolution, and of European imperialism. All these forces fueled the expansion of Christianity across the globe. It was often a sordid business with the Bible following the British flag and the barrels of trading goods. Nevertheless, the result was a web of Christian fellowships that include the most rapidly growing churches in the Anglican world today. The Lord works in mysterious ways.

After Napoleon's army was defeated at the Battle of Waterloo in 1815, Europe enjoyed a space of relative peace for several decades. England in particular saw the explosion of forces that had been inhibited for a generation. Christian

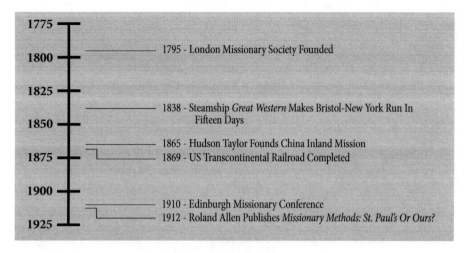

1775

1800 — 1795 - London Missionary Society Founded

1825

1850 — 1838 - Steamship *Great Western* Makes Bristol-New York Run In Fifteen Days

1865 - Hudson Taylor Founds China Inland Mission
1875 — 1869 - US Transcontinental Railroad Completed

1900

1910 - Edinburgh Missionary Conference
1925 — 1912 - Roland Allen Publishes *Missionary Methods: St. Paul's Or Ours?*

revival, industrial growth, and overseas conquest all took off together. Let's look at these three movements and their contribution to the spread of Anglican Christianity throughout the world.

The evangelical revivals in Britain and America had their roots in the 1740s, as we have seen. The Wesley brothers built the Methodist network of small societies for Christian growth and multiplication. George Whitefield's evangelistic genius drew vast crowds to his outdoor sermons in Britain and America, putting Christian revival at the top of the headlines throughout the mid-1700s. At the end of the century, William Wilberforce and his allies began to transform British politics and society, leading to the abolition of slavery in 1833. They inspired more than five hundred voluntary societies for the reform of education, health care, prisons, factories, alcoholism, and countless other causes. Meanwhile in America, the Second Great Awakening in New England, the southern tent meeting revivals, and the urban evangelism in the northern cities all combined in a "Protestant empire" of evangelistic activism in the early nineteenth century. On both sides of the Atlantic, mission societies proliferated. The American Episcopal Church was too small and weak to do much missionary work until after 1811, but gradually it began to awaken—sending Jackson Kemper as missionary bishop to the "Old Northwest" in 1835, and William Boone as "bishop of Amoy and Other Parts of China" in 1844.

Anglican and Episcopal missions were a small part of the wave of evangelical church-planting efforts that spread overseas after 1815. Some evangelical groups recruited from a single denomination, like the Church Missionary Society (CMS) in England. Others were interdenominational, like the London Missionary Society (1795). Still other voluntary societies had no ties to specific denominations, like the so-called faith missions that proliferated after the 1850s. The most famous of these latter was the China Inland Mission (CIM), founded by Dr. Hudson Taylor in 1865. These faith missions enjoyed greater flexibility than their denominational counterparts, and often showed the most creativity, as in the CIM's adoption of Chinese dress and living conditions.

Evangelical mission societies exhibited several strengths in the nineteenth century. They recruited people who were wholly committed to Christ, who knew the risks, and who were ready to die. One Alexander MacKay said to the CMS board in 1878, "Within six months you will probably hear that one of us is dead. When the news comes, do not be cast down, but send someone else immediately to take the vacant place." English missionaries traveling to East Africa famously packed their belongings in the coffins that they reckoned on needing very soon.

Likewise the evangelical missions were dedicated to serving the whole person. Schools and hospitals were as central to their strategy as were preaching stations. Christians opened 270 hospitals in China, for example. This was not a large number in a population of about 500 million, but it represented half the hospitals in the land.

The missionaries came not only to serve and to teach but also to learn. Despite all their European blind spots, missionaries did study local cultures and help build bridges of understanding between the races. Baptist pioneer William Carey spent most of his life in India working on linguistics, translating the Bible into six local languages, and the Hindu classic *Ramayana* into English. S. M. Williams's brilliant *The Middle Kingdom* interpreted Chinese civilization to the English-speaking world. We could add many other examples.

Finally, many missionaries genuinely loved the people they came to serve. One Indian preacher said of the man who had taught him many decades before, "He loved us. He loved us very much. Yes, very much he loved us." Despite all the narrow-mindedness and the condescension and the racism of so many Western missionaries, the love of Christ shone sufficiently clear through them that millions came to the Lord.

Of course there were obvious failures in the missionaries' attitude and conduct, Anglican missionaries not least. All too often they failed to distinguish between the gospel and the Western packaging in which they brought it. There was no need for Christian native women in the Pacific Islands to wear the hot, uncomfortable Mother Hubbard dresses that the missionaries prescribed. There was no need to build thirteenth-century English Gothic parish churches in China. And there was no need for Inuit choir ladies in Pangnirtung to wear blue cassocks, white cottas, and four-cornered black caps—perfect vestments for an English cathedral.

Likewise the missionaries often identified too closely with the Western colonial governments, whose aims were hardly spiritual. Mission schools often taught their students to be submissive junior clerks in the colonial administration. The missionaries—looking down at these junior clerks—were generally loath to raise up strong indigenous leadership, or to turn over control to them. Paternalistic attitudes lasted long into the twentieth century. The assumption was that "Father knows best" and that the local Christians were simply not ready to shoulder the task of leading Christians in their own native lands. This nearsighted paternalism would nearly spell ruin for the Anglican churches of the Global South, when the tide of colonialism began to recede in the mid-twentieth century, and country after country in Africa and Asia won their independence.

But not all the missionary leaders clung to paternalistic control in the nineteenth century. In 1865, the CIM raised Western eyebrows by insisting that its workers wear Chinese dress, live in Chinese houses, and eat Chinese food. Likewise, Taylor ordered that the headquarters of the CIM be located in China, not in London, so that the directors might know the local situation intimately and devise appropriate strategy. Many other missionaries were convinced that the CIM would "go native" and the English lose control. Another radical Westerner was Dr. John Nevius, who in 1890 convinced the Methodist and Presbyterian missionaries in Korea that local Christians should choose their own leaders, design and build their own churches, and raise their own funds. Finally, Anglican clergyman Roland Allen wrote the classic work supporting rapid indigenization, *Missionary Methods: St. Paul's or Ours?* (1912). All these "radical" ideas needed to wait almost a century before their acceptance by the Western churches.

Meanwhile, evangelical missionaries could not have made their way to Africa, Asia, and South America in such numbers after 1815 without the revolutionary advances in transportation that steam power made possible. In 1815, the voyage from England to India could take as long as six months. Steamships began to greatly shorten ocean voyages, bringing distant shores closer. The paddlewheel steamer *Aaron Manby* crossed the English Channel in 1822, the first all-iron ship to make the trip. Sixteen years later the *Great Western* (an oak-hulled paddlewheel ship) made the run from Bristol to New York in fifteen days, instead of the ninety days that a sailing vessel might have required. The China run was of course more challenging, for until 1865 no ship could carry enough coal for the journey round the southern tip of Africa, and have any room for commercial cargo as well. The *Agamemnon* made the run in 1865, thanks to a coaling stop in Mauritius. The opening of the Suez Canal in 1869 brought India and China still closer to England. Missionaries could now travel around the globe without months at sea, where disease and shipwreck took a great toll. But of course the challenge remained of surviving once they reached China, India, or Africa. Tropical diseases accounted for the huge death rates among Western missionaries until twentieth-century medicine began to supply vaccines and treatment.

The technological shrinking of the globe also enabled the Western powers to carve out continental empires on a scale hitherto impossible. The first commercial railroads had appeared in America in 1826 and in England in 1829. Since the fifteenth century, European states had planted coastal trading depots like Bombay in India. Spain had successfully moved inland in Central and South America, and thanks to the St. Lawrence River, the French had done likewise in Canada. But the British in India first took full advantage of steam railroads, in gradually establishing the Empire in India, the British *Raj* (1858–1947). At the same time, railroads enabled America to move its frontier westward to the Pacific. On May 19, 1869, the "golden spike" joined the Central Pacific and Union Pacific railways at Promontory Summit, Utah Territory, establishing the first transcontinental rail system in America.

The Great Century of Western missions came to a symbolic close in 1910, with the famous World Missionary Conference in Edinburgh. Major Protestant denominations and missionary societies sent some twelve hundred delegates to the meeting. Only eighteen were invited from the non-Western world. The conference thus exhibited both the achievements and the failures of the previous century. Most major language groups had some Christian presence by then. Only a few areas like Afghanistan, Nepal, and Tibet remained obstinately closed. But the transition to fully self-supporting, self-governing churches had hardly begun. Only 1.5 percent of the delegates were indigenous Christians! And the Western missionaries were still deeply dependent on the colonial governments and their military presence.

These continental empires grew at an enormous cost both in suffering and in lives. Missionaries were often complicit in the evils of colonialism, as we have seen. Missionary access to the Yangtze Valley in China still depended heavily on Western gunboats as late as the 1930s. The case against Western missions has been made over and over, in terms of military, political, cultural, and religious aggression. There is no need to rehearse it in detail here. Suffice it to say that both original sin and amazing grace were profoundly at work in the growth of the Anglican Communion, to which we now turn our attention.

Let's Pause and Reflect

1. What were the primary strengths and weaknesses of European global missions during the Great Century of 1815–1914?

_____

_____

_____

_____

_____

_____

_____

_____

_____

_____

_____

_____

_____

The Growth of the Anglican Communion

The American Episcopal Church was the prototype for all the subsequent provinces of what became the Anglican Communion. Originally founded as an extension of the established Church of England, in the period 1783–1789 it reinvented itself as an independent national body, despite how deep its roots were in the story of the mother church across the Atlantic. The Episcopal Church encompassed both Reformation/Evangelical and High Church traditions. It derived its episcopacy from British roots in Aberdeen and Canterbury (however estranged the Aberdeen non-Jurors were from the latter). But following its generation of quiescence between 1789 and 1811, it started to turn its attention away from England and toward the young American nation and its expansion westward. Philander Chase was planting congregations in Ohio soon after the War of 1812 made it safe to do so (but significantly, he had to raise money in England to pay for his work). Then of course Jackson Kemper took up the task farther west in 1835. Kemper included missions to the Native Americans in his brief. At his consecration he said, "The needs of the red men are a weight upon my soul." His foundation at Nashotah Lakes in 1841 deliberately

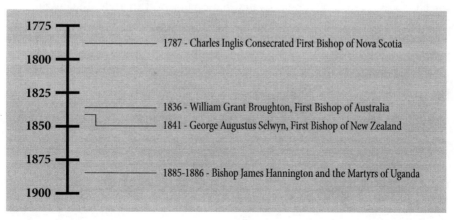

listed native evangelism among its goals. His successor in Minnesota, Bishop Benjamin Whipple (in office 1859–1901), ordained a number of native clergy and became a strong advocate of native rights. The Ojibwa people named him Straight Tongue in their language. Nevertheless, the Episcopal Church grew into a denomination that was largely Caucasian. Parishes in the eastern cities were sometimes large and rich (like Trinity, Wall Street, in New York). Parishes in small towns were often lower in attendance, with seventy-five or fewer worshipers on a Sunday. Membership in the national church peaked at 3,615,643 in 1965, falling off sharply thereafter.

Like the American Episcopal Church, other provinces in the nineteenth-century Anglican world first developed to meet the spiritual needs of English colonists. The Anglican Church of Canada received its first bishop in 1787, Charles Inglis (in office 1787–1816), who had been the loyalist rector of Trinity, Wall Street, in New York, and had prayed for King George III while George Washington was in the congregation. (Mobs then broke into Inglis's home and plundered it.) He became bishop of Nova Scotia, where many American loyalists had migrated in the 1780s. That diocese and its neighbors, New Brunswick and Prince Edward Island, were established by law, though the large Roman Catholic population in Quebec and Ontario made establishment impossible there. Funding for the established dioceses came initially from Parliament in Westminster, while the Society for the Propagation of the Gospel and the CMS paid for missionaries further west. Then a judicial decision by the English Privy Council (*Long v. Gray,* 1861) declared that all Anglican regional churches in the empire should be self-governing and self-supporting. The Anglican Church in Canada held its first national synod in 1893. Meanwhile, its attempts to evangelize native populations had failed to achieve much. It had cooperated with provincial and national authorities in gathering First Nations children into residential schools, a policy that led to abuses that would haunt the Church in the late twentieth century. Despite a lively ministry to the Inuit in the north (supported by the Arthur Turner Training School in Pangnirtung), the Church remained predominantly Caucasian.

The same held true for the Anglican Church in Australia. The Aborigines there were hesitant to join the religious body that was blessing the seizure of their lands. By the early twenty-first century, the Anglican Church in Australia claimed just over three million adherents, in twenty-three dioceses among five archdioceses. Sydney is the largest of the latter, and is at some odds with the rest of the Australian church over modernist theology.

The Church in New Zealand likewise suffered in its ministry to the Maori people when the colonial government repeatedly broke treaties that the missionaries had encouraged the Maori to accept. A century and a half later, the Anglican Church in New Zealand had incorporated parts of Polynesia and established three cooperative "streams" (each a *tikanga*)—for Polynesia, for the Maori, and for the English. Each has its own archbishop and its own assembly, and each is committed to refrain from any action to which another *tikanga* objects. Whether this cooperative polity can survive Western modernist theology remains to be seen.

The Anglican Church in South Africa was another case in which outreach to the indigenous population had an equivocal record. Originally the Anglican presence there was to serve the British soldiers who were defending the white settlers who were expanding into lands occupied by Xhosa and Zulu peoples. Bishop Robert Gray (in office 1848–1872) organized a province of five dioceses, which he intended to be multiracial. His intentions were foiled by the incessant Kaffir Wars and the expansionist policies of the colonial government. In 1852, he organized a new diocese in Natal, to which Bishop John Colenso was appointed. Colenso was a fierce and tireless advocate for the Zulu people in particular, which, of course, ran him afoul of the British commissioner for native affairs in Natal. Colenso was unable to prevent the destruction of the Zulu kingdom in 1878, but his example did encourage the anti-apartheid movement in South Africa a century later. This heritage was more significant than Colenso's excommunication by Bishop Gray for heresy, in part for trying to understand Scripture through Zulu culture. (The "Colenso affair" was one reason for the first Lambeth Conference of Anglican bishops in 1867, as we will see.)

Other regions of the world saw Anglican missions enjoy better long-term success in birthing indigenous churches. We'll look at Nigeria as an example. Evangelism in West Africa benefited enormously from the British abolition of the slave trade in 1807, and the efforts of the Royal Navy to capture slave ships and to free their captives. Freetown in Sierra Leone became the great center for the rehabilitation and resettlement of freed slaves from all over West Africa.

One such freedman there would be Samuel Ajayi Crowther, pioneer bishop of Nigeria. Another advantage for evangelism in West Africa was the election of Henry Venn as secretary of the CMS in 1841. Venn was a lonely pioneer of the missionary strategy that Roland Allen later advocated, namely, the establishment as soon as possible of a "self-governing, self-supporting and self-propagating native church." With this in mind, Venn persuaded Crowther to accept appointment as bishop "on the Niger . . . beyond the Queen's dominions" in 1864. He was consecrated to this office in Canterbury Cathedral. A complicated ministry followed, focusing on the Yoruba people, some of whom were within the queen's dominions in West Africa and some were not. Crowther had no jurisdiction over the former, though his efforts focused on the Yoruba as a whole people group (for whom he oversaw the translation of the Yoruba Bible). Of course, the English missionaries along the Niger resisted Crowther's work. After his death in 1891, there were no native diocesan bishops in Nigeria until 1951, and the missionaries retained control of the work there. Fortunately after Nigerian independence in 1960, the now indigenous Anglican Church has undertaken a vigorous program of evangelization, and its numbers are now estimated at some 20 million (or 10 percent of the total national population). The province of Nigeria is also a strong proponent of classical Anglican theology among the indigenous provinces in the Global South, about which we will see more in the next chapter. (The term "Global South" has come to replace such phrases as the "Third World" or the "Two-Thirds World" or the "developing world," in reference to those parts of the Anglican mosaic—principally in Africa and Asia—that remain largely orthodox in theology, and resistant to the modernism exported by the Western churches.)

Uganda is another large and rapidly growing province in the Anglican Communion today. Its foundation was sealed by the blood of martyrs, both English and African. In 1883, the Rev. James Hannington, a CMS missionary, responded to calls for help from East Africa, and set out to plant churches inland from Zanzibar on the coast. He immediately fell ill and almost died from dysentery and malaria, and had to return to England. Once recovered, he was consecrated bishop for Eastern Equatorial Africa and set out once again. The political situation in Uganda was complicated. German efforts to expand their East African conquests in Tanganyika had angered King Mwanga, and he deeply suspected Hannington of aiming to undermine his rule. Hannington persisted, and Mwanga had him captured and put to death. Hannington's last words were, "Go, tell Mwanga that I have purchased the road to Uganda with my blood." Soon thereafter Mwanga—fearing the cultural and imperial aspirations of England and Germany—resolved to make an example of certain young men (twenty-three Anglicans and twenty-two Roman Catholics) who had refused to provide the conventional homosexual services expected of pages at his court. Mwanga had these "Martyrs of Uganda" burned to death. None of this held back the evangelistic efforts of the survivors, and five years later there were enough Anglican converts in Uganda to justify the consecration of Alfred Tucker as bishop in 1891. In 1897, an English and African translation team rendered the whole Bible into Luganda, and it quickly took root in the ambient culture. Uganda is the African Anglican province where the indigenous population most deeply "owns" the Church. When its initial fervor began to flag in the 1920s, what has come to be known as the East African Revival (more next chapter) swept through the Church, with a strong focus on repentance and "walking in the light" with transparent honesty. It is no surprise that the Anglican province of Uganda now numbers over 12 million, a growth of 1000 percent since independence in the 1960s.

We could recount many more stories similar to those of Nigeria and Uganda, featuring muddling missionaries and long-term successful and growing indigenous churches, as in India and South America and the Far East. The modern Anglican Communion—the outcome of all this complicated Anglican evangelization—is now organized into thirty-nine independent provinces, claiming some 85 million adherents. Its provinces vary widely in population, from Bangladesh (sixteen thousand) up to Nigeria (20 million). The Church of England claims 25 million members; but with an average Sunday attendance of 703,000 in 2018, that larger number needs to be viewed with considerable skepticism. Of course, the preponderance of the Anglican Communion's membership is now in the Global South. Provinces like Nigeria and Uganda continue to grow exponentially, and the growth rate shows no sign of slowing at present. Meanwhile the Western provinces (especially the United Kingdom and the United States) continue to shrink, with average Sunday attendance well below a million apiece. Whether the Global South's numerical superiority will translate into leadership of the Anglican Communion remains to be seen.

Let's Pause and Reflect

2. What is the Anglican Communion, and what are its fastest-growing provinces?

_____

_____

_____

_____

_____

_____

_____

_____

_____

Instruments of Communion

As the number of overseas Anglican bodies gradually grew in the mid-nineteenth century, the need for some kind of unifying structure began to emerge. If the American and Canadian and Australian churches and the rest were not parts of the Church of England—as it was obvious that they were not—then what were they? The American Episcopal Church had declared independence in 1789. The British Privy Council had ruled in 1861 that the other offspring should be self-governing. They all had originated in the Church of England, but what held them together now?

The first of four "instruments of communion" took shape in the 1860s. The Canadian church was feeling isolated, and its Provincial Synod appealed in 1865 to Archbishop of Canterbury Charles Longley, asking for a General Council to deliberate the affairs of the Anglican diaspora. The Canadians had also condemned Bishop Colenso of Natal for heresy, and wished to see their judgment vindicated. Archbishop Longley responded by inviting the world-

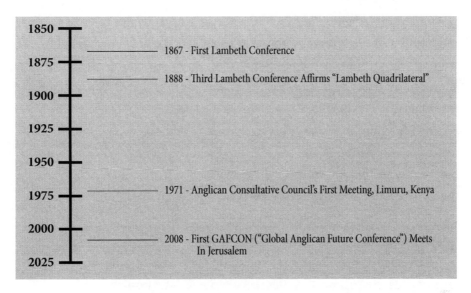

1850

1875 — 1867 - First Lambeth Conference

— 1888 - Third Lambeth Conference Affirms "Lambeth Quadrilateral"

1900

1925

1950

1975 — 1971 - Anglican Consultative Council's First Meeting, Limuru, Kenya

2000

— 2008 - First GAFCON ("Global Anglican Future Conference") Meets In Jerusalem

2025

wide Anglican bishops to Lambeth in 1867. He avoided the word "council" with its implications of jurisdiction and sovereignty, simply using the word "meeting" in his letter of invitation, later amended to "conference." Seventy-six bishops made their way to Lambeth Palace (the Archbishop of Canterbury's residence in London). Colenso was originally on the list, but he wisely stayed away. Bishop Crowther was also invited, but likewise did not come. (His CMS friends and allies smelled a whiff of "popery" in the notion of a worldwide council.) Archbishop Longley steered the conference away from condemning Colenso, and established the precedent that the meeting should be for consultation and deliberation, with Canterbury as *primus inter pares* ("first among equals") but emphatically not as pope.

Here was a second "instrument of communion," the primacy of Canterbury. The archbishop had the authority to invite bishops to Lambeth, and gradually the idea emerged that being in communion with Canterbury (and hence being eligible for invitation to the Lambeth Conference) certified a bishop to be authentically Anglican. This general understanding persisted until the early twenty-first century, when a group of mostly Global South bishops met in Jerusalem in 2008 to symbolically challenge Canterbury's primacy. More about this in the next chapter.

In 1878 Archbishop of Canterbury Archibald Tait convened a second Lambeth Conference. About a hundred bishops attended, discussing such matters as the nature of Anglican unity and the theological challenges to the faith from modernism. These meetings proved so useful, and so encouraging to bishops from lonely missionary outposts, that they agreed the Lambeth Conference should meet every ten years. In 1888, Archbishop Edward Benson called a third meeting, at which the Lambeth Quadrilateral was affirmed as the basis of Anglican unity, as we saw back in chapter 1. With the exception of an eighteen-year gap during World War II, the Lambeth Conferences continued to meet every ten years through 2008. But Archbishop Justin Welby postponed the 2018 meeting because a substantial number of Global South bishops indicated that they would not attend for theological reasons. As of this writing, the future of the Lambeth Conferences is unclear.

Two other instruments of communion took shape in the later twentieth century. The 1968 Lambeth Conference proposed the formation of a triennial Anglican Consultative Council (ACC) composed of bishops, clergy, and laity to coordinate worldwide Anglican mission work and ecumenical relations. The first ACC meeting took place in Limuru, Kenya, in 1971. Likewise, since 1979 Canterbury has invited the "primates" (archbishops or presiding bishops or moderators) of the thirty-nine worldwide provinces to gather every two years or so for mutual consultation. This Primates Meeting and the ACC, like the leadership of Canterbury and the Lambeth Conferences, have been largely organized and paid for by the Western world. There have been occasions when the voice of the Global South has been muzzled. The outcome of the meetings has often been predetermined by staff members serving the interests of Canterbury and New York. But the voices of the now-preponderant Global South majority first broke through at Lambeth 1998, which passed the now-famous Resolution 1.10 describing homosexual behavior as "incompatible with Scripture." The vote was 526 bishops to 70, with 45 in abstention. Resolution 1.10 was advisory and not legislative for the whole Communion, in keeping with Lambeth practice. The refusal of modernist Western provinces to follow Lambeth's advice has occasioned much strife in the Communion, the outcome of which is not yet certain. We will consider this struggle in the next chapter.

Over the Anglican Communion's century and a half of existence, the great question has been whether the Western provinces will permit the independence of the Global South. Initially the issue was whether the indigenous churches were ready to assume self-government and self-support. With the exception of a few prophets like Henry Venn and Roland Allen, English and American Anglicans almost invariably said "no." Likewise in the 1950s, when the former English colonies in East Africa were about to declare independence, many missionaries mourned that the local Christians "weren't ready" for leadership. Alfred Stanway (later the founding dean at Trinity School for Ministry) was bishop of Central Tanganyika from 1951 to 1971, and labored tirelessly to see that an able Tanzanian named Yohana Madinda should succeed him. However stoutly resisted by the white missionaries, the handover to indigenous leadership happened throughout the Communion. A series of group photographs taken of the bishops at four successive Lambeth Conferences (1958, 1968, 1978 and 1988) demonstrates this shift. In 1958, the group was almost entirely Caucasian. By 1988, the non-Western faces vastly outnumbered the whites. The independent self-government of the Global South Anglican provinces is an established fact in the twenty-first century.

But the Western provinces are still loath to allow the Global South its independence or the leadership in the Communion that its numbers would justify. The issue now is theological and cultural, rather than blatantly paternalistic, as before. The Western Anglican world is almost exclusively Caucasian, despite the Episcopal Church's African American presiding bishop, and it has embraced the worldview and social values of modernism. It has used its considerable wealth to press these views on the non-Western Anglican churches. Western leaders assert their confidence that the Africans and the Asians and the Latin Americans will soon exchange their "primitive" beliefs for a more "progressive" Western modernist outlook. Nevertheless, most of the Global South holds fast to the orthodox and biblical Christian faith. A meeting of mostly African and Asian bishops in Jerusalem (the Global Anglican Future Conference, or GAFCON, in 2008) found it necessary to issue a statement affirming the central Christian doctrines like the resurrection of Christ and the authority of Holy Scripture. What made this declaration necessary? In the following chapter, we will consider the return of the Western Anglican provinces to modernist theology in the late twentieth century, and the resulting estrangement between those mother churches and their daughters.

Let's Pause and Reflect

3. Summarize briefly how the demographic tide in the Anglican Communion has shifted from Global West to Global South in the last fifty years.

_____

_____

_____

_____

_____

_____

_____

_____

Review

A. What features of global evangelism in the Great Century have proved to be the most successful and long-lasting in making the Anglican Communion a truly global movement?

_____

_____

_____

_____

_____

_____

_____

_____

_____

_____

_____

For Thought and Application

B. Western missionaries clearly played a vital role in the expansion of Christianity during the period 1815–1914. Many educated Westerners today assert that the age of the missionary is over. How would you respond to such an argument?

_____

_____

_____

_____

_____

_____

_____

_____

_____

_____

_____

C. Nineteenth-century English and American missionaries strongly believed that unless the peoples of Asia and Africa heard and received the gospel, they would go to hell. Do you believe this today? Why or why not?

_____

_____

_____

_____

_____

_____

_____

_____

_____

_____

_____

_____

Chapter 12

Two Churches: West and South

(1938–2018)

Our understanding of the Bible is different from them.
We are two different churches.
—Archbishop of Kenya Benjamin Nzimbi

O ver the past eighty years, the Anglican provinces in the Global South have become independent. Many of those provinces are growing rapidly, especially in Africa, where during the twentieth century the numbers of all Christians grew from 10 million to 360 million. Meanwhile the Anglican churches in the Global West are all shrinking. The American Episcopal Church slipped from 3.5 million members in 1965 to about 1.8 million in 2018, with an average Sunday attendance of about 560,000. The Church of England, despite the 25 million members it claims, has an average Sunday attendance of about 703,000, as we saw in the previous chapter. Other Anglican provinces in the Global West have seen similar membership trends. The reasons for this disparity between South and West are complex, and we will examine them in this chapter.

It looks as if the Anglican story as we have been tracing it may be about to end—the tale of an orthodox threefold English tradition, with similarly orthodox daughter churches overseas. However, a new story is beginning, a story of a network of Global South churches whose roots were planted by Western missionaries, but whose theologies and church cultures remain distinctly biblical, in contrast to the contemporary Anglican churches in the West that once planted them.

In the period immediately following World War II, however, a brief generation of Christian renewal in the Western churches raised the hope that those Anglicans had seen through the naïveté of modernism and returned to classical biblical orthodoxy.

C. S. Lewis and a Generation of Renewal in the West (1938–1963)

When we last considered the Church of England, we noted that William Temple (to be Archbishop of Canterbury 1942–1944) had responded to the crisis of Nazi aggression by renouncing his optimistic Hegelian theology of upward human progress. The approaching storm clouds of war, said Temple, forced him to hope exclusively in God's supernatural intervention in the cross and resurrection of Jesus Christ. The horrors of World War II—coming on the heels of the Great Depression—inspired a similar, more realistic, more biblical perspective throughout most of the Western Anglican churches for a generation. Church attendance and church membership also saw a brief uptick. For example, confirmations in the Church of England ran at 251 per 1,000 fifteen-year-olds in 1940; 279 in 1950; and 315 in 1960. The Church of England was adding about 15,000 new confirmed members per year. The American Episcopal Church likewise shared in the postwar religious boom in the United States. The 1950s were a golden age for the Episcopal Church when families had lots of children and their parishes built Sunday school wings to accommodate them.

England at mid-century was the period when C. S. Lewis' wartime BBC talks were heard and generally approved, all the more when they were compiled and published as *Mere Christianity* after the war. Many observers noted a general feeling of religious revival when Christianity was almost respectable and could even be discussed in polite company. In America, too, Lewis' works were widely read, his portrait appearing on the cover of *Time* magazine as a cultural icon. Let's consider Lewis for a moment as a symbol of modern Western Anglican culture in the postwar generation. What might his example teach us?

Lewis was born in Belfast, Northern Ireland, of transplanted Welsh Protestant stock. He rejected Christianity as a teenager, all the more bitterly for having suffered the horrors of the trenches in World War I. He later described

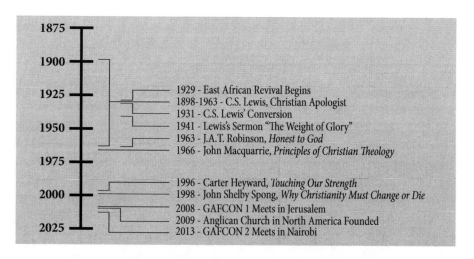

1875
1900
1925
1950
1975
2000
2025

1929 - East African Revival Begins
1898-1963 - C.S. Lewis, Christian Apologist
1931 - C.S. Lewis' Conversion
1941 - Lewis's Sermon "The Weight of Glory"
1963 - J.A.T. Robinson, *Honest to God*
1966 - John Macquarrie, *Principles of Christian Theology*
1996 - Carter Heyward, *Touching Our Strength*
1998 - John Shelby Spong, *Why Christianity Must Change or Die*
2008 - GAFCON 1 Meets in Jerusalem
2009 - Anglican Church in North America Founded
2013 - GAFCON 2 Meets in Nairobi

his return to faith in his autobiography, *Surprised by Joy*. Typical of many modernist Anglicans, he was convinced intellectually that God existed, but held out against accepting Jesus Christ as the Son of God. But as a young don at Magdalen College, Oxford, Lewis had a rich circle of Christian friends. Late one evening in 1931, Lewis strolled with J. R. R. Tolkien and Hugo Dyson up and down Addison's Walk, on the college grounds. Lewis wondered if the story of Jesus wasn't simply another version of the ancient hero myth, found in most human cultures? And weren't all myths basically lies, even when "breathed through silver"? Tolkien and Dyson took up the challenge. What if human myths (like the dying-and-returning hero) were actually "good dreams" that God gave to mortals to prepare them to recognize the *true* Story of when myth finally became history in Jesus of Nazareth? Nine days later Lewis took a trip with his brother Warnie to Whipsnade Zoo north of London. Lewis rode in the sidecar of Warnie's motorcycle. As Lewis later wrote, "I was driven to Whipsnade one sunny morning. When we set out I did not believe that Jesus Christ is the Son of God, and when we reached the zoo I did."

Lewis was in the midst of establishing a distinguished career as a scholar of medieval and Renaissance English Literature. His *The Allegory of Love* (1936) was hailed as a masterpiece on both sides of the Atlantic. But Lewis harbored an "expository demon" (as he put it) and felt driven to defend the Christianity he had recently adopted. Initially he adopted a style of argumentation that was vigorous and lucid. *Mere Christianity* still reads as a winsome and highly readable defense of the faith today. But Lewis concluded that England had not simply lapsed into incredulity during the depression and the war—and needed not simply to have its memory jiggled by lively talks. In fact, for the past century, Christianity had been leaching out of the English consciousness, and needed to be planted afresh. Lewis could not presuppose in his lay audiences even a dim awareness of right and wrong. No matter if church attendance was up slightly in the 1940s, England had lost the Plot; it had forgotten the Story.

How then to reintroduce the Christian story? Lewis decided that left-brained, rational, cognitive argument wouldn't change hearts (even though he was very good at it). People learn what they love. And people love stories. They love stories that fascinate, enthrall, catch us up into beauty and danger, and good and evil.

In June 1941, Lewis preached a sermon called "The Weight of Glory" at St. Mary the Virgin, Oxford, in which he laid out the problem. He began by deploring modern people's satisfaction with feeble and fleeting pleasures.

> *Our Lord finds our desires, not too strong, but too weak. We are half-hearted creatures, fooling about with drink and sex and ambition when infinite joy is offered us, like the ignorant child who wants to go on making mudpies in a slum because he cannot imagine what is meant by the offer of a holiday by the sea. We are far too easily pleased.*

Lewis went on to ask,

> *Do you think I am trying to weave a spell? Perhaps I am; but remember your fairy tales. Spells are used for breaking enchantments as well as inducing them. And you and I have need of the strongest spell that can be found, to wake us from the evil enchantment of worldliness that has been laid upon us for nearly a hundred years.*

Here was the genesis (and genius) of the Narnia tales for which Lewis remains best known. All his life, Lewis had found that worlds of fantasy or enchantment offered him breathtaking moments of pure joy. He met that world first in Longfellow's *Norse Ballads.* Lewis later discovered that he could describe a world of danger, savage beauty, noble faithfulness, ultimate hope—that could spark in his readers the same transcendent moments of joy. A mighty Lion rules in Narnia. What if angels appeared in England? Through such stories we are changed.

Our whole expectation of what's possible opens out to heavenly horizons. And joy sweeps us up.

> *All the trees of the world appeared to be rushing toward Aslan. But as they drew nearer they looked less like trees, and when the whole crowd, bowing and curtsying and waving long thin arms to Aslan, were all around Lucy, she saw that it was a crowd of human shapes. Pale birch-girls were tossing their heads, willow-women pushed back their hair from their brooding faces to gaze on Aslan, the queenly beeches stood still and adored him, shaggy oak-men, lean and melancholy elms, shock-headed hollies (dark themselves, but their wives all bright with berries) and gay rowans, all bowed and rose again, shouting, "Aslan! Aslan!"*

The impact of Lewis's stories and essays was powerful in his generation and the generations to follow, up to today. Yet Lewis was under no illusion that his stories alone would bring the entire nation back to the Story, or that the respectability of Christianity in the postwar generation would last very long. He wrote in the magazine *Cherwell*,

> *Perhaps no one would deny that Christianity is now "on the map" among the younger intelligentsia as it was not, say, in 1920. . . . We must remember that widespread and lively interest in the subject is precisely what we call a fashion. . . . Whatever mere fashion has given us, mere fashion will presently withdraw. The real conversions will remain, but nothing else will. In that sense we may be on the brink of a real, permanent Christian revival: but it will work slowly and obscurely in small groups. The present sunshine . . . is certainly temporary. The grain must be got into the barn before the wet weather comes.*

And come it would in the 1960s.

Let's Pause and Reflect

> 1. What was the heart of Lewis' strategy to bring the Christian Story alive again in secular postwar England? Do you think that kind of strategy can work in Western society today? Why or why not?

_____

_____

_____

_____

_____

_____

_____

_____

Believing the Bible in the Global South

Philip Jenkins' important book *The New Faces of Christianity* (2006) adopted the phrase "Believing the Bible in the Global South" as its subtitle to describe the piety that has emerged in the non-Western world since World War II. The center of gravity of Christianity has shifted southward. No longer is it a Western religion, to be exported in judicious doses to "the lesser breeds without the Law," in Rudyard Kipling's words. The sea of non-Western faces at the recent Lambeth Conferences shows clearly the tilt in the Anglican Communion toward Africa, Asia, and Latin America. Yes, this new majority had its roots in England and America, in the *Book of Common Prayer* and the King James Bible, but how does its faith compare now with the Anglican provinces in the West today?

It is impossible to generalize accurately about so disparate a phenomenon as Anglican Christianity in the Global South today. The best summary can be found in Philip Jenkins' work, especially in the volume mentioned above. Jenkins notes, first of all, that the churches of the Global South are living in poverty and the constant threat of violence. Issues of wealth and poverty in the Bible speak loudly to people whose crops are destroyed by warfare and climate change.

For example, sub-Saharan Africa is home to some 40 million Anglicans who live with the daily reality of violent death. Fulani raiders burned the house and killed the friends of Archbishop Ben Kwashi of Jos in Nigeria. Further east, Ugandan Anglicans hallow the memory of Archbishop Janani Luwum, who was shot to death by the dictator Idi Amin in 1977. Likewise, Kenyan Anglicans recently lived through the violence incited by rival candidates for president. Anglican Christians in South Sudan number about 3.5 million, many of whom have been torn from their homes and forced into exile by the Muslim rulers to the north and by civil war in their own failed state. A Sudanese hymn laments the desolation of their life.

> *The Father of our Lord, who has power,*
>
> *Help us for we are all worried.*
>
> *Don't allow the evil spirit to crush us.*
>
> *Help us, we are mourning, we are mourning, all of us are mourning.*
>
> *The sin of the world is preventing us from taking your path.*
>
> *We are left alone, we are left, we are left, we are left . . .*
>
> *Father of our Lord, who is able to help,*
>
> *Allow us to sit at your right hand.*
>
> *Your Truth I have heard, O Lord.*
>
> *Release us from sin for we are falling in the fire.*
>
> *The sin of this world has divided us and thrown us into the fire, O Lord,*
>
> *We are burning, we are dying,*
>
> *we are burning, we are burning, we are burning.*

These are the Christians who make crosses of the aluminum they harvest from downed MIG fighter-bombers that have destroyed their villages. It is no wonder the book of Lamentations is the Sudanese prayer book.

Anglicans in the Global South are not only viscerally aware of the visible evil wrought by MIG bombers in the Sudan, or by death squads in Honduras, or by Western corporations that have persuaded mothers in India to bottle-feed their emaciated babies instead of nursing them. They are also keenly aware of the invisible powers of evil, the devil and his demons, witchcraft and curses, and all the allied forces of darkness. Christians in the Global West skim over Jesus' ministry of exorcism, often assuming modern psychiatry has rendered this kind of superstition obsolete. Christians in Africa are under no such illusion. One hymn from South Africa proclaims,

> *Jesus Christ is conqueror*
>
> *By his resurrection he overcame death itself*
>
> *By his resurrection he overcame all things*
>
> *He overcame magic*
>
> *He overcame amulets and charms,*
>
> *He overcame the darkness of demon possession*

He overcame dread
When we are with him
We also conquer.

In the Anglican diocese of Nunavut in arctic Canada, many older believers still remember the animism of their childhood when people lived in fear of malicious spirits that haunted their steps. One old hunter said, "Before the missionaries came, we lived in darkness and we feared the spirits. But now we walk the Jesus way and all is light." Likewise, in southern Chile, a witch threatened to curse a young Christian. (Jesus was obviously invading the *bruja's* territory.) The Christian confronted her and said, "I belong to Jesus and I cannot be cursed. You know what happens when a curse cannot touch its intended victim. It rebounds on the one who spoke the curse." The witch turned and ran.

Anglican Christians in the Global South live not only in rural African or Southeast Asian villages, but in vast cities as well. Lagos in Nigeria—home to around 25 million people—is one of the largest cities in the world, and the center of an Anglican province with thirteen dioceses. Urban or rural, Anglicans in the Global South live amid poverty and violence, not so different from the Roman Empire in the New Testament. So it is not surprising that the majority of Anglicans in the world read the Bible with different eyes than modernist Anglicans in the West. They find that the Bible speaks directly to everyday issues like poverty and debt, famine and disease, the squalor of urban life, warfare between religions and between races, the corruption and the brutality of predatory thugs in failed states. Global South Anglicans take the Bible seriously as the text inspired and authorized by God—not the purely human artifact of German higher criticism. Anglicans in the Global South accept the historic Anglican principle that while ancient ceremonies and church structures may be adapted to changing times, biblical theology and morality are timeless and nonnegotiable. They are especially interested in the supernatural dimension in Scripture for it describes the world in which they live. The Bible prescribes the antidote to witchcraft and cursing. Anglicans in the Global South likewise reckon with the present reality of prophecy, both true and false. God's revelation still breaks forth from the Bible, through its inspired preachers (and is parodied by its demonic imitators). For Anglicans in Africa, Asia, and Latin

America, the Bible is fresh, pertinent, authentic, and authoritative as our guide for daily living.

One other feature of Global South Anglican churches is their "pentecostalization." This does not mean that they subscribe to Western Pentecostal theologies such as the dogma that speaking in tongues is the necessary sign of having received the Spirit. Nor does it mean that Anglican leaders support the "prosperity gospel" teachings that have invaded the Global South from America. Rather this pentecostalization seems to be a return to the early church's expectation of God's intervention in our daily life by signs and wonders, by radically changed lives, and by the empowerment of ordinary Christians to do extraordinary works of evangelism and self-sacrifice.

One example of pentecostalization in the Anglican South was the East African Revival. On Sunday, September 23, 1929, two friends met in front of the Anglican cathedral in Namirembe, part of the city of Kampala, the capital of Uganda. Dr. Joe Church was an English medical doctor, and Simeon Nsibambi was an official in the Ugandan medical service. They had met previously at a Bible study led by CMS missionary Mabel Ensor. Both men had been sensing that the spirit in the Ugandan churches had grown cold, and they longed for revival. They agreed to pray together for the Spirit to touch the nation. Soon Nsibambi gave up his government job and began to work as a lay evangelist, roaming the streets of Kampala and talking to anyone who would listen. The center of his message was salvation through Christ, and the power of the Holy Spirit to make this word come alive in people's hearts. Dr. Church, for his part, had read a book on revival by Charles Finney, the American evangelist in the 1830s and 1840s. Finney described a "second blessing" that would empower believers to live a "victorious" life. Before long, another theme emerged in the revival, namely "walking in the light," confessing one's sins publicly, and seeking reconciliation with one's enemies. (Bishop Alfred Stanway, Church Missionary Society missionary and bishop of Central Tanganyika 1951–1971 remembered that he needed to caution converts not to describe their sins too specifically— testimony by one converted thief led to a rash of robberies carried out in exactly the same way!) The East African Revival soon spread to other churches as well—the Anglicans had no monopoly on the Holy Spirit. But many of its leaders were Anglican in the next half century, including Archbishop Erica Sabiti of

Uganda and Bishop Festo Kivengere, whose evangelistic preaching in England and North America reached tens of thousands in the late twentieth century. This pentecostalization of Global South Christianity has been one more reason for the estrangement of the Anglican South from the West, and for Archbishop Nzimbi's observation (quoted at the head of this chapter) that the Anglican Communion now represents two different kinds of Christianity.

Let's Pause and Reflect

2. Summarize the most important features of Anglican piety in the Global South that distinguish it from most of the Western provinces.

_____

_____

_____

_____

_____

_____

_____

_____

_____

Modernist Theology in the Anglican West (1963–Present)

In contrast to the vibrant Christianity in the Anglican South, the Western churches saw a resurgence of modernist theology in the later twentieth century. After the generation of generally orthodox teaching during World War II and its aftermath, the 1960s saw a return to the optimistic confidence in human progress that had lost its credibility in the 1930s. In the midst of the postwar economic boom, some theologians in the Western world misconstrued a few snippets from the letters of Dietrich Bonhoeffer to the effect that modern man had "come of age" and was ready for a "religionless" Christianity. Bonhoeffer's misinterpreters were simply promoting a regression to the German Romantic theology of the 1800s, with its rejection of the supernatural and its confidence in the upward spiral of human subjective "God consciousness."

The first salvo in this modernist resurgence came from John A. T. Robinson, the Anglican bishop of Woolwich in South London. Titled *Honest to God*, Robinson's book claimed that "modern man" could no longer believe in the old supernaturalist Christianity, with its story of a Creator God who personally entered time and space in Jesus of Nazareth. In fact, Robinson announced that he no longer believed in a "personal" God at all, but rather that the universe was in some general way "personal" at its deepest level. We can hear the echoes of Hegel and Schleiermacher sounding through his prose.

> To say that "God is personal" is to say that "reality at its very deepest level is personal," that personality is of ultimate significance in the constitution of the universe, that in personal relationships we touch the final meaning of existence.

Honest to God sold hundreds of thousands of copies, and occasioned much uproar at the spectacle of a Church of England bishop publicly denying the faith. He kept his job.

An impersonal "Force" or "Essence" similar to Robinson's appeared as God in the theology of John Macquarrie, at the time professor of theology at Union Seminary in New York and subsequently Lady Margaret Professor of Divinity at Oxford University. Macquarrie was later hailed as the most influential Anglican theologian in the late twentieth century, and his textbook *The Principles of Christian Theology* (1966) shaped the belief of Anglican seminarians for years to come. Like his modernist predecessors, Macquarrie rejected the Christian story of a Creator God who spoke and acted in history. He characterized God as "Being" with a capital *B* in contrast to "beings" with a lower-case *b*. "Being" is the ground and source of all "beings" but *not* a personal being among other beings in the world (whereas classical Trinitarian theology would affirm that God is both). "Being" was manifest in the disciples' experience of Jesus' resurrection, although in Macquarrie's view the resurrection was not an actual historical event.

> It is obvious that the resurrection *is not an historical event in the same way that the cross is, that is to say, not a publicly observable event*. . . .

> *Stories of the empty tomb and of accompanying marvels look like the usual mythologizing tendency.*

Given the authority of Macquarrie's teaching in Anglican seminaries and theological colleges, it is easier to understand how Bishop John Spong thrived in the American Episcopal Church in the late twentieth century. The church's House of Bishops had failed to correct Bishop James Pike in the 1960s, when the latter had described the Trinity as "excess baggage." But Spong's rejection of Christianity was much angrier and more comprehensive than Pike's. In over twenty-five books, Spong successively denied every major Christian doctrine. In *Why Christianity Must Change or Die* (1998), he described how he had come to hold the positions he did.

> *The God [that I discovered] was the infinite center of life. This God was not a person, but rather like the insights of the mystics, this God was the mystical presence in which all personhood could flourish. This God was not a being but rather the power that called forth being in all creatures. This God was not an external, personal force that could be invoked but rather an internal reality that, when confronted, opened to us the meaning of life itself.*

Impersonal, inactive, mute, unresponsive—here was the seed of Schleiermacher's God consciousness come to fruition in the late twentieth century. Despite his energetic rejection of Christianity, Bishop Spong retained his office as bishop of Newark and his seat in the House of Bishops, where he was much lionized and was invited to address the House on matters of faith on a number of occasions. As new bishops were consecrated in the 1980s and 1990s, who had been nurtured in seminary on the theology of Macquarrie, the number of Episcopal bishops dwindled who could (or would) resist their colleague Spong's fiery rhetoric.

If "God" was an impersonal essence who could be encountered in the depths of one's subjective consciousness, it was not a great step to identifying "deity" with the ecstasy that one felt in the throes of any profound experience—including sexual experience. In the late 1990s, the Rev. Carter Heyward (professor at the Episcopal Divinity School in Cambridge, Massachusetts) made that connection explicit. She argued for homoerotic ecstasy as the doorway to "deity" in her 1996 book *Touching Our Strength*: "The erotic is our most fully embodied experience of the love of God. . . . Our erotic experience of the power of God is the root of our theological epistemology. It is the basis of our knowledge and love of God." At the parish level, most Episcopalians were quite unaware of these theological trends among the leadership in the late twentieth century. Many pockets of orthodoxy remained, where faithful parishioners kept the "faith once delivered to the saints." The same was true in England and in the other Western Anglican provinces, but with modernist teaching once more ascendant among the Church's leaders, it is easy to understand why those provinces were unwilling (indeed unable) to critique the ideology of the sexual revolution that swept the Western world from the 1960s onward.

Let's Pause and Reflect

3. What were the central features of the modernist theology that swept through the Western Anglican churches in the late twentieth century?

_____

_____

_____

_____

_____

_____

_____

_____

_____

_____

The Three Traditions and the Two Churches

It seems as if the Anglican story has come to the end as we have been telling it. Hitherto, we have seen that three orthodox traditions (Evangelical, Anglo-Catholic, and Charismatic) developed in the Church of England and spread throughout the world. Then modernist theology, based on axioms alien to the Bible, captured the Western provinces of the Anglican world—first in the late nineteenth century and then decisively in the late twentieth. The moral corollaries to these axioms, though emphasizing certain aspects of social justice, increasingly prioritized self-realization and self-expression as the highest religious and social ideal—resulting in what Christian Smith has termed a "moralistic therapeutic deism." But the daughter churches in the Global South kept the faith, and began to recognize how far their Western cousins had drifted from the Christian story. The schism was manifest at the Lambeth Conference of 1998. Since then the tectonic plates have been grinding further apart, and the Global South provinces are beginning to develop their own network of Anglican institutions. The next chapter of the Anglican story will be theirs to tell.

As we saw in the previous chapter, at the Lambeth Conference of 1998 a resolution on sexual behavior came to the floor, despite resolute behind-the-scenes opposition from English and American factions. This Resolution 1.10 clearly rejected "homosexual practice as incompatible with Scripture," and carried by a vote of 526 to 70, with 45 abstentions. True to precedent at Lambeth Conferences, this vote expressed the conviction of its adherents, but did not bind any province to compliance. Nevertheless the margin of victory showed how the tectonic plates were shifting.

The American Episcopal Church responded five years later by confirming the election of a practicing homosexual as bishop of New Hampshire. The Rev. Gene Robinson had been Canon to the Ordinary (assistant to the bishop) for seventeen years in New Hampshire. Earlier he had been married to a woman for fifteen years, and they had two daughters. The couple had separated when Robinson declared his homosexual orientation, and he had since taken a male partner (whom he married in 2010 and divorced in 2014). The bishop of New Hampshire scheduled the diocesan election in 2003 in such a way that General Convention would have to approve it, instead of the usual procedure of polling bishops and standing committees one by one. The intention was to put the Episcopal Church on record in the clearest way, as favoring the sexual revolution. Which it did.

In response, some twelve bishops and over two thousand clergy and laypeople gathered at Christ Church, Plano, Texas, the following January, to protest the Robinson consecration and to find ways out of the quandary. Bishop Robert Duncan of Pittsburgh emerged as the leader of this remnant, in which all three orthodox strands in the American Episcopal Church combined. No longer were the issues dividing them sufficient to keep them apart (though the question of women's ordination would continue to be an issue). Party issues gave way to a united front opposing the modernist agenda and its embrace of the sexual revolution in the West. Out of the Plano meeting came tentative steps to form a new Anglican province in North America, which would come to fruition six years later.

Meanwhile Global South leaders had shown their willingness to intervene and help beleaguered Episcopal conservatives. In January 2000 in Singapore, Archbishop Emmanuel Kolini of Rwanda and Archbishop Moses Tay of South East Asia had consecrated two Episcopal priests as bishops in a new "Anglican Mission in America," the Rev. John Rodgers and the Rev. Charles Murphy. After the Plano conference, additional Global South provinces offered refuge to other conservative American bishops, giving them "canonical residence" in their own colleges of bishops. An alliance of American Episcopal leaders and parishes with Global South bishops (for example from Kenya, Uganda, Nigeria, and the Southern Cone of South America) was both strengthening the resistance in America and keeping their allies overseas up to date as to what the theological and sexual revolution in the West entailed. This cooperation with the Global South bore fruit in June 2009 with the founding of the Anglican Church in North America. Bishop Robert Duncan of Pittsburgh was elected as Archbishop of this body. Archbishops and provincial assemblies in Africa, Asia, and Latin America hastened to recognize this new province as the authentic Anglican body in the United States and Canada. Though formal schisms did not immediately follow in England, Australia, or New Zealand, the tectonic gaps continued to widen.

In the years following the Robinson consecration, leaders on both sides tried to mend the Anglican network using the extant instruments of communion. Archbishop of Canterbury Rowan Williams appointed a committee on unity, which produced the Windsor Report in 2004. This document urged the creation of an "Anglican Covenant" that would commit all sides to consultation before initiating any more sexual innovations. (In 2012, the Church of England would reject this proposal, ending its chances.) Meanwhile in 2007, a Primates' Meeting in Dar Es Salaam actually called the Episcopal Church to accountability, saying that unless it performed certain specific acts of repentance, its bishops should not be invited to the Lambeth Conference in 2008. Archbishop Williams and Episcopal Presiding Bishop Katherine Jefferts Schori both gave verbal assent to this motion. Both reneged immediately upon returning home.

The historic instruments of communion had manifestly failed to hold West and South together. Recognizing this fact, a number of Global South leaders called for a Global Anglican Future Conference in Jerusalem for 2008 (GAF-CON, as it came to be called). Archbishop Peter Akinola of Nigeria gave particularly strong leadership in this direction. In June 2008, in Jerusalem, some 1,148 delegates gathered from 29 different countries. Included were 7 primates, 291 bishops, and 850 clergy and lay representatives.

The GAFCON meeting addressed a wide range of issues of particular concern to the Global South, such as poverty and HIV/AIDS. But the major work of the meeting was to address the theological and moral apostasy of the Western Anglican churches, and to clarify the identity of the Southern provinces over against their erstwhile founders. The Jerusalem Declaration reaffirmed the historic basis of Anglican Christianity in the Bible, the historic creeds and councils, and the founding documents of the Reformation: the *Book of Common Prayer,* and the Thirty-Nine Articles. The declaration even found it necessary to restate "the Lordship and atoning death of Jesus Christ for our redemption"—so far had the West forgotten the Christian story. The Jerusalem Declaration went on to address specific issues, such as the Great Commission and the stewardship of creation. But at the top of that list was "the creation of man in God's image male and female and the primacy of Christian marriage." The conference also announced the formation of a Primates' Council, composed of the leaders from the provinces represented in Jerusalem. With the old instruments of communion rendered impotent by their captivity to the West, the new council could speak with authority for the member provinces.

A second GAFCON meeting occurred in Nairobi in October 2013 with a larger attendance (10 primates, 1,003 clergy, 1,358 total), and a second Jerusalem conference in 2018 was larger still (9 primates, 38 other archbishops, 333 bishops, 660 other clergy, 1966 total). This latter conference announced the creation of nine new networks, coordinating the ministries of the member provinces in such areas as church planting, theological education, and youth work. At this point the GAFCON movement stood forth clearly as the successor to the Western-dominated Anglican Communion that had birthed it. As one leader put it, "We are not leaving the Anglican Communion; we *are* the Anglican Communion." At the end of the conference, nearly two thousand delegates gathered on the southern steps of the Temple Mount in Jerusalem for a dramatic photograph. African, Asian, and Latin American faces were all in the majority: a foretaste of the kingdom.

> *After this I looked, and behold, a great multitude that no one could number, from every nation, from all tribes and peoples and languages, standing before the throne and before the Lamb. (Revelation 7:9)*

Let's Pause and Reflect

5. How would you describe the Christianity believed and practiced widely in the Global South today?

_____

_____

_____

_____

_____

_____

_____

_____

_____

_____

6. What were the major events that displayed the growing separation between the Anglican South and the Anglican West from the late 1990s onward?

_____

_____

_____

_____

_____

_____

_____

_____

_____

_____

_____

_____

Review

A. What are the main theological differences between Anglicans in the West and Global South that have been a source of division?

_____

_____

_____

_____

_____

_____

_____

_____

_____

_____

_____

_____

For Thought and Application

B. How has the modern Christian revising of theology led to the modern Christian revising of sexual ethics?

C. "Progressive" Western Christianity often affirms the Bible's call to social justice and ignores the Bible's call to self-denial and holiness, while "conservative" Christianity often does just the opposite. Can both be affirmed together? Explain your answer.

_____

_____

_____

_____

_____

_____

_____

_____

For Further Reading

J.R.H. Moorman, *A History of the Church in England, Third Edition.*

- Chapters 22-23

Robert W. Prichard, *A History of the Episcopal Church, Third Revised Edition.*

- Chapters 8-11

Notes

1. The Anglican Way

Pages 5-7   All quotations from the Lambeth Quadrilateral are taken from the 1979 *Book of Common Prayer* (Church Publishing Incorporated, New York, 2016), 877-878.

3. The English Reformation (1525–1603)

Page 60   Articles 6, 11: See the *Book of Common Prayer,* 868, 870.

4. The English Civil War and the Scientific Revolution (1603–1736)

Page 85   *...and all was light:* quoted in James M. Byrne, *Religion and the Enlightenment* (Westminster John Knox Press, Louisville, KY, 1997), 150.

Page 90   *...no need for that hypothesis:* quoted in Nancy R. Pearcey and Charles B. Thaxton, *The Soul of Science* (Crossway Books, Wheaton, IL, 1994), 92.

5. Holiness and Evangelical Revivals in England (1735–1791)

Page 95   *...excites nothing but laughter:* quoted in G.R. Balleine, *A History of the Evangelical Party in the Church of England* (Church Book Room Press, London, 1951), 17.

Page 96   *...I thank God, No:* quoted in Kenneth J. Collins, *A Real Christian: The Life of John Wesley* (Abingdon Press, Nashville, TN, 1999), 40.

Page 101   *...three thousand people:* quoted in *Ibid.,* 69.

Page 106   *...rope of sand:* quoted in *Ibid.,* 81.

6.   The Church of England in Colonial America (1607–1789)

Page 129   ...*shot heard round the world:* from Ralph Waldo Emerson, "Concord Hymn," poetryfoundation.org.

7.   Anglican Evangelicals in England and America (1787–1873)

Page 146   ...*reformation of manners:* quoted in Ernest Marshall Howse, *Saints in Politics: The 'Clapham Sect' and the Growth Of Freedom* (George Allen & Unwin, London, 1976), 32.

Page 148   ...*the great century:* Kenneth Scott Latourette, *The Great Century* (Harper, New York, NY, 1941).

Page 155   ...*he doesn't know it:* quoted in E. Clowes Chorley, *Men and Movements in the American Episcopal Church* (Charles Scribner's Sons, New York, NY, 1946), 38.

Page 158   ...*United States together:* quoted in Diana Hochstedt Butler, *Standing Against the Whirlwind: Evangelical Episcopalians In Nineteenth-Century America* (Oxford University Press, 1995), 164.

8.   Anglo-Catholics in the Church of England (1833–1867)

Page 171   ...*with thy Holy Spirit:* This form of words goes back to Archbishop Cranmer's second *Book of Common Prayer* in 1552: "We yelde thee heartie thankes, most merciful father, that it hathe pleased thee to regenerate this infant with thy holy spirite..." *The First and Second Prayer Books of Edward VI* (J. M. Dent & Sons, London, 1910), 398. The use of the word "regenerate" persisted through the 1928 BCP in America.

Pages 172-173   ...*virtue residing in them:* quoted in Owen Chadwick, *The Mind of the Oxford Movement* (Stanford University Press, 1967), 191.

Page 177   ...*painted and frescoed:* Geoffrey Rowell, *The Vision Glorious: Themes and Personalities of the Catholic Revival in Anglicanism* (Oxford University Press, 1983), 104.

9. The Episcopal Church in the United States (1789–1873)

Page 194   ...*Scarlet Woman:* quoted in Chorley, *Men and Movements,* 203.

Page 195   ...*errors of individuals:* quoted in *Ibid.,* 220-221.

10. Modernism in England and America (1860–1940)

Page 203   ...*of the skies:* quoted in Jeremy Morris, editor, *The Oxford History of Anglicanism,* Volume 4 (Oxford University Press, 2017), 30.

Page 208   ...*O Nature! O my Mother!* Jean-Jacques Rousseau, *The Confessions* (Penguin Classics, Harmondsworth, Middlesex, 1985), 594.

Page 210   ...*consequent emotions:* Friedrich Schleiermacher, *On Religion: Speeches to Its Cultured Despisers,* translated by John Oman (Kegan, Paul, Trench and Truebner, London, 1893) 48. Available online.

Pages 216   ...*clash by night: The Norton Introduction to Literature,* Fifth Edition (W.W. Norton & Company, New York, NY, 1991), 698-699.

Page 217   ...*within the limits of the Church of England:* quoted in Bernard M.G. Reardon, *Religious Thought in the Victorian Age,* Second Edition (Longman, London, 1995), 237.

Page 218   ...*claim and meaning:* quoted in *Ibid.,* 319.

Page 220   ...*the Holy Ghost:* quoted in Arthur Michael Ramsey, *An Era in Anglican Theology* (Charles Scribner's Sons, New York, NY, 1960), 160-161.

Page 221   ...*the glory of them:* Phillips Brooks, *Sermons for the Principal Feasts and Fasts of the Church Year* (E.P. Dutton & Company, New York, NY, 1895), 181.

Page 223   ...*criterion is within us:* quoted in Richard H. Schmidt, *Glorious Companions* (William B. Eerdmans, Grand Rapids, MI, 2002), 201.

Page 224   ...*museum piece:* quoted in Robert W. Prichard, *A History of the Episcopal Church* (Morehouse Publishing, New York, NY, 2014), 269.

11. The Anglican Communion (1789–2018)

Page 233   ...*vacant place:* quoted in J. Herbert Kane, *A Concise History of the Christian World Mission* (Baker Book House, Grand Rapids, MI, 1978), 97-98.

Page 241   ...*with my blood:* quoted in *Lesser Feasts and Fasts,* 4th Edition (Church Hymnal Corporation, New York, NY, 1988), 382.

12. Two Churches: West and South (1938–2018)

Page 249   ...*two different churches:* quoted in Philip Jenkins, *The New Faces of Christianity* (Oxford University Press, 2006), 1.

Page 251   ...*breathed through silver:* quoted in Philip Zaleski and Carol Zaleski, *The Fellowship* (Farrar, Strauss and Giroux, New York, NY, 2015), 188.

Pages 252-253   ...*nearly a hundred years:* the two quotations from the sermon are found in C. S. Lewis, *The Weight of Glory* (William B. Eerdmans, Grand Rapids, MI, 1973), 2, 5.

Page 253   ...*Aslan! Aslan!* C.S. Lewis, *Prince Caspian* (Harper Trophy, New York, NY, 1994), 166.

Page 253   ...*wet weather comes: Time: The Weekly Newsmagazine,* September 8, 1947, 74.

Page 255   ...*we are burning:* quoted in Mark Nikkel, *Why Haven't You Left? Letters from the Sudan* (Church Publishing, New York, NY, 2006), 45.

Page 255-256   ...*we also conquer:* quoted in Jenkins, *The New Faces of Christianity,* 104.

Page 256   ...*all is light:* I remember being told this story when I was teaching at the Arthur Turner Training School in Pangnirtung on Baffin Island in the 1980s. There is a useful chapter on Pre-Christian Inuit religion, "Of Myths and Angakoks," Archibald Lang Fleming, *Archibald the Arctic* (Appleton-Century-Crofts, New York, NY, 1956), 187-202.

Page 259   *...meaning of existence:* John A. T. Robinson, *Honest to God* (The Westminster Press, Philadelphia, PA, 1963), 48-49.

Pages 259-260   *...mythologizing tendency:* John Macquarrie, *Principles of Christian Theology* (Charles Scribner's Sons, New York, 1966), 265-266.

Page 260   *...life itself:* John Shelby Spong, *Why Christianity Must Change or Die* (Harper One, New York, NY, 1999), 64.

Pages 260-261   *...love of God:* Carter Heyward, *Touching Our Strength: The Erotic As Power and the Love of God* (Harper San Francisco, CA, 1989), 99.

Page 262   *...moralistic therapeutic deism:* Christian Smith and Melina Lundquist Denton, *Soul Searching: The Religious and Spiritual Lives of American Teenagers* (Oxford University Press, New York, NY, 2005), *passim.*

Page 264   *...Christian marriage:* "The Complete Jerusalem Statement" *(gafcon.org)*, #8.